Contractors' Handbook

The expert guide for UK contractors and freelancers

To order more copies of this book or to obtain further information about ContractorCalculator's future publications, please contact:

The Marketing Department
ContractorCalculator
An imprint of Byte-Vision Ltd
112c Roman Road
Basingstoke
Hampshire RG23 8HE

Tel: 01978 368808
Fax: 01978 368809
Email: info@ContractorsHandbook.co.uk
Web: www.ContractorsHandbook.co.uk

Contractors' Handbook

The expert guide for UK contractors and freelancers

Dave Chaplin

First published in 2008 by ContractorCalculator

ContractorCalculator
An imprint of Byte-Vision Ltd.
112c Roman Road
Basingstoke
Hampshire RG23 8HE
United Kingdom

British Library Cataloguing in Publication Data:

A catalogue record for this book is available from the British Library

ISBN 978-0-9560745-0-8

Contents

Foreword

By John Brazier
Managing Director
Professional Contractors Group (PCG)

Contractors and freelancers represent the inherent flexibility of the UK's workforce to adapt to the challenges of the national and global economy, with the unique ability to respond effectively to major opportunities and threats.

When the economic cycle is at its peak, contractors and freelancers are a vital additional skilled labour resource to increase the capacity of organisations and complete vital projects, where their independent perspective and fresh insights can add huge value. During downturns and at times of crisis, contractors and freelancers offer a low risk and flexible solution to organisations that need to maintain and improve the provision of their products and services in an uncertain climate.

It takes a special kind of person to thrive as a freelance contractor – the kind who embraces risk in return for potentially greater rewards. And the kind who, in addition to maintaining high quality professional and technical skills, is also able to seamlessly integrate into their client's organisation. Successful contractors and freelancers are those who recognise they must also focus on their business skills, because it is not necessarily the best qualified who win contracts, but those who most effectively apply a range of skills to market and sell their services.

As the stakeholders in the economy increasingly recognise the validity, effectiveness and strength of the contracting and freelance model, PCG is confident that the number of contractors and freelancers active in the economy will increase. Globalisation will also play its part in the growth of the sector, with an increasing number of cross-border opportunities available. The challenge is to ensure that the flexible models that we know work in the UK can be constructively combined with the best international working practices, thereby preventing international barriers from reducing flexibility.

The influx of new blood will need guidance, particularly as many workers in permanent roles who are considering a freelance career are dissuaded by the uncertainties of the regulatory regime imposed by government. Such guidance will come from representative industry bodies, such as PCG and its guides to contracting and freelancing, as well as through websites like ContractorCalculator.co.uk and, of course, publications like the *Contractors' Handbook*.

Such expert guidance will ensure they get the best start and continue to trade successfully and profitably throughout their contracting and freelance careers.

John Brazier

Preface

The *Contractors' Handbook* is the expert guide for all contractors and freelancers in the UK – whether you're just considering the move into contracting, or have many years of experience, this book can help you. It's a resource that pulls together in one place: my first-hand experience; the wisdom of many contractors built up over nearly two decades; the specialist knowledge of dozens of expert contributors; and over 350 carefully researched and regularly updated guides available on ContractorCalculator.co.uk.

Scratch the surface of every great economy and you'll find that the hard work, cutting-edge skills, broad experience and flexibility of the key members of its workforce are the drivers of its success – in other words, contractors are the pathfinders of growing businesses and economies. Vital to the success of UK PLC for centuries, highly skilled and flexible contractors have always been found in every sector – from science, engineering and medicine, through crafts and trades, to education, the arts and media.

No matter what the state of the economy, from times of plenty through to recession, one thing remains consistent: the ongoing demand for contractors to achieve results for their private, public and not-for-profit sector clients. Demand may dip and soar, but it will always be there.

So, for those of you who have desperately longed to take control of your destiny and move into contracting, I offer you encouragement and practical 'how to' guidance for your journey. For experienced contractors, you'll find information on advanced techniques to really 'up your game'. And when things go wrong, which they probably will at some point in your contracting career, I'll share with you solutions that have been effectively used by others.

Most successful contractors remain successful because they recognise that their market is always moving, and maintain their skills accordingly. This book provides another opportunity to do just that, but for the skills that feature less highly on most contractors' radars, but can be even more important than the letters after your name when it comes to winning the best contracts: things like CV writing, contract law, negotiation techniques and key sales and marketing skills.

As a maths graduate, my ambition was to become a teacher; but the lure of the City and its rewards to IT contractors have ensured my goal remains unrealised. However, through the website ContractorCalulator.co.uk and the *Contractors' Handbook*, I have found other channels to pass on what I have learnt. If I have achieved this, even in a very small way, I will have given back some of what I have taken over the years as a successful contractor. But if you don't find what you're looking for in this book, would like to take issue with anything I've written, or have any questions about contracting, then please do get in touch with me through www.contractorshandbook.co.uk.

Dave Chaplin

Dedicated to my parents, for all their love and support.

1.

Why go contracting?

1.1 The main reasons people do it

The decision to move from being a permanent employee to becoming a contractor seems to have been endlessly dramatised. In fact, it's not that big a decision at all. Choosing to become a contractor ranks well below decisions like getting married or deciding on which career to choose.

In fact, if you are reading this, you've probably already made some fairly important decisions about your career, which is why contracting sounds attractive. You may be a programmer with years of experience and already earning good money in a job. Or you may be a recently qualified engineer and wondering whether you should give contracting a try.

After reading on, the choice can only be yours. The question is, do you always want to be asking yourself 'what-if?'. Don't forget that you can always return to the permanent workplace if contracting doesn't suit you. But if you don't take the plunge, you'll never know what you've missed!

Most contractors go down the contracting road for three typical reasons:

- To do the things they really want to do, and this includes taking more time off
- To avoid the things they really don't want to do
- For the money.

'It's not what I want to do anymore'

Actually, it is the second reason that drives many wannabe contractors into the sector, and then keeps them happily embedded in the contractor lifestyle. In their last role as a permanent worker, or permie, something happens to make them think: 'Surely there must be something better out there?'

Many of us get to the stage in our careers when we become as experienced, skilled and technically proficient as we are likely to get in our chosen skill set. This could be in programming, engineering, medicine, marketing or many other disciplines.

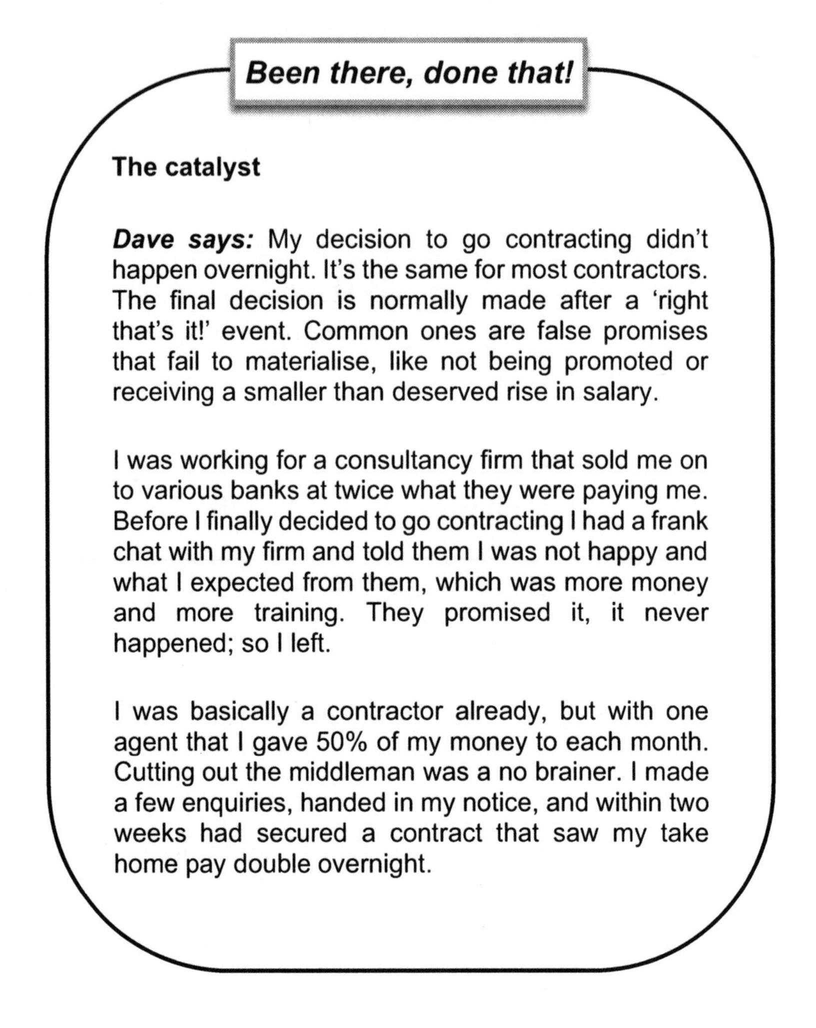

Been there, done that!

The catalyst

Dave says: My decision to go contracting didn't happen overnight. It's the same for most contractors. The final decision is normally made after a 'right that's it!' event. Common ones are false promises that fail to materialise, like not being promoted or receiving a smaller than deserved rise in salary.

I was working for a consultancy firm that sold me on to various banks at twice what they were paying me. Before I finally decided to go contracting I had a frank chat with my firm and told them I was not happy and what I expected from them, which was more money and more training. They promised it, it never happened; so I left.

I was basically a contractor already, but with one agent that I gave 50% of my money to each month. Cutting out the middleman was a no brainer. I made a few enquiries, handed in my notice, and within two weeks had secured a contract that saw my take home pay double overnight.

The common theme, however, is that for most the next stage of progression after reaching a professional or technical pinnacle is into management, which tends to raise two big questions:

1. Do I really want to be a manager? It typically means learning lots more of the soft skills that are essential to effectively manage people. After all, that is what managers do; their role is generally to manage people.

2. Having become the most qualified person at what I do, would I want to start at the bottom again, learning a new skill set and being the smallest fish in a bigger pond?

So many potential contractors find themselves being promoted, or not being promoted, either of which can prove frustrating. And typically many highly qualified professionals find themselves sidelined into 'special projects' or doing tasks they really don't enjoy. This then makes them think about what it is they really want to do.

Now, what can I do that I have always wanted to?
So, having been given a reason to think about taking the contracting route, we then think about the first reason – contractors who go contracting because they get to do what they want to do.

Here is a really important point: contractors are not employed by the organisation that pays them for what they spend their time doing. There is a big difference between being paid as an employee to perform a task and being paid to do a task without being employed. This will be explained in more detail in section 1.3.

The major point of difference is that, as a contractor, as long as you perform, you can do a lot more of what you want to do. It varies between different types of clients and different sectors, but the common theme is that you take control of your work and your work-life balance.

If you are a software developer and have been allocated specific sections of software to develop during the week, and you finish early on Thursday, you could take Friday off. The developer sat next to you who is an employee has to find something else to do to finish their week. Or, to be more precise, they will either be found something else to do or will try and stretch out the job to last the week.

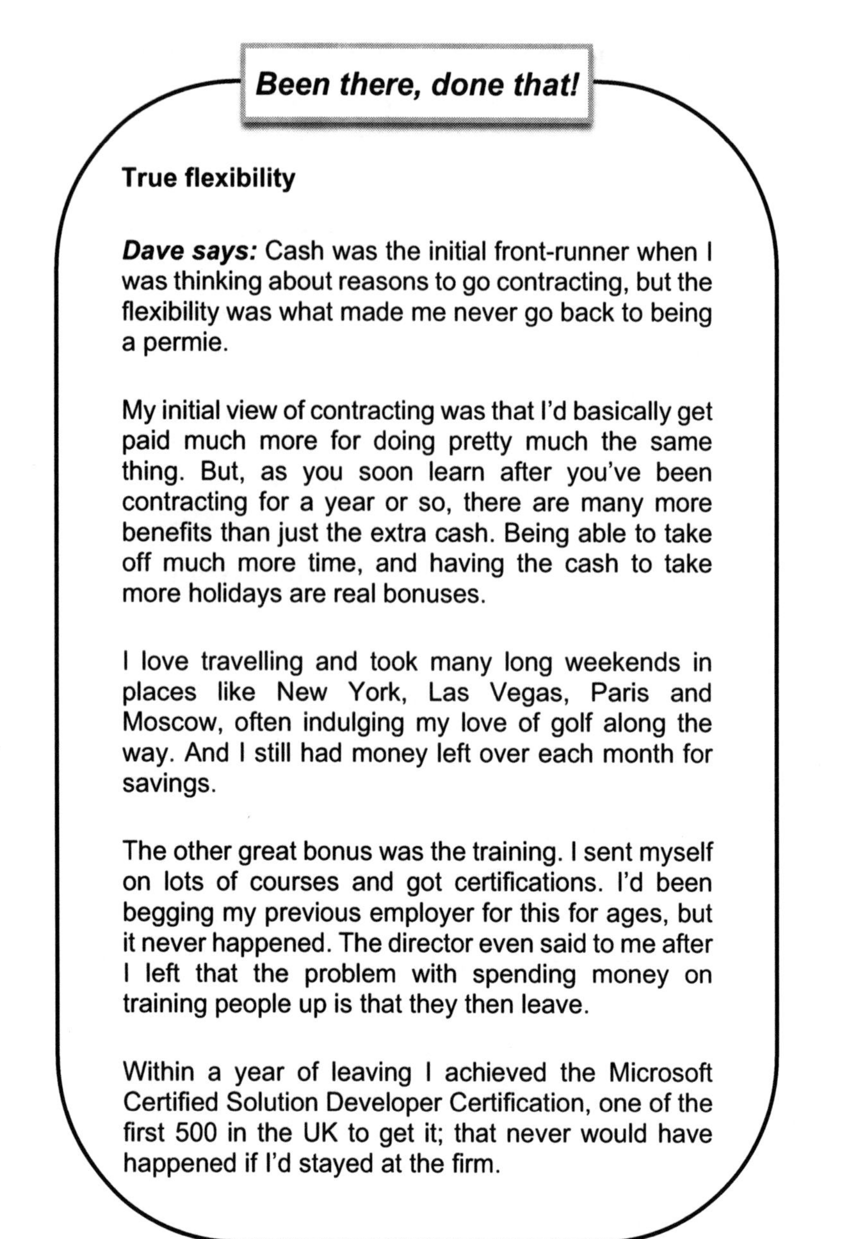

However, it does not always work like that. If a contractor is an offshore safety specialist working on an ongoing drilling project, for instance, they can't just leave for the weekend until their safety role is covered. But you can bet that what they are being paid more than compensates them for working some weekends!

Contractors have a level of flexibility that permanent employees simply do not have. If they can afford it – and many can – contractors can take long periods of time away from work, or they can choose to work particularly hard for a few years to earn enough to retire early. The keyword is choice; a contractor really can choose what work to do, when to do it, and how to do it.

This can also work well for contractors with families who want to be able to choose to spend more time with them, particularly if they have young children or perhaps they want to spend time as a carer for a parent or other relative. The increased money contracting brings can make flexible working possible for many with family commitments who might otherwise not be able to work at all.

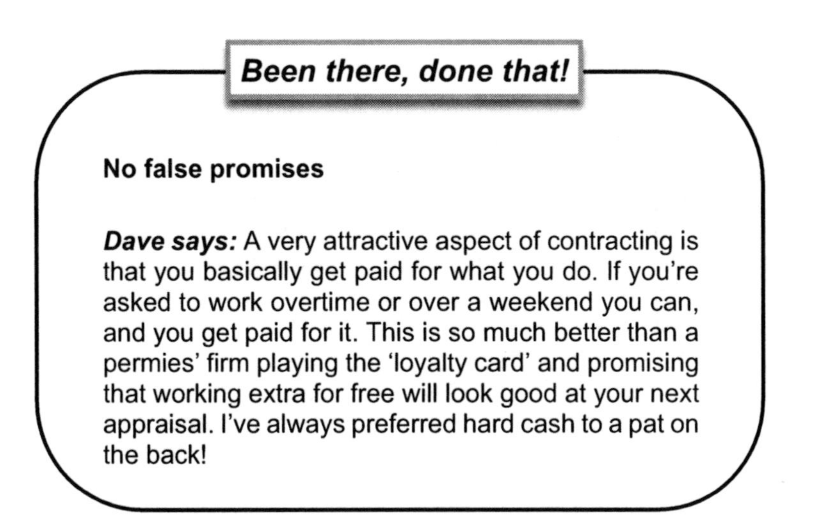

For the money

In addition to the flexibility contracting gives, and the ability to leave behind the world of office politics, another important reason people choose to become contractors is for the money. And that's not surprising, because contractors typically earn between 20 and 150% more than permanent employees.

Why do they get paid so much more? It is generally because they are not employees but also because they may, particularly in some key sectors and disciplines, be highly skilled and very rare, in which case market forces contribute to their high rates. As an employee with such skills, even if they're well rewarded, it is not often that an employee's true market value is paid to them, particularly if they have been with a company for a long time.

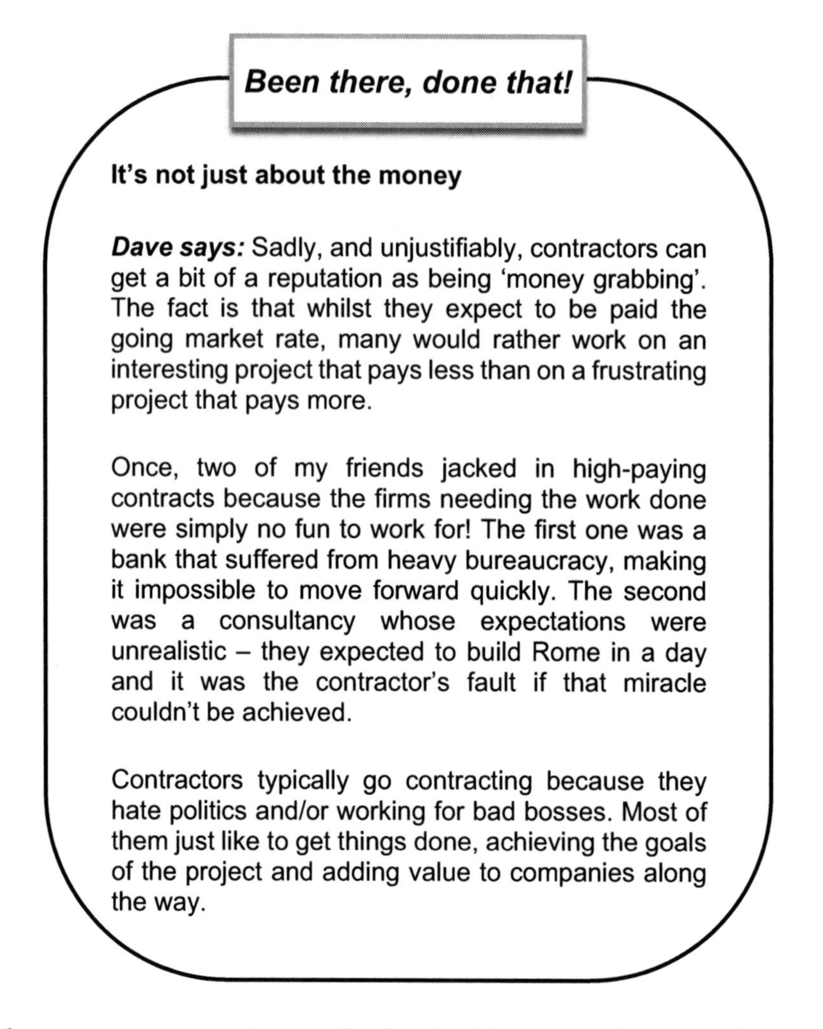

Been there, done that!

It's not just about the money

Dave says: Sadly, and unjustifiably, contractors can get a bit of a reputation as being 'money grabbing'. The fact is that whilst they expect to be paid the going market rate, many would rather work on an interesting project that pays less than on a frustrating project that pays more.

Once, two of my friends jacked in high-paying contracts because the firms needing the work done were simply no fun to work for! The first one was a bank that suffered from heavy bureaucracy, making it impossible to move forward quickly. The second was a consultancy whose expectations were unrealistic – they expected to build Rome in a day and it was the contractor's fault if that miracle couldn't be achieved.

Contractors typically go contracting because they hate politics and/or working for bad bosses. Most of them just like to get things done, achieving the goals of the project and adding value to companies along the way.

Employees are expensive and a high risk to employers. They insist on having reasonable wages, pensions and a whole raft of benefits, yet even if they become too ill to work or the work itself dries up for a while, they still have to be paid. Employers also have to pay additional National Insurance Contributions on top of everything else.

Contractors are cheap by comparison and almost always highly cost-effective to use. They are not employed by the company they are contracting for, so don't have the overheads associated with permanent employees. And if they don't work, they don't get paid, whatever the reason. So the result is that contractors get paid more for taking the risk of not being employed. And, as we'll see in later chapters, that need not be much of a risk at all.

But contractors also have a bit of a trick up their sleeves that makes the contracting option so rewarding for so many. As they are not employees, contractors can pay much less tax, meaning that more gross income finds its way into the contractor's bank account. The tax advantages are explained in greater detail in section 1.3.

Contracting can be a great way of life and, with the help of this book, you too can pick up the tips and tricks to make a real success of it.

Why do contractors choose the contracting lifestyle?

- They want to earn more
- They love the hands-on work they do and want to carry on doing it
- They have become disillusioned with permanent work
- They don't like office politics, have heard one too many false promises, and are fed up working for sometimes unappreciative management
- They don't want to move up the ladder by going into management and finding themselves doing a job they do not enjoy
- They don't want to move into a role they don't want
- After many years working really hard, obtaining their valuable skills, they would like to have more holiday than the 20-25 days a year they currently get
- They'd like to have more time to pursue other interests, hobbies and business opportunities outside of the 9 to 5, including spending more time with families and children
- They see contracting as a way of earning more money, taking more holidays, and continuing to do what they love doing.

1.2 Profile of the typical contractor

Actually, there is no such thing as a typical contractor. But there is a collection of skills, experience and attributes that makes it possible for people to choose to become a highly successful contractor.

Firstly, there are the hard skills a person must have before they consider going contracting. A successful contractor needs to have a transferable skill that has a proven market demand from clients who need this skill on a one-off basis to complete a specific project.

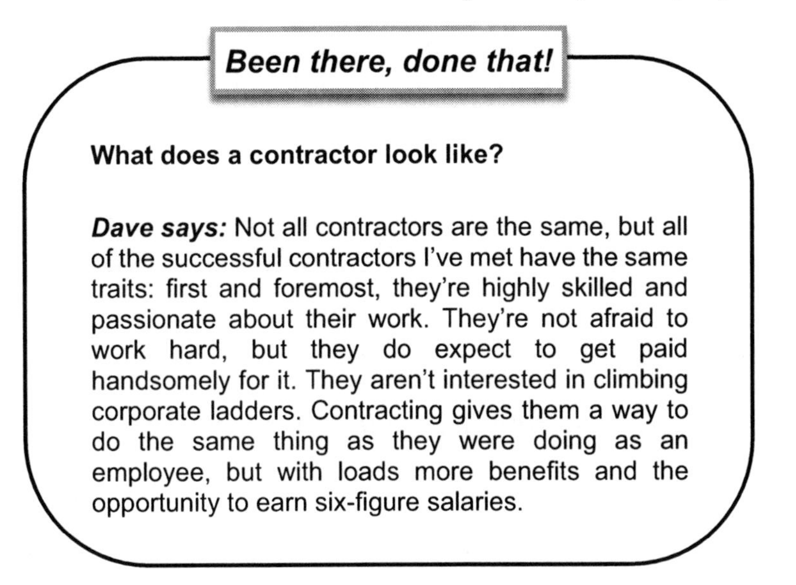

Most IT, engineering, construction and technical skills, for example, are transferable. So too are those skills, particularly in engineering, surveying, architecture and medicine, where a professional qualification is required to practice.

Although less common now, many IT professionals in the past became highly skilled at developing major organisations' legacy systems. You can be sure that this made them highly respected within their business. But their skills were not in a common computer language and thus not transferable to wider industry.

So the potential contractor's skills must also be in demand by a wide market. In other words, there must be plenty of potential clients out there who need that skill and are therefore prepared to pay well for it. A budding contractor must also have some hard business skills, although these can be developed, not least through reading books like this one.

However you go about contracting, and however you feel you dislike the thought of it, as a contractor you have to make some business choices for yourself, otherwise you might just as well remain as a permanent employee.

A grasp of marketing, sales, finance and taxation are needed to be a successful contractor, but they are remarkably easy to pick up. We'll cover all of these subjects later in the book.

Softer skills, such as managing and motivating people, also start to become more important, because as a contractor you have to:

- Act as 'account manager' to your client
- Hit the ground running when starting a new contract
- Work with employees of the client, some of whom may feel the higher wages and better conditions contractors enjoy are not deserved
- Work with other contractors, who may well become your best friends and a great source of future contracts.

Most importantly, you have to want to be a contractor. There are so many benefits to the contracting lifestyle, and sometimes hard work is required to maintain those benefits. But there are several hundred thousand people in the UK who have chosen to work as contractors and wouldn't go back to being a permie. Not all of them can be wrong!

1.3 Contracting compared to being a permanent employee

Contracting as we know it today had its roots in the IT boom of the 1980s, although it has now spread to cover virtually every sector. Back then it was typical for someone to leave work on the Friday as a salaried employee and return on the Monday as a full-blown contractor. They could be doing exactly the same job, at the same desk and for the same company, but finding themselves being paid three or more times as much as they had been the week before!

Nowadays the same happens, but the contractor should be working with a different company. That's because contracting with a former employer immediately after leaving them puts the contractor at risk of still being seen by the taxman as 'employed', with the risk of being caught by nasty tax legislation.

But there are some important differences when comparing the situations of contractors versus permanent employees, as can be seen in table 2. The contractor may get paid a larger sum, but the permanent employee enjoys a range of benefits that have a hidden cost to the employer. At a glance, table 2 does not appear to greatly favour the contractor. But in the key categories of pay, hours, holidays and tax, being a contractor can far outweigh all the other benefits combined.

Pay

Contractors get paid a gross sum, usually weekly or monthly, and by the hour or day. Day rates can be typically up to £500 per day, increasing to £1,000 per day at the top end of the market. Some very specialist roles can be even more.

	Permanent employee	Contractor
Pay	Standard market rates - much less than contractors or consultants	20-100% more than employees
Type of contract	The employer is required to supply paid work during the contract of service and the employee is obliged to accept it	The employer is not required to provide paid work; the contractor only has to do work previously agreed to
Hours	Usually fixed or limited flexibility	Flexible
Holidays	Paid, 20-30 days	Unpaid, flexible
Notice	Usually weeks	No subject to contract
Redundancy	Minimum statutory	No
Sick pay	Yes/statutory	No
Maternity	Yes/statutory	No
Pension	Yes/stakeholder	No
Private health	Potentially	No
Company car	Potentially	No
Mileage allowance	Potentially	No
Health club	Potentially	No
Staff canteen	Potentially	No
Crèche	Potentially	No
Social events	Potentially	No
Company politics	Yes	No
Promotion worries	Yes	No
Tax and expenses	PAYE, NIC, few allowances	Salary, dividends, high allowances

Table 2 Permanent employee versus Contractor

Type of contract

The difference between the types of contracts an employee has with their employer and the contract a contractor has with their client is significant:

- An employee-employer contract is a contract *of* service
- A contractor-client contract is a contract *for* services.

Basically, the contractor's contract is just the same type, one for services, as if the client were hiring, say, a grounds maintenance company.

They come in, cut the grass, get paid and move on to their next client's site. The contractor is just another service provider and, as long as the work is completed to the agreed standard, according to budget and schedule, they get paid.

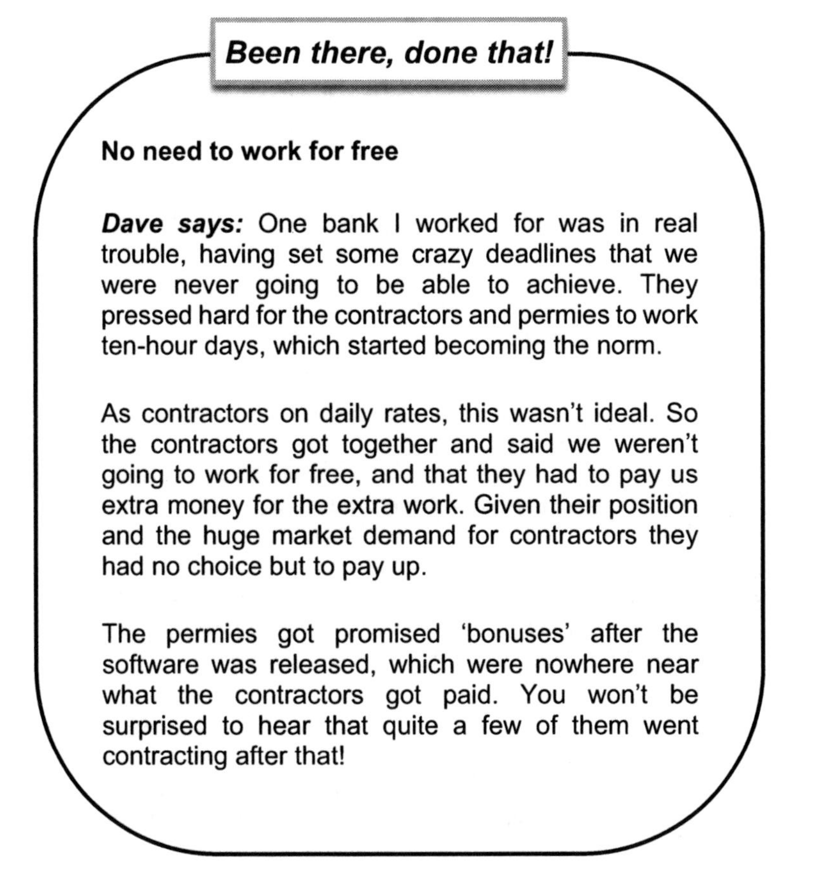

Been there, done that!

No need to work for free

Dave says: One bank I worked for was in real trouble, having set some crazy deadlines that we were never going to be able to achieve. They pressed hard for the contractors and permies to work ten-hour days, which started becoming the norm.

As contractors on daily rates, this wasn't ideal. So the contractors got together and said we weren't going to work for free, and that they had to pay us extra money for the extra work. Given their position and the huge market demand for contractors they had no choice but to pay up.

The permies got promised 'bonuses' after the software was released, which were nowhere near what the contractors got paid. You won't be surprised to hear that quite a few of them went contracting after that!

An employee, with a contract of service, on the other hand, is controlled by their employer. Most permanent employees would not consider themselves as controlled by their employer, but in practice they have signed a contract that says they will do a job, which the employer, within certain limits, can change. They also have to be present at a specific place between certain hours and for certain minimum days of the year.

Another crucial difference is that the employer has what is called a 'mutuality of obligation' with their employees, but not with their contractors. What mutuality of obligation, or as it is referred to in the contracting sector 'MOO', means is that if the employee keeps their part of the bargain and turns up to work, the employer has to find them some work to do and pay them regardless.

This often means that the permanent employees get a great deal of the less exciting and satisfying work, because contractors rightly refuse to do the work as it was not in the original agreement with the client. An employee can't do this, even if it's not in their job description, because in the real world employees do what they must to secure their next promotion or pay rise, or perhaps even to keep their job.

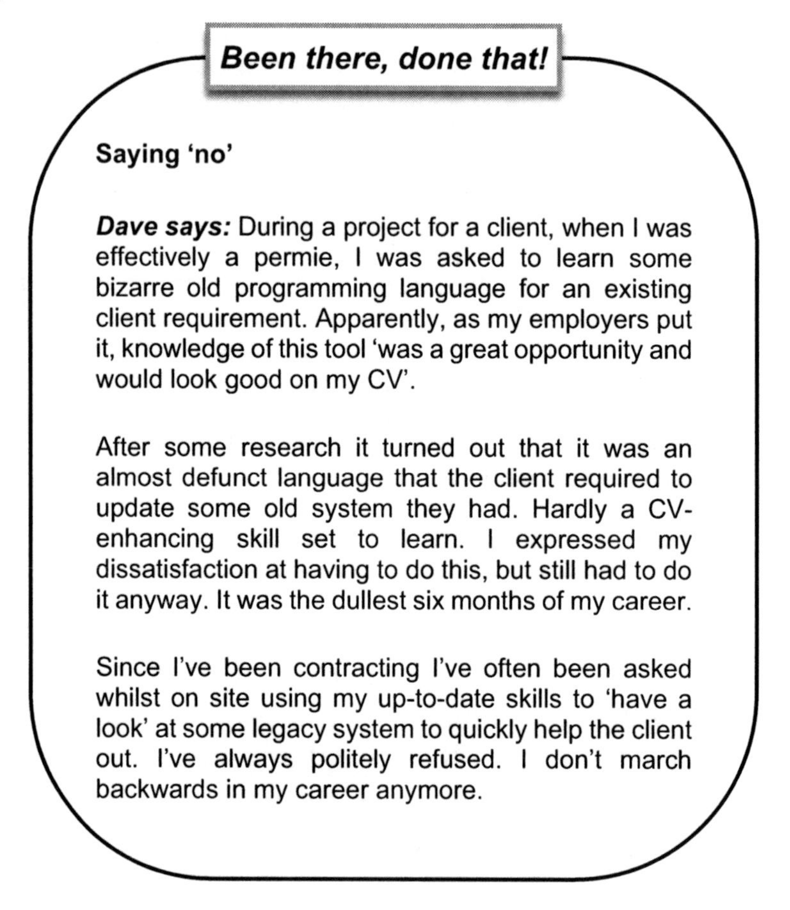

Been there, done that!

Saying 'no'

Dave says: During a project for a client, when I was effectively a permie, I was asked to learn some bizarre old programming language for an existing client requirement. Apparently, as my employers put it, knowledge of this tool 'was a great opportunity and would look good on my CV'.

After some research it turned out that it was an almost defunct language that the client required to update some old system they had. Hardly a CV-enhancing skill set to learn. I expressed my dissatisfaction at having to do this, but still had to do it anyway. It was the dullest six months of my career.

Since I've been contracting I've often been asked whilst on site using my up-to-date skills to 'have a look' at some legacy system to quickly help the client out. I've always politely refused. I don't march backwards in my career anymore.

Whilst it might seem odd to be going into these nitty gritty details so early in this book, it is necessary because these key contract points are of vital importance for establishing a contractor's tax status and therefore how much more or less tax they may be liable for.

Hours

Employees are required to work at a specific place or places for a specific number of hours on specific days. Although many employers operate some form of flexi-time, in practice, for most employees, there is little flexibility.

Contractors have no set hours, although there are reasons why contractors may be restricted to working certain hours on some contracts. If for example, key members of the client team were only present during traditional office hours, then the contractor might have to be present during some of those hours to get their work done.

Holidays

Employees, and even temporary workers, have a statutory right to holiday pay. It can vary above the statutory minimum, depending on the generosity of the employer, but is rarely more than 30 days. Contractors, on the other hand, do not get holiday pay; in practice, most simply save some of the extra money they earn as contractors to tide them over the periods they choose not to work, or may not be able to work through illness.

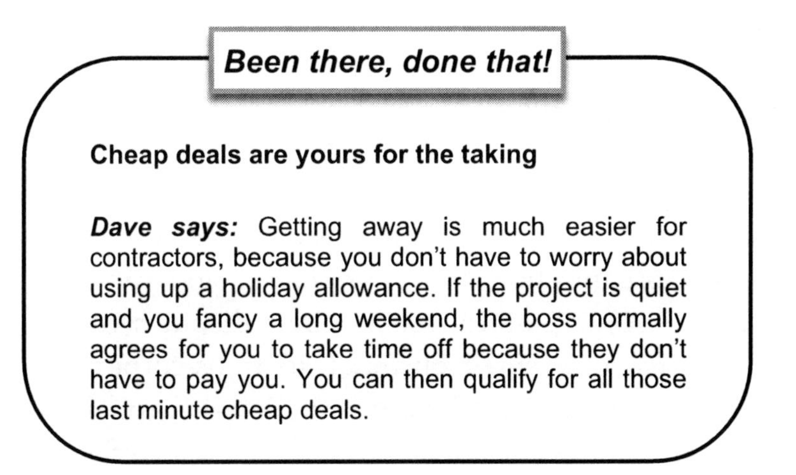

Contractors may have to plan their holidays around the requirements of clients, particularly workflows associated with the contracts on which they are working. With some planning, this is very easily done; we cover holidays for contractors in chapter 11.

Without a doubt contractors, if they choose, can take off much more time than permanent employees.

Notice and redundancy

Neither applies to contractors, although they do to employees. But many contractors would not want the loss of flexibility that comes with being an employee, and therefore entitled to notice and redundancy. Conversely, many employees feel the need to have the cushion of a redundancy payment – no matter how small – if they lose their job. The key lesson for contractors is to put by enough to survive the usually short periods between contracts.

Benefits

As they are not employed by the client, contractors receive no employee benefits. This should not matter, however, as the contractor's extra pay is more than enough to cover these benefits. It also means contractors get to choose the benefits they want, whereas many employees find themselves paying tax on benefits, such as cars and gym membership, that they don't particularly want or need.

Providing some financial cover for periods of sickness is a sensible approach, and not an expensive one, for a contractor to take, and we cover this topic in chapter 12.

Company politics

Every organisation, whether large or small, has politics. If you're a part of that organisation as an employee, you can't help being dragged into office politics. From minor disputes over the right brand of coffee in a small business, to trans-corporation battles between departmental leviathans over billions in capital investment, for most of us politics are a pain that causes untold stress inside and outside work.

Contractors, of course, do not work for the company and, except for minor things like understanding job requirements and getting timesheets signed, do not take orders from, or come under the thumb of, the company's management.

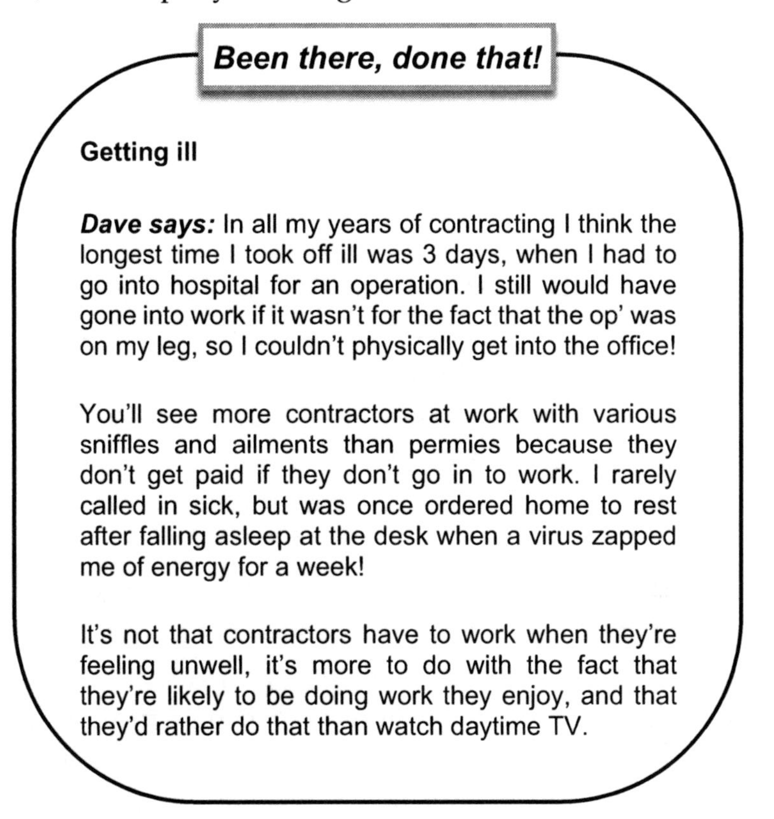

During the research for this book, company politics was one of the most common reasons cited by contractors as to why they left their full time permanent job to become a contractor.

Promotion worries

Most organisations base pay and benefits on some form of rank within their infrastructure. Promotion for most employees is often the only way to improve their lot. But there can never be more managers than workers, so promotion opportunities are generally hard-fought contests, frequently with good doses of constant pressure and unpleasantness.

Why should contractors worry about promotion if they don't work for the client? They'll be off to the next higher paying contract in a few months anyway, so there is no need at all to get involved in anyone's power play or disputes.

Contractors who want to promote themselves can simply take the opportunity to win a contract with a better rate, and buy the 'manager's perks' with the difference.

Tax

Employees generally work on the Pay as You Earn (PAYE) tax scheme with their employer arranging to pay their income tax and National Insurance Contributions at source. There are very few deductions employees can claim to reduce their tax payments, so they often face the double whammy of not only earning less than contractors, but also paying more tax than them.

One of the major advantages that most contractors enjoy is that they do not collect pay taxed at source under a Pay As You Earn, or PAYE, scheme. Contractors who opt to provide their services through a limited company can divert the income from the company in a variety of beneficial ways, such as dividends for themselves and payments into their pension funds, which employees are unable to do.

Another major advantage for contractors using their own company is that they can charge expenses against the business, which means that technically they make less profit, but as a result they also pay less tax. Plus, if they earn enough, which most do, they can register for VAT and claim VAT back on their costs.

Tax advantages

Here's a classic example of the tax advantages of buying work equipment as a contractor:

To buy £2,000 of new computer equipment would, for a higher rate tax paying contractor, only result in their net income reducing by £100 for that month. Why? Because the company has bought the equipment and claimed the VAT back. If they took the money out of the company to buy it themselves it would cost them a great deal more than £2,000!

Some contractors find themselves better suited to working through what are known as umbrella companies, which give them official 'employee' status and therefore deduct tax and National Insurance Contributions at source. Such contractors do take home less net income than they might otherwise, but there are some tax advantages with expenses, which means they're still quids in compared to permies.

Chapter 6, How to set up and run your business, takes you through your trading options in detail. It also gives example calculations showing how financially better off contractors can be compared to employees.

1.4 Common contracting myths

Not surprisingly for a sector that has grown so rapidly in such a short time, there are many myths about contracting and contractors that might discourage a permanent employee from taking the plunge. However, like most myths, they can be debunked. Here are some of the more common contracting myths:

Contractors' income is not much higher than permanent workers get
The fees earned by contractors should always be more than permanent employees earn; much more. Provided you take a professional approach to finding contracts you will avoid gaps between contracts and should, if you follow the steps in this book, make considerably more money than you could in permanent employment.

If your skill set is heavily in demand then you could at least double or even triple your current take home pay by going contracting.

Your skills will become outdated

A common fear is that after a year or so your skills will become outdated or even redundant. Some worry that without the training an employer might arrange for an employee, it will not be possible to update the contractor's skills and that contractor will then find it hard to get work. Some contractors do have this problem, but no more so than permanent employees who also don't invest time in training.

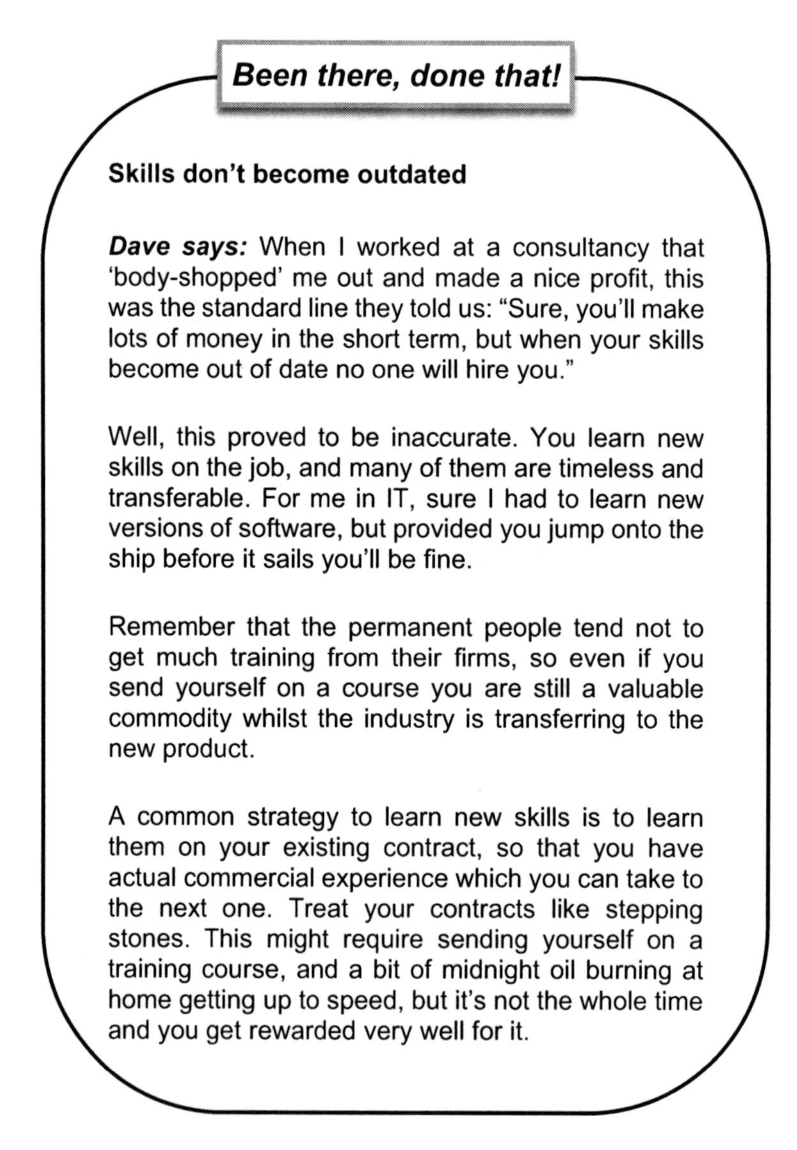

Been there, done that!

Skills don't become outdated

Dave says: When I worked at a consultancy that 'body-shopped' me out and made a nice profit, this was the standard line they told us: "Sure, you'll make lots of money in the short term, but when your skills become out of date no one will hire you."

Well, this proved to be inaccurate. You learn new skills on the job, and many of them are timeless and transferable. For me in IT, sure I had to learn new versions of software, but provided you jump onto the ship before it sails you'll be fine.

Remember that the permanent people tend not to get much training from their firms, so even if you send yourself on a course you are still a valuable commodity whilst the industry is transferring to the new product.

A common strategy to learn new skills is to learn them on your existing contract, so that you have actual commercial experience which you can take to the next one. Treat your contracts like stepping stones. This might require sending yourself on a training course, and a bit of midnight oil burning at home getting up to speed, but it's not the whole time and you get rewarded very well for it.

Contractors who work hard to keep their skills updated rarely experience problems finding work. Contractors also have the luxury of being in complete control of their professional development. They can attend as many courses as they wish, in addition to investing regularly in the latest professional books and manuals, whereas permies frequently have to beg managers for training with all sorts of restrictions and payback clauses added to their contracts in the event they leave their employer.

Plus, of course, contractors have all the benefits of having developed their skills at a number of different companies, so they often have knowledge and abilities way in advance of permanent employees who have mainly worked for one or two companies for a long time. Permanent employees who have had only one or two jobs over many years are the ones who find it hardest to make the transition to contracting. Change is very healthy, for contractors and permies alike.

You get given all the boring work to do

It is true, there are some contracts that nobody would want to do, but the simple solution is not to apply for the contract, or not to accept it when it is offered to you. Remember, contractors don't get told what to do by the manager, like permanent employees. On the contrary, contractors choose what projects they want to work on.

Should a contractor get asked during a contract to complete something that is outside the bounds of the original contractual agreement, then the contractor is not obliged to do it and, in most cases, shouldn't even think about doing it. If things become untenable (which is very rare) the contractor can simply leave, then sue the client for breach of contract, which is not as difficult or expensive as it sounds!

You do not get benefits - sick pay / holidays / health insurance / company cars

We've already covered this topic and we know that it is true. However, as their own employer, contractors can buy all the benefits they want. And, interestingly, many contractors find themselves taking fewer days off sick; not because they're working through their illness, but because they're enjoying what they do and don't tend to get the 'Monday blues'.

Health insurance is available for contractors, and can guard against long periods of time off work due to sickness. Company cars benefit employees who would not normally be able to afford such a model themselves, and therefore cost significant amounts of extra tax. But it is much cheaper for an individual to purchase and fund their own car, and most contractors very quickly amass the disposable income to buy exactly the model they want.

You cannot get a mortgage without two years worth of accounts

Contractors can get access to the same high street mortgages as permanent employees, even if they're first-time contractors. With the amount of extra money contractors are earning, they can also make overpayments and clear mortgage balances in a few years instead of paying loads of interest over twenty-five years.

In addition, when a contractor can approach a lender with a high deposit of 20-30%, they tend to get much better offers than would be available with a lower deposit.

You are liable for costly errors in your work.

It is true that contractors, as service providers, are liable for any errors they make, but so are professionals like lawyers and accountants. To mitigate this risk, most contractors simply purchase their own professional indemnity (PI) insurance, which is not expensive. Just like any other insurance, it is there to protect the contractor in case a client makes a claim against them.

It's a hassle setting up a company and doing all the accounts
A contractor can buy a new company online in less than half an hour for under £30. Most contractors work with accountants or umbrella companies that handle the vast majority of record keeping, accounting and tax return preparation.

Contractors usually only have to keep accurate invoicing, timesheet and expenses records, not much more than they would as a permanent employee. In fact, some contractors might find running their own company simpler and less painful than extracting expenses from their former employer!

The hardest part about contracting is making the decision to leave the perceived comfort and security of permanent work to go and get that first contract.

Once that decision has been made, most wonder why they didn't choose to become a contractor years before. Perhaps they were waiting for this book to be published!

2.

Markets for contracting

2.1 Why do clients like contractors?

The UK has relatively relaxed employment laws compared with most of the other European Union member states. The last few years have seen a wealth of new employment laws – some argue these empower employees; others see them as reducing the UK's flexibility and competitiveness on the world stage.

There has been a mixed impact on the lot of the contractor as a result of legislation but, on balance, contractors still compare very favourably to employees when organisations are looking for highly skilled, task-based work to be completed. That's because:

- Contractors do not have to be employed and therefore
    - Contractors are cheaper and more cost effective over time
    - Contractors are more flexible
    - Contractors are the low risk option.

In addition, contractors also bring other benefits to an organisation, such as:

- New skill sets (although contractors are not normally there to train the company's employees)
- Lessons from other organisations
- The ability to focus entirely on completing the project, without getting sucked into other areas
- Greater productivity and motivation to get the job done
- Objective viewpoints, untarnished by office politics.

Different client organisations place a different emphasis on how they use contractors compared with their employees. The contracting sector has matured since it took off in the 1980s, with contractors having proved their worth time and again. There are a lot of organisations in the marketplace that not only like using contractors, but also see it as a long-term business model, basing their future development and growth on actively encouraging the greater use of contractors throughout their businesses.

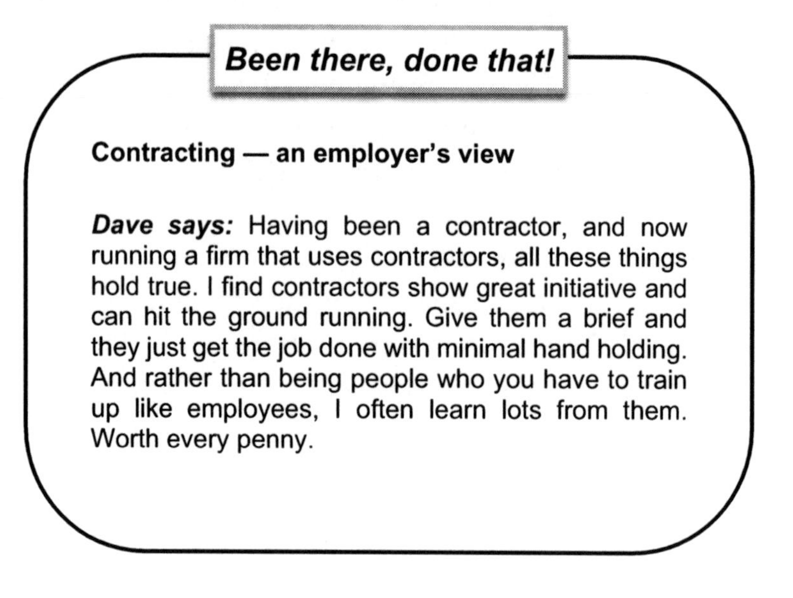

Many companies use contractors as a flexible workforce and might have a ratio of permanent employee headcount to contractors of 80/20. This allows them to shed staff when times are tough without the expense of redundancy.

However, contractors in these kinds of firms need to be careful not to take any 'random' work assigned to them by the client – which is called work 'coming down the pipe' – rather than specific projects as detailed in their contracts as this may impact adversely on their tax status.

It has been known for contractors to stay with client firms for ten or more years, earning the nickname 'permtractors'. Contractors who work like this are clearly employees and have strong cases to claim employment rights; they will also be subject to the taxation employees pay.

2.1.1 Saving money and paperwork

Organisations always have tasks that need to be completed, but which only have to be done once – so they naturally don't want to take on someone permanently to do the task. Contractors are there to complete such projects, and when the project is finished, they go on to another one at another company.

On an annual basis, working with contractors also costs less. Hiring a permanent employee costs the salary plus many hidden costs (see table 2.1). With contractors the situation is much simpler and cleaner, without the strings attached. The client can pay the contractor what will generally be more than the salary for a permanent employee, but they get a highly skilled and motivated expert who can hit the ground running.

Permanent employee	Contractor
Visible costs	Visible costs
Salary	Fee
Invisible costs	Invisible costs
Benefits	None
Employer NIC	
Risk	
HR	
Training	

Table 2.1 Total costs of employees versus contractors

From the client's perspective, if the contractor does a bad job they can be taken to court for breach of contract, or not paid, which is not the case with a permanent employee. In practice, though, the client knows their contractor will almost certainly deliver the goods, because they've brought on board an expert who has every motivation to get the job done, get it right and get it finished on time.

In some organisations, the invisible costs of employment, as shown in table 2.1, can be as high as the employee's gross salary, particularly if they are a senior employee with many benefits. Employees also attract employment risk, which we cover in the next section, and that is another key reason why clients like contractors.

Permanent employees also need to have their benefits administered, which requires a whole functional department, human resources management, or, in a smaller business, takes up the time of senior managers and directors. Canny clients recognise this as an overhead – it is not a productive, business generating, fee earning part of an organisation. Employees also expect to be trained, and not only to be trained, but also to have the course fee paid for by their employer, plus the costs of their time whilst training, plus travel, sustenance and accommodation expenses.

Is it any wonder that clients prefer contractors?

2.1.2 Flexibility

Permanent employees of the typical grade and skill levels that contractors work at are generally not very flexible. Of course it is not that most well paid, highly skilled workers and professionals won't work long hours, weekends and travel great distances. They are not flexible in the sense that they cannot be recruited very quickly, in a matter of days or weeks, and they cannot be 'divested', asked to leave the organisation, very quickly either.

Contractors can be recruited within a matter of days, complete a project over three months and then leave. No baggage and no risk, no redundancy, no golden handshakes or parachutes, and no endless negotiations over benefits. All the company gets is a series of invoices from the contractor or the agency that is acting on the contractor's behalf. Easy, simple and quick.

Employees also come with employment rights. These have certainly enormously improved the lot of most workers and labour relations in general over the years. Unfortunately, they have also removed a great deal of flexibility from the labour market; the sort of flexibility that allows companies to adapt quickly and take advantage of new opportunities.

Contractors are not employees and therefore do not have employees' employment rights. So they can start and finish specific contracts very quickly.

Why does this help? Well, it offers companies enormous flexibility. For example, when a portion of IT security needs to be rapidly overhauled at a bank, it simply calls in a squad of specialist contractors who do nothing else until the job is done. And when it's finished, they go away and the company doesn't have to worry about them anymore.

Similarly, when a nuclear power station needs a rapid and specific repair; a specialist contracting engineer comes in, identifies the fault, rectifies it and goes away. Their highly expensive skills do not need to be paid for over 52 weeks of every year, just to make sure they are on hand for the few weeks every couple of years that their skills might be needed.

The Confederation of British Industry (CBI), the employers' group that includes most major companies with a base in the UK, has completed study after study showing that the ability of contractors to provide flexibility offers savings of 30 - 40% in costs over comparable employment.

As can be seen in table 2.2, there are a significant number of financial and legal barriers to hiring and firing permanent employees. With the exception of short notice periods, contractors do not have any of the barriers that permanent employees have, which makes them particularly attractive to employers.

Permanent Employees	Contractors
Starting	Starting
Notice from previous job – months	Notice from previous job – maximum weeks
Agency fee – up to 40% gross salary	Agency fee – included in fee
Joining bonus – possible	Joining bonus - no
Joining costs – yes (new car etc)	Joining costs - no
Leaving	Leaving
Notice – several weeks to months	Notice – maximum weeks
Redundancy – usually months	Redundancy – no
Golden parachute – possibly	Golden parachute – no
Gardening leave – possibly	Gardening leave – no

Table 2.2 Hiring and firing – a comparison between employees and contractors

2.2 Contractor markets

There is a market for contractors wherever a client needs a highly skilled and flexible worker. In fact, in 2008 a thoroughly researched report estimated that there are 1.4 million contractors in the UK whose commercial activities contribute 8% of total private sector turnover.[1]

These workers tend to be IT and telecoms specialists, engineers, technicians and in the construction-related professions and trades. But the contractor net spreads much wider, too, taking in management, medicine and virtually every sector.

Not surprisingly, the 'hottest' contractor markets tend to be found in these sectors:

- IT and telecoms
- Engineering
- Construction
- Other sectors requiring highly skilled, flexible workers.

[1] Kitching J and Smallbone D. Defining and Estimating the Size of the UK Freelance Workforce Kingston University Small Business Research Centre, 2008. This report was commissioned by the Professional Contractors Group

It is not just commercial companies that use contractors: the public sector is also a major consumer of contractors' services. This includes HM Revenue & Customs, as well as the behemoths of health and defence. The latter both spend huge sums on all of the major contractor skills areas. Styles of work may differ with public sector clients, but as they are in a seller's market, where contractors are generally holding the balance of power, they have to pay market rates, just like private sector clients.

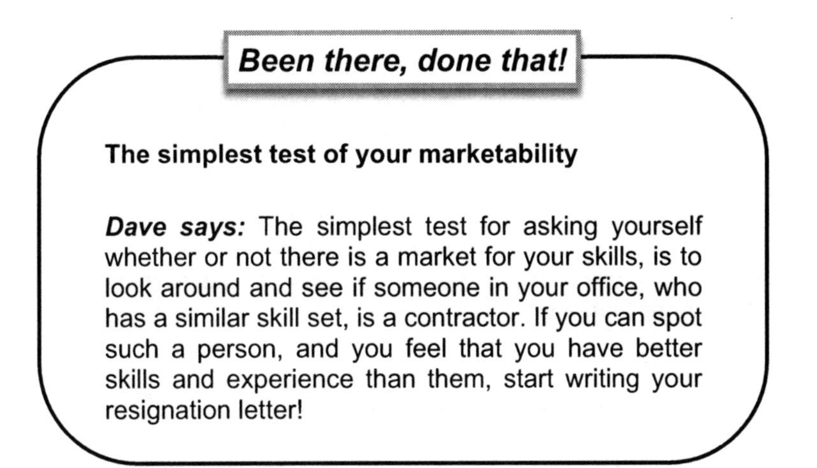

Contractor clients are looking for a specific type of worker. At one end, they do not want consultants who spend a few days a week lending advice but not generally completing major tasks on an ongoing basis for a single client. At the other end, contractor clients do not want low skilled workers, or 'agency workers' as they are often called, who can perform a wide variety of low skill roles, albeit on a flexible basis.

And that's a key point to bear in mind, because contractors are neither consultants nor temps or agency workers – they are contractors. Contractors tend to work for one client at a time on one project, then move onto another contract with a new client.

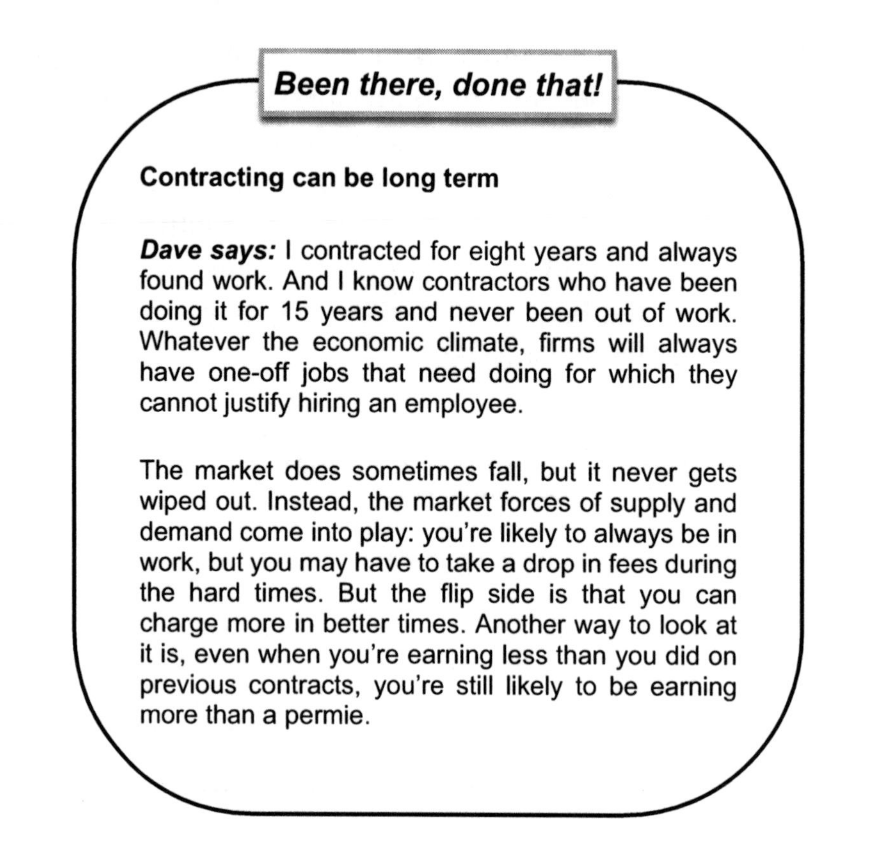

Contractors are different from consultants because they tend to work for only one client at a time, rather than many, and actually perform ongoing tasks to complete a project, rather than just offering advice.

Contractors are different from agency workers because they are highly skilled and tend to work in a particular sector, rather than moving from one lower skill occupation in one sector to another and under the direct control of the client.

Sectors like film, music and journalism are generally not considered to be contracting areas although, confusingly, many in this sector do work on a contract basis. But whilst, for example, creative professionals in the film industry work on a project basis, usually for a fee rather than being employed, these sectors are much more specialised and work to their own rules.

2.2.1 IT and telecoms

The market for IT contractors in the UK is very large for two reasons:

- There is a major shortage of skilled workers in this area
- Businesses can't neglect their IT departments, because their companies simply won't run without them!

There are simply not enough IT workers in the UK to go around. The British Computer Society (BCS) maintains a close watch on how many university students take up computing and year after year it reports that there are never enough to meet demand.

Despite the substantial rewards a career in computing offers, fewer and fewer young people choose it. There are small fluctuations, but the BCS suggests an ongoing total shortage of IT workers of around 25%. That means most of the time, UK organisations have only three quarters of the IT people they need. And, perhaps more controversially, it is also likely to mean that those with mediocre or even poor IT skills are able to find permanent employment. These companies often rely on highly skilled contractors to come in and clean up the mess after them.

There is a great deal of media coverage about offshoring to help solve this problem. But after the first great wave of interest in outsourcing to India, Eastern Europe and elsewhere, organisations rapidly discovered that a large part of the work simply cannot go abroad.

Why? Well, the offshore centres can do the rote work, but not the higher level development work. That is when managers need to work closely with IT departments and it is just not practical to do this when your IT department is abroad. We won't go into a detailed look at how offshoring works, but most of the experts agree that it will not have a major impact on IT contracting in the UK. The proof is in the pudding, and the pudding is the resiliency of the UK contracting sector for IT professionals.

Much of the demand for IT and telecoms contractors in the UK comes from one square mile: The City. Financial services in London account for a substantial proportion of IT and telecoms contracts in the country. Work in banking and insurance is tremendously demanding and not all contractors can take the pressure, but the rewards are considerable.

After financial services, service companies of all types engage the largest groups of IT contractors. Companies that offer extended marketing and delivery tend to need great IT support to help them keep costs down.

In the high-tech sector, demand tends to remain high no matter what the wider economic picture is. And demand tends to remain steady for contractors in manufacturing business in the UK, which is still the fifth largest manufacturer in the world.

2.2.2 Engineering

Engineering contractors can be as diverse as the disciplines within engineering. The very nature of many engineering projects is that they are just that – projects, with a beginning, a middle and an end. And that is ideal for engineers who want to work on a flexible basis.

In fact, if it was not for contracting engineers, who, many would argue, have been around a lot longer than IT contractors, very little engineering would actually get done. There is an ongoing, desperate shortage of engineers worldwide, not just in the UK. There are, therefore, many overseas contract opportunities for engineering contractors who want to spread their wings and explore the world.

Although all engineers tend to be in demand all of the time, there are peaks and troughs of availability, according to the types of infrastructure projects ongoing at any one time, and their geographical spread.

There is no overarching trade association for engineering contractors. They are split into groups like the British Chemical Engineering Contractors Association and the Civil Engineering Contractors Association. It is therefore difficult to obtain accurate statistics about how many engineering contractors there are in the country.

Unlike many IT contractors, nearly all engineers require a professional qualification in order to practice. There are levels within these; for example an incorporated engineer does not have quite the same professional status as a chartered engineer, regardless of how well they do the job. Pay rates tend to reflect this.

2.2.3 Construction

Contractors in construction have, in many respects, separate rules to other areas of contracting, and there are also special conditions that apply to the industry. Legislation is often specific to the sector, and there is even a special court for construction issues.

The construction sector experiences periods of great demand and periods of relative stagnation, with opportunities for contractors following these trends.

Where there is any kind of demand for construction, there are also contractors – whether it's for building railways, schools, office blocks or retail units. The industry completely depends on small companies and even single workers who are available whenever they are needed.

The recent increase in demand for projects, at the time of writing driven by mega-projects like the London 2012 Olympics, has proven a boon to contractors in construction. But it is a sector that is particularly sensitive to the economy. In fact, the sector is notorious for shedding tens of thousands of workers when times are bad, although when things pick up there are generally skills shortages and fantastic opportunities for contractors. Feast or famine!

At the time of writing, the use of workers from elsewhere in Europe has attracted much media attention. However the huge increase in workers from other EU, mainly Eastern European nations, coupled with the constant demand for labour, demonstrates how much need for construction contractors there is. There is no evidence that these migrants are replacing indigenous labour, only that there is room for all.

2.2.4 Other highly skilled flexible workers

There are other types of contractor in the marketplace who work for periods of time on a contract for a single client on a flexible basis. These tend to be in smaller numbers than the sectors mentioned previously. They typically include:

- Professionals, like accountants and solicitors
- Paralegals
- Interim executives
- Marketing and sales professionals
- Medical personnel.

Although from a diverse range of sectors, all these types of contractors do share the same profile: they are highly skilled at what they do and prefer to work on a flexible basis, earning more than their permanent contemporaries and making the most of the flexibility the lifestyle affords. In other words, they are typical contractors!

2.3 Contractor earnings

When it comes to gross earnings and take home pay, contractors have a number of advantages over their permanent employee equivalents:

- Payment is gross, pre-tax and much higher
- Contractors can factor in business expenses and items like pensions
- Contractors can use various perfectly legal techniques to become more tax efficient, i.e. paying less tax and having more cash in their pocket.

You should consider how much more of the money earned will come to you through tax efficiency, rather than being taken in deductions like income tax and National Insurance Contributions.

2.3.1 Rates

As a general rule, the rates a contractor can expect to command are significantly higher than those of a permanent employee in an equivalent role. Almost certainly, the extra percentage they're earning should be in double digits.

Rates range from £15 per hour for more junior roles up to £125 per hour and even higher for technical consultants with years of in-depth experience in a particular specialism or product. Experienced project managers get around £75 per hour.

But again, those rates are purely indicative and, by the time you read this, will be out of date. No matter what your skill, if a client needs you urgently, or others in your field are busy on a major project elsewhere, you could find the rates you are offered rising sharply.

Hourly and daily rates fluctuate across sectors and in each area rates can vary depending on level of experience and the current market demand for that skill.

Like most jobs, the general rule is that if your skills took a long time to master and are in short supply, then you will command more money than someone who acquired their skills relatively easily and in a much shorter space of time.

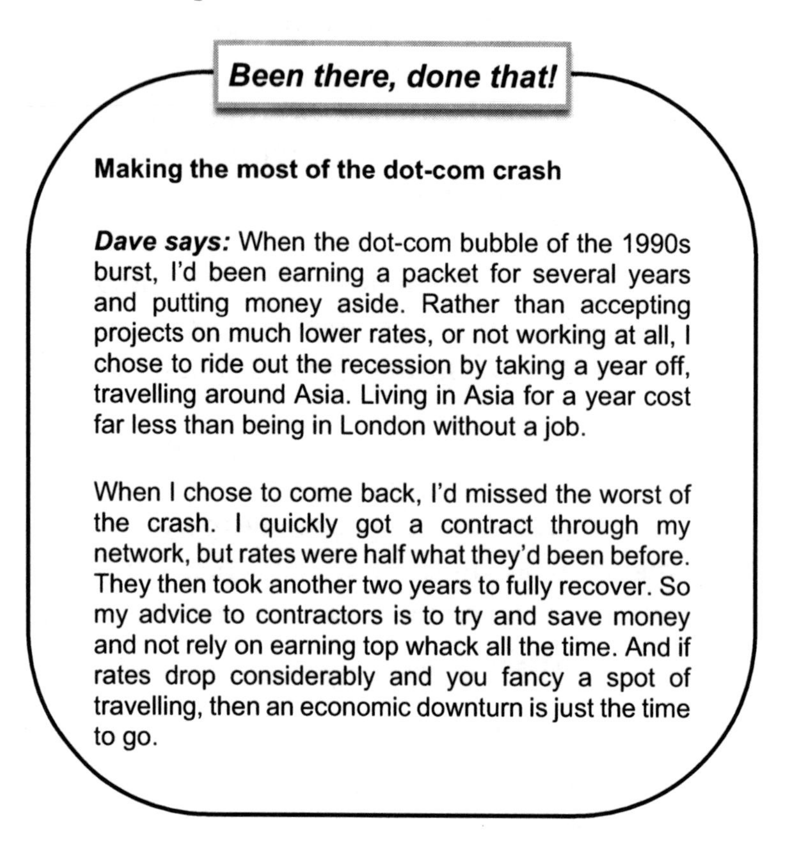

Been there, done that!

Making the most of the dot-com crash

Dave says: When the dot-com bubble of the 1990s burst, I'd been earning a packet for several years and putting money aside. Rather than accepting projects on much lower rates, or not working at all, I chose to ride out the recession by taking a year off, travelling around Asia. Living in Asia for a year cost far less than being in London without a job.

When I chose to come back, I'd missed the worst of the crash. I quickly got a contract through my network, but rates were half what they'd been before. They then took another two years to fully recover. So my advice to contractors is to try and save money and not rely on earning top whack all the time. And if rates drop considerably and you fancy a spot of travelling, then an economic downturn is just the time to go.

2.3.2 Tax efficiency

Everything changes when you become a contractor and bill your client using your own limited company. In chapter 1, we explained that employees pay income tax and National Insurance Contributions (NICs), which are taken out of their salary, usually monthly, by their employer.

Contractors working through a limited company don't work this way. Tax does get paid, but in significantly reduced amounts. This is what is known as tax efficiency. Do not mistake tax efficiency, which is a perfectly legal practice of mitigating tax liabilities (or reducing your tax bill) with tax evasion, which is illegal and involves defrauding HMRC, the government and your fellow citizens who pay tax legally. Tax evasion can, in the worst case scenario, land you in prison, and at the very least is likely to wipe you out financially when you get caught.

There are alternatives to using a limited company, particularly if you have a contract that is judged by the taxman to be inside the IR35 legislation, which is covered extensively in chapter 8. One alternative is to trade through an umbrella company, which, although not as tax efficient as working through a limited company, for those contractors working inside IR35 it can still be more tax efficient than permanent employment.

There are a number of ways contractors can pay themselves and a wide range of tax payment timings. Generally, instead of being paid a monthly salary that gets taxed at source, contractors pay tax after their end of financial year accounts have been completed and tax returns filled in. After the first year of contracting they are required to make an interim payment on account once the taxman can estimate how much tax you should pay each year.

After calculating the profits in their limited company, and setting aside the money for corporation tax, contractors will then typically pay themselves:

- A small salary that attracts either no or very little income tax and little or no employee's NICs
- Dividends, which often form the bulk of a contractor's earnings; these can only be paid out of profits, and although they attract income tax, there are no NICs to pay.

In addition, whilst expenses do not form a part of a contractor's income, contractors are often better off because they are allowed to claim certain travel, subsistence and other expenses that permanent employees cannot. Plus, these are deducted before tax is calculated, helping reduce contractors' tax bills.

All of this amounts to considerably more than contractors would have been paid if their gross earnings were paid as a salary and taxed at source.

Permie salary	£50,000
Cost to employer	£55,701
Employers NI	£5,701
Employees NI	£3,902
PAYE	£10,386
Net income	£35,711
Net income % of cost to employer	64%

Contractor revenue	£55,701
Salary	£6,500
Employers NI	£133
Employees NI	£114
PAYE	£93
Corporation tax	£10,304
Distributable profit	£38,764
Further tax on divs	£1,965
Contractor takes home	£43,090
Net income % of revenue	77%

For the same monetary cost to the employer of £55,701, the contractor takes home over £7,000 more per year.

But beware…
Don't skip chapter 8 about IR35, which we mentioned earlier; it might sound dull, but it is important to get your head around IR35, because understanding it is the best way to ensure your take home pay is as high as it possibly can be.

2.4 Contractor skills

A contractor has to have something specific to sell. In the job market, that something is a skill or set of skills. The skill could be highly specialised and technical, like thin film section analysis or finite element modelling; or it could be a management skill, like project or programme management, which has to combine a detailed knowledge of the technical with knowing how people and projects tick.

So, to become a contractor you have to have a skill to start with. However, as later chapters in the book will reveal, it is not just possible, but in many cases easy and worthwhile, to develop your skills and make yourself even more of a hot property than you already are!

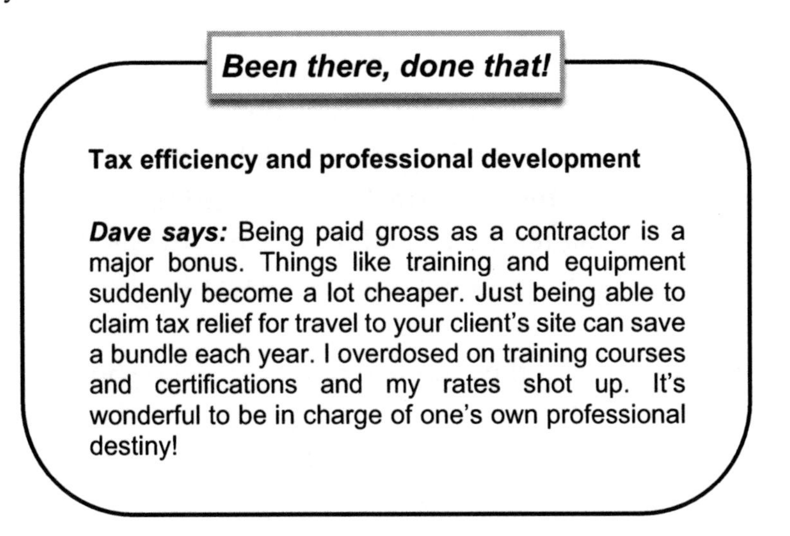

The Trick to Hot IT Skills – insights from an IT contractor

The shifts of demand in IT contracting depend less on economics and more on the specific skills required. Some skills areas, like SAP, for example, are really hot and seem to stay that way.

Others, like the entire web development area, have seen a massive increase in rates of pay and demand. These have been driven by new areas like Web 2.0 and social networking, and, without doubt, new areas in web development will constantly occur.

The trick to keeping on top of the job is to make sure that you have at least a handle on the hottest skills. This can be challenging as a contractor, when you don't really get as much training support as you might if you worked in a permanent role. So you need to use downtime on the job to study and stay at the cutting edge, or to find other ways to keep from slipping back.

But the real point to remember in all this is that businesses need IT contractors, regardless of economic conditions. So contractors don't really have to worry about shrinking IT departments. Indeed, when they shrink, the companies call in contractors to fill in the gaps.

To give another example in the IT sector, during the booming dot-com era between 1995 and 2001, everyone who could became a contractor, even those with poor IT skills or only one year's experience. Many of these contractors were getting paid £100,000 a year and it didn't matter if they had two heads, dressed like a tramp, and hadn't washed for a month – someone would hire them.

As reality dawned and the bubble burst, those who should not have entered the contracting market in the first place were soon forced back into permanent employment. As a general rule, those with the top skills continued to get work.

However some did not and an interesting observation and powerful lesson was that those who continued to find contracts were not always the ones who were most suited to the roles, but the ones who were better at securing contracts – which means better at marketing themselves. Self promotion and sales are covered in greater detail in chapters 5 and 10.

2.5 The future of contracting

One thing is quite clear: most of the contracting industry is not cyclical. With the exception of many but not all parts of construction, there are no real boom and bust times for contractors in the UK.

Certainly there have been periods of unbelievably intense demand, like during the dot-com boom. But, so far, we haven't really seen periods of very low demand. There are a few good reasons for this.

2.5.1 The UK economy and contractors

Whether business is booming or slack in the UK, businesses need to make their IT departments work, utilities need engineers to keep supplying essentials and machines still have to be kept running. Our public services will not be allowed to shut down and the international financial markets keep dealing, no matter how rosy or ropey the economy is looking.

There is, at all times, a shortage of skilled high-technology workers and engineers in the UK. Each year the media mourns the shrinking graduate intake figures in subjects considered to be 'difficult': engineering, IT, physics, mathematics, etc.

As highlighted earlier in the chapter, IT and engineering workers are in desperately short supply and the situation is not improving. Yet both the private and public sectors are increasingly dependent on IT and engineering for their critical infrastructure.

So the inexorable laws of supply and demand will kick in and contractors who can work flexibly to fill gaps at short notice and patch up what may start to become an increasingly leaky machine will find themselves in high demand. Probably very high demand.

The caveat, and to an extent paradox, to the supply and demand equation is that in major economic downturns the demand for engineers and IT contractors tends to be at the very least maintained, but perversely rates can drop; in some cases dramatically.

2.5.2 Insulated from trends

Contractors have, for the most part, been insulated from economic trends. The Association of Professional Staffing Companies

(APSCo), formerly known as the Association of Technology Staffing companies, which keeps track of contractor demand through its membership, shows no significant decline from 1985 to 2008.

Another reason for this continued demand is simply that businesses have to stay competitive and high-technology is an ever-increasing component of that competitive edge.

There was a time, until very recently, when you still met executives who didn't know how to log on or needed their PAs to print out their emails for them, but that time has gone. Nowadays, IT and technology experts sit on the board alongside the finance and sales directors, and they play an integral, often central, part in developing corporate strategies.

There are parallels in the engineering sector. The shortage of engineers in the UK is so acute that non-EU engineers are allowed to come and work in the UK with significantly fewer barriers than most other job roles.

But what about the companies that engage the services of contractors? Contractor clients do experience the peaks and troughs of business alongside the economic cycles. The market demand in those times suggests that contractors are needed as much during economic downturns as during prosperous years. Sometimes more.

So, why is this? Because companies have to stay competitive, and if investment in key areas falls, then, in most sectors, so does business. There is one other piece of business logic worth noting. When times are bad, companies downsize employees. But they still need the jobs done, so contractors get called in to do them.

2.5.3 How will contracting evolve?

In the short term, allowing for fluctuations in the economic cycle, it is likely that little will change, although the construction sector is always more sensitive to economic downturns. However, a number of global macro-economic and socio-economic factors suggest that the number of contractors is likely to increase, and not just in the UK, but worldwide too.

The Geneva-based International Labour Organisation (ILO) confirms this, having on numerous occasions reported that there is far less need for highly specialised employees and a much greater need worldwide for highly skilled contractors who can adapt to industry and cyclical changes. The ILO predicts that within the next decade the percentage of contractors in the workforce will rise to nearly half, from the current estimate of 15%.

Not everyone believes in this trend, and noises coming from the UK Government and European Commission would not support this view, as the labour market within many European countries becomes ever more closed. But the likelihood is that global market forces will pull the contracting market in the direction that is needed. After all, the clients, many of them global trans-nationals, will still need flexible highly skilled workers like contractors.

So there is little doubt that contracting will grow, but at a pace dictated by the marketplace.

3.

Making the transition

3.1 Preparation – an introduction

When you're ready to make the move from being a permanent employee (or 'permie') to becoming a contractor there are a number of steps that could give you a flying start. The process recommended here is tried and tested – it has worked again and again, been refined over years and led to many successful careers in contracting.

Parts of the process will also tell you if you're ready for contracting. For example, if you can't make the numbers add up at the start, maybe now is not the right time to move into contracting. Perhaps you need to spend a couple of months saving some more cash to ensure the transition goes smoothly, so that you have a financial safety net in place in case things don't go exactly to plan.

This chapter is just an overview of some of the key topics. We include creating a curriculum vitae here because it is an important part of the transition process, but it is also such an important part of successful contracting that we dedicate the whole of chapter 4 to the subject.

Similarly we touch here on the tax issue of IR35; but, as it is so fundamental to anyone considering becoming a contractor, it is also covered more comprehensively in chapter 8.

3.1.1 Market research

The first thing that any prospective contractor should do is to get online and visit the job boards that cover their target industry. Professional market researchers use the phrase 'desk research', although most of us think of it as surfing the net!

Job boards have really become *the* place to find new work. The chances are you're probably already very familiar with them – maybe you won your last permanent job through one.

Browsing the job boards will give you a sense of what's out there and how you fit in. Are your skills marketable? Do you see lots of demand for people who do what you do? Answer a few of the ads on the job boards and see how quickly it takes for you to get a response. Don't be discouraged if you aren't getting calls; just continue looking and, instead of just searching for your specific area of expertise, try looking for something similar to what you do. This is all about testing how marketable your skills are.

Of course you need to create a CV, which is your primary 'sales tool', and post it on the relevant job boards. You should also upload it to any online databases that your market research has shown are used by agencies who have the types of contracts and clients you want.

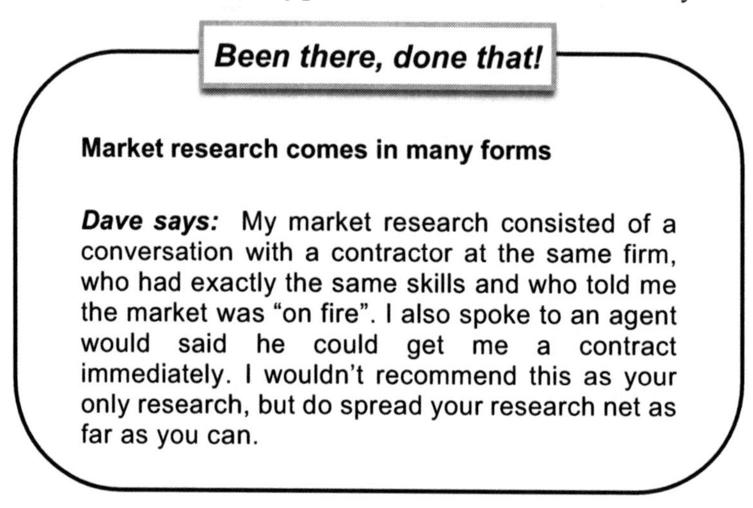

One word of warning – because you're looking for a job and you're a first timer you'll get lots of agents 'phishing' by calling you on the premise that they have a position you might be interested in. The truth is they probably haven't, and are just trying to find out who your last boss was and the name of key people in other companies where you've worked.

Recruitment advertisers are increasingly using social networking sites as a source of jobs, including contracts. Check out all the most popular sites and join relevant forums – you may get feedback from other site members, although take care not to place too much trust in unsubstantiated claims.

Advice you get from forums

It pays to be very careful about the advice you take, particularly legal advice. Forums are notorious hangouts for people who want to have a view on everything regardless of whether or not they are experts. Taking advice from someone who isn't an expert could land you in lots of trouble.

Particularly in legal and accounting areas lots of people have opinions about how they think things should work, often based on their own moral principles and their views of 'fairness', but typically their opinions don't actually align with the law.

Golden rule: Make sure you get expert advice from qualified people.

The other major source of information about jobs and your sector is the trade media. Most sectors have a huge range of niche websites and trade magazines. Plus many professions and disciplines have their own professional bodies, producing their own media, which can sometimes be the best source of market data.

There are also a number of sites dedicated to contracting professionals. Whilst these vary considerably in the quality of information available, there are some that are likely to become essential to your contracting. Probably the best place to start is the independent site run by this book's publisher, www.ContractorCalculator.co.uk, which produces a monthly market report on the current state of the UK contracting sector.

3.1.2 Setting rates

The next stage in the transition to contracting process is to establish rates for your skills, so you have a starting point for negotiations with a client or agency. Again, browsing the job boards, and the internet generally, will help you research rates, which is the next stage in the transition process.

For first-time contractors it is hard to know what rate to quote for your skills. Many first-timers are nervous about asking what they're worth, because their new rates seem so high when compared to previous permanent roles. But all successful contractors learn to better understand their value in the marketplace as their contracting career builds. The following, in addition to the research you have done, will help you get it right.

Getting Started: The Minimum Rate

Remember that contracting pays more than permanent employment, because you generally not only get a higher gross income, but will also benefit from lower tax payments. You can determine a minimum starting point for your contracting rate based on what you get paid as a permanent employee, by using ContractorCalculator's free web-based services.

To do this, start with your permanent salary and add in your benefits, such as healthcare and pension contributions, until you get to a 'total package' figure. Put that figure into ContractorCalculator's **Permanent to Contracting Calculator** to determine your minimum starting rate. The calculator can be found at:

http://www.contractorcalculator.co.uk/PermanentToContractingCalculator.aspx

For example, if you type in a total package of £50,000, the results show that you need a minimum rate of £28 per hour outside IR35, or £39 per hour inside IR35 (IR35 is explained briefly later in this chapter and then in more detail in chapter 8).

Table 3.1 shows some basic comparisons between what hourly rate would be required to match annual gross salary and benefits.

Salary	Hourly rate		Daily rate	
	Outside	Inside IR35	Outside	Inside IR35
£25,000	£15	£19	£118	£149
30,000	£18	£24	£139	£175
£35,000	£21	£27	£156	£202
£40,000	£23	£30	£177	£230
£45,000	£26	£34	£196	£254
£50,000	£28	£39	£213	£289
£75,000	£44	£56	£338	£427
£100,000	£60	£76	£437	£553
£125,000	£75	£93	£565	£707
£150,000	£89	£111	£670	£837
£175,000	£108	£134	£775	£968
£200,000	£123	£152	£925	£1,145
£250,000	£152	£188	£1,145	£1,417

Table 3.1 Minimum hourly and daily rates

Although you need to be aware of your likely IR35 status within a contract, it is not the basis for negotiation. You state your daily, or hourly, rate and talk about IR35 issues later. The inside IR35 rate is ideally the minimum rate to accept, for your desired annual salary.

Minimum rate is the operative word, because for example most contractors earning £75k per year are senior enough to command rates of £500 per day, and these are generally rounded-up during negotiations to the nearest £25. Hourly rates tend to be rounded-up to the nearest £5. Over £35 per hour and you will generally be working on days rates anyway.

Search the internet

During your market research, you should have found some sites that offer useful survey results stating what rates certain skills can command in the current market.

While these figures provide some good overall guidelines they can be a little limited, since they do not take into account combinations of skills, the level of experience, and market sectors. Use your current salary as the baseline for the rate you should expect and ask your colleagues.

The other thing to accept is that on a few occasions you may discover that the agent has been less than fair with the rate they are paying you out of the gross fee from the client. Don't take this personally – agents are there to make money and you must ensure you negotiate at the next contract renewal or new contract.

Ask Other Contractors

'Human intelligence' is generally the best source of information. Make sure you talk to as many colleagues and friends as you can, although be careful to manage relationships in the workplace of your current permanent employer.

Existing contractors and permanent employees who have worked with contractors will know the work and will understand the value of specific skills. Simply ask an experienced contractor you know or work with who has similar skills and experience to your own.

Been there, done that!

Better than you

Dave says: Dave says: Some contractors worry about whether they are good enough to be contractors, assuming all contractors to be experts. Contractors don't have to be experts, but they can't be rubbish. Requirements are driven by the flexible needs of the market, not by the need for experts.

I was working on a client site for a consultancy who took half my fees, and sitting two desks down from a contractor who used the same skill set as me. After weeks of working with him and teaching him how to use the advanced aspects of the product, I figured that if he was a contractor then I could be too!

It is highly unlikely, although not impossible, that you will be able to charge the same amount as the contractors you talk to. Their experience and skill sets will differ from your own. You should establish a range by talking to a few contractors, and then try it out in negotiations.

Establish a minimum, for example £400 per day and a maximum like £500 per day. Aim for £450, and the £25 less or more is likely to be the agent trying to increase their margin rather than the client's limit.

Different Markets – Different Rates

Some markets can pay more than others, although you can never be certain that this is the case. There may be regional variations or timing factors that can skew rates both up and down.

In IT contracting, banking is generally known to pay higher rates. But in the same way that not all bankers earn those eye-watering City salaries we hear about, your particular part of the banking market may differ too.

Talking to friends and colleagues who do very similar work to your own is a good method of benchmarking variations.

What Kind of Rate: Hourly Rate or Daily Rate?
Varying types of contracts with different types of clients tend to use different pay periods. In anticipation of talking to potential clients and agencies that might have all types of expectations, you need to have a rate proposal prepared for each scenario. Rates tend to be on an hourly or daily basis. Payment is weekly or monthly.

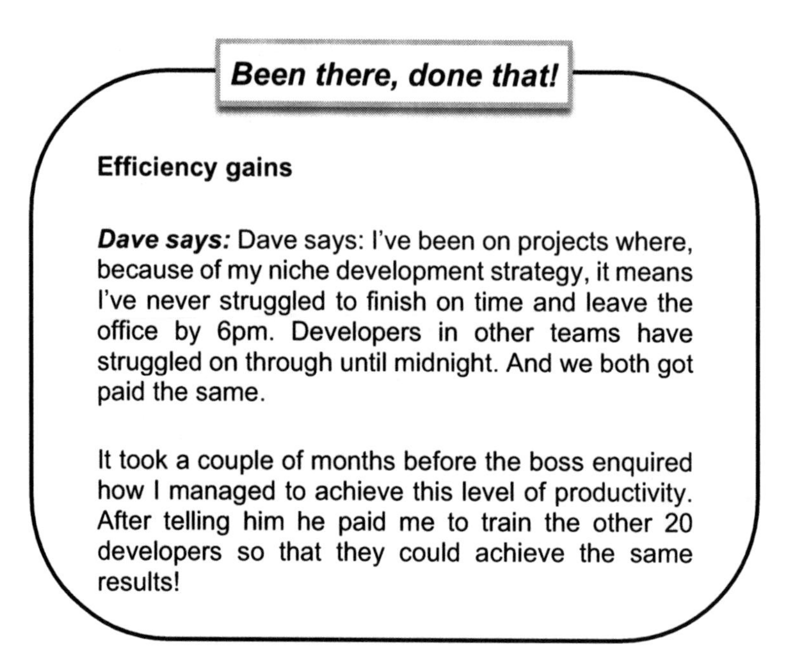

The Hourly Rate - You are paid for the number of hours you work. This type of rate is more common than the daily rate and is normally for rates below £40 an hour.

The hourly rate can be better than the daily rate. Both the client and the contractor know exactly where they stand. Clients may cap weekly hours accumulated to avoid problems, but may demand more hours at busy times.

The Daily Rate - You are paid for the number of days you work. This type of rate tends to be favoured by clients in the finance sector and is more commonly offered to those earning rates of about £400+ per day.

Many clients like the 'day rate' because they can keep tighter control of budgets. They might occasionally ask you to work late to hit a deadline without adding the extra hours they would if you were on an hourly rate. But typically you would get the hours back another day when work was not so busy and you could leave the office early.

Most contractors should be prepared to put in the occasional long day or week to get something finished, provided it is not being demanded all the time. However, the willingness of professional contractors to do this does sometimes get abused by clients and we cover this issue in chapter 9.

Weekly, monthly and calendar month periods tend to be negotiated as a package, with a contract schedule detailing hours per week, and days of the month to be worked.

3.1.3 Crunch the numbers

This is the stage of the transition process when you find out whether you are kidding yourself about wanting to become a contractor. The key question is: can I afford to go contracting?

It is always best to err on the side of caution. So work on the assumption that it might take between two and four months for you to win your first contract. This might seem like a long time, but when you are up and running as a contractor, all your fellow contractors will tell you to build up a fund of six month's living expenses to cope with the unexpected. And of course because you are earning twice as much, saving six months money will only take you, six months!

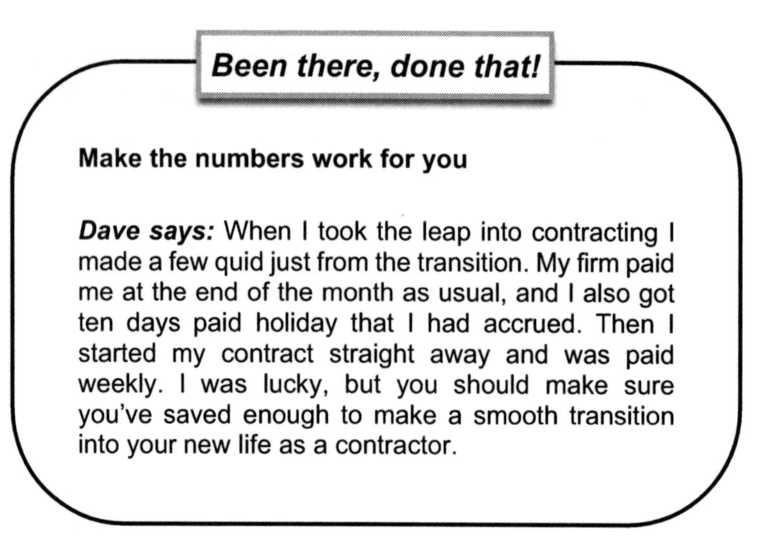

If you work in a high demand sector, you could find a role within days or weeks. Ideally, you should always start working on finding a contract in the final weeks of your permanent job or current contract.

Calculate your monthly outgoings and be honest with yourself, making allowances for the luxuries you enjoy over and above the basics like housing costs, utilities, food, clothing, transport costs and so on.

Set aside a budget to pay for professional advice from accountants, at around £100 per month, and solicitors. This may be needed for things like contract reviews at a maximum of £200 per review, accounting advice and starting up a company. Add to this some costs for travel and subsistence, including for hotel accommodation, as you may have to travel for interviews.

Work out much cash you have in the bank and do the calculation – if you left your permanent employment tomorrow, could you exist for long enough to secure your first contract? Take into account any holiday not taken that the firm will also have to pay you when you leave.

If not, would three to six more months's saving make the difference? If so, consider deferring the transition to contracting while you save up the cash you'll need to be able to make the switch comfortably, with minimum risk.

Also, bear in mind the timings of payments. You might finish work and get a month's money, and when you get a contract you could get paid weekly. This will certainly help the cash flow. But it might not always go so smoothly and having savings can help tide you over.

If you are paid monthly on your first contract, remember you'll have to work the thirty days and then invoice. Most agents pay within five days of the invoice, and they shouldn't drag it out thirty days.

3.1.4 Timing the transition

Each element of the contracting market, whether it's IT, engineering, construction or something else, has its own cycles you need to become aware of. It also has two annual cycles, driven by the financial year and holiday seasons.

January to February – after the Christmas holidays, clients are spurred into action. New budgets are approved and hiring starts. This is the equivalent of *spring*.

March to April – this is the equivalent of *summer*. Arguably the best time to look for a new contract.

May to June – As the summer holidays approach, this is the equivalent of the *autumn*. If you can secure a three-month contract in March, you'll be in a strong negotiating position in June.

July to August – Holidays break the rhythm of the market, and hiring becomes a low priority. If you're not in a contract by the end of June, you may end up unemployed until September – contractor's *winter*.

September – *spring* again! After the summer holidays, children return to school, decision makers are back at their desks and the human resources department awakens from its slumber.

October to November – another contractor *summer* brings better paid contracts. This is a good time for contractors to be monitoring job boards and calling contacts looking for contract opportunities.

December – *autumn* and *winter* come around quickly. Many projects are scheduled to deliver in the week before Christmas, which means that this is the perfect time to renegotiate. By 24th December, the market goes dead until the New Year.

The key is to ensure you don't finish a contract in November or December and June to August as you could find yourself out of work. By juggling initial contract periods and renewal timings, you can ensure your contracts do not end during those months.

In addition, shorter renewal periods mean greater opportunity to renegotiate and the right to add renewals to your CV, the importance of which is covered later in this book.

3.1.5 Handing in notice

If you're still working in a permanent job, it's time to hand in your notice. Hopefully your employment contract does not require you to wait out an excessively long notice period before you can move on to something else.

Legally, there is almost nothing you can do to challenge a long notice period. You do not want to breach your contract by violating the notice period terms, especially as your employer could hold you responsible for any losses incurred because of your early departure. So, when handing in your notice, you may find yourself in one of two situations:

A good relationship with your employer

If you're in this happy position, you are likely to be able to constructively negotiate an earlier departure date. The employer may be willing to do this for several reasons.

Some employers who are good managers will not want personnel who are leaving working on their projects. Management experts say that this employee is the most liable to be careless, and not likely to be motivated to provide their best work. In addition, departing employees can be security risks. Your employer may be sorry to see you go, but may wish to see you leave without delay.

It may also be possible to offer your employer a deal involving remuneration or benefits that will allow you to depart early. Knowing that you are about to depart, employers may be happy to save a little money on your pay and benefits, as they will no longer have their intended effect of motivating you to work.

A poor relationship with your employer

If you find yourself in this situation, there may be other possibilities for leaving your job early.

An employer who does not like you may, of course, be glad to see you leave. In this case make sure that all the formal details involving your termination have been checked and respected, so that the firm can never come back to you with demands or liabilities in respect of your early departure.

Sadly, but quite often, your unfriendly employer wants to keep you, because replacing you is a nuisance, even though the employer has made it clear that you are not liked. In this case, ask yourself if there is any way in which your employer has not respected the terms of your contract?

Have all of your holiday benefits been paid? Have the conditions in terms of the workplace been respected? Is there any area in which the employer has been remiss? If so, you could claim breach of contract and terminate the contract immediately. You could even sue for constructive dismissal if the breach is a serious one.

Unfortunately, this happens much more often than one might expect. It is wise to take professional advice if you choose to pursue the breach of contract route, for, as we highlighted earlier, leaving early without justification could cost you a great deal.

3.1.6 Preparing a Curriculum Vitae

Unless you're fortunate enough to be recommended directly to a client, the next key stage in the transition process is to create a good Curriculum Vitae (CV) to be sent out to prospective clients and agencies and uploaded onto relevant sites and job boards. We will be covering writing your CV in more detail in chapter 4, but here we cover some suggested approaches for contractors.

Under no circumstances should you ever, ever lie on your CV. You will get found out, lose the contract, damage lots of work relationships and quite possibly never work in the sector again. However, it is possible to emphasise the positive elements of your CV to help you attract the attention of the agent or client.

A good CV will immediately grab the attention of the reader, who is probably looking for any excuse to bin your CV and go on to others in the pile. So the trick is to make the first thing visible exactly what the reader is looking for, saving them a miserable hour trawling through dozens of poorly presented efforts.

To ensure that you grab that attention, you need to tailor each CV you send out so that, right at the top, you maximise the value of the experience and skills you have that makes you right for the contract being offered. What you want to avoid is a laundry list of what you've been doing since you left full-time education.

The ideal CV, of course, would be one where you seek position X and, right at the top, you can say that you've been working at X for the past ten years.

If only life were that simple! When applying for position X, explain right at the top of your CV the experience you have that makes you right for position X. You can do this in a short profile at the beginning, which you can then follow up with a list of your directly relevant work experience.

Each CV you send out should be tailored with the idea of matching your work and education to exactly what the agency or client is looking for. This really is very important: the agent or client will not spend much time in putting the few useful CVs on one side and the big pile of rejected CVs on the other. Even if you have the ideal background, if you haven't spent enough time on your CV it will find its way onto the wrong pile time and again.

An example: if you worked on more than one type of skill in your past job, you can list just the one that the agent or client is looking for first in your profile. You can mention the others later. You have most definitely not told a lie on your CV; you have simply presented the pertinent information in the best light and helped the agent or client to identify you as a likely candidate.

If you are applying for a contract through an agent, it is the agency's job to send your CV to the end client, once you have agreed to allow them to do so. Some agents frequently abuse this privilege and send out your CV without your permission.

Others will even obtain your CV without your permission and you will be surprised to find that a client you have never heard of is considering you for a job you've not asked to be considered for!

Chapter 9 details what you should do in either of these scenarios, but you should know that you own your CV. No one, under any circumstances, has the right to view it or send it out without your permission.

3.2 Securing a contract

Having done all your market research, prepared your rates and handed in your notice, the next vital stage in the process, and the ultimate reason for embarking on this exercise, is to secure a contract. Searching for a contract, compared with finding a permanent position, is a very different process. Recruiting a contractor typically takes only one interview, compared to sometimes up to five or six for a permanent position.

The timescales are much shorter, too; a contractor is usually hired within a week of the interview and there are few, if any, contractor candidate tests. Applicants to a permanent post may endure weeks or even months of waiting and intensive candidate testing before they are awarded a position.

The motivation behind this very different recruitment process is that the decision by the client to hire a contractor is typically made only a few weeks before they are needed, so the contractor is wanted on-site 'yesterday'.

Plus, as we have mentioned earlier, contractors are not employees and have no employment rights. So, if the client doesn't like the contractor for whatever reason, the contractor can get fired immediately, subject to the terms of the contract. Trying to remove a permanent employee, on the other hand, can be a lengthy, stressful and expensive process, so employers want to know they have the right candidate before they employ them.

For first time contractors it is advisable to only commit to a maximum of a three to six month contract, so that you can see what it is like on the job, talk to other contractors, and learn how to determine what you really have a right to ask for.

3.2.1 Applying for contracts

If you have handed in your notice but are still working out your notice period, you may have time constraints, but keep to as much of the following process as you can during your spare time. Whilst it might be tempting to start applying for contracts during the working day, don't do it if you can avoid it, although most agents don't work in the evenings and so some calls will be necessary.

But always do this in your own time. Not to do so is unfair to your current employer (who may at some point think of hiring you back as a contractor); is probably against the terms and conditions of your contract of employment; and might have an adverse effect on your reputation, which is a key tool in any contractors' marketing toolbox.

So, once at home and totally devoted to finding work, make applying for contracts your 'other' full time job until you've won your first contract. We devote the whole of chapter 5 to finding and securing contracts, but what follows is a useful overview that will help you put in context some of the other information you'll be reading.

Initial Activities

You should send your CV to all the relevant agencies you've found during your market research so that you are entered onto their databases. Agents make use of huge databases of contractors when they are attempting to match someone to a position; if you're not on it, you'll never be contacted for a potential interview.

The list of key agencies can be found on one of the main sites, JobServe, which at the time of writing offers a service with which your CV is distributed to other agencies. Do this at least one month before you're planning to start contracting, as it can take a few weeks for your CV to be entered into all the major agency databases.

Daily Activities for Securing a Contract

Having prepared to enter the market, and left your full time position, following the daily schedule below will ensure you are optimising your job search activities. It also means you have a routine – being at home after years of the structured life of permanent work can be disorientating, but working at finding your contract is your job, for now.

Morning:

- Call agencies that you applied to yesterday afternoon.
- Chase up any other positions you have applied to and have not yet spoken to the agent about
- Search the job websites for suitable positions that have been added since yesterday
- Send off email applications.

Afternoon:

- Call agencies that you made applications to in the morning
- Chase up any other positions for which you have applied and have not yet spoken to the agent about
- Search the job websites for suitable positions that have been added since you last looked
- Send off email applications.

Unfortunately, the contract search process can be quite dull and often frustrating, but the harder you work at it, the sooner you'll get a position.

Locating Positions – Using online job boards

As the job boards are such an important source of potential contracts, it is vital you monitor these websites regularly. Most contracts are advertised on the internet via job boards. There are some specialist job boards for specific sectors, but at the time of writing the most important job boards are:

- Jobserve
- Jobsite
- CWJobs
- Monster.

These are so dominant in the recruitment sector that agencies will frequently post the same position on all three boards.

The main jobs boards have a free alerts facility that you can set up to automatically email you when a new job is advertised that matches your specified criteria, for example, "C# Developer London". You can set up multiple alerts with different criteria, and with a bit of tweaking should find a way to refine the results. But don't 'refine' them so much that you miss potential opportunities – it's better to have to delete a few emails through the day than to not get an email for a contract you're perfectly suited to.

Make sure you keep a log of what roles you have applied for in a format that you can call up instantly on your home PC or laptop when an agent or client calls, so you know instantly which role the call refers to. A log will also prevent you from submitting multiple applications for the same role through different agents.

Targeting your Application
It is likely that you will be applying for different roles that might focus on different aspects of your skill set. As we explained in section 3.1.6, to give yourself the best chance of success you need to target your application and your CV accordingly. Remember to:

- Tailor your CV to the position
- Write a targeted email for the position.

Writing many different versions of your CV can be time consuming to start with, but you'll soon build up a collection of different versions. For example one might paint the picture of you being a great C# Programmer, while another might focus on you being an experienced Project Manager.

3.2.2 Staying with your current firm but as a contractor – warning!

A common occurrence when permanent employees decide to become contractors and they have a good relationship with their manager is for the manager to offer the new contractor their first contract.

This is of course very tempting. You know the work, the people and the workplace. You could suddenly be earning a lot more money for doing the same work you did before.

There is, unfortunately, one very serious problem with this arrangement. You will almost certainly fall into the tax law constraint, which is loosely referred to as 'IR35'. It's a term you will become very familiar with as a contractor, because it makes such a difference to how much you can potentially earn as take home pay, after tax. That's why there's a whole chapter about IR35 in this book.

But for now, here's what you need to know: HM Revenue & Customs will almost certainly assume that if you move from being a permanent employee one week, to doing exactly the same job as a contractor the next, you are really an employee disguised as a contractor.

That means that you will have to pay PAYE and National Insurance Contributions on your pay, and that will considerably reduce what you would earn if you were contracting 'outside' IR35, even through your own limited company. You could try to claim you are 'outside' IR35, but you would find it difficult to prove.

The safest route is to politely decline, ensuring you explain why and about IR35, because you never know when you might come across your manager again in the future; then move on to another company where you will be able to benefit fully from your new contracting lifestyle and increased earnings.

And also remember you decided to leave your last employer for a reason that is unlikely to have gone away simply because you have changed status – old habits die hard!

3.2.3 Working with agencies

Recruitment agencies are responsible for brokering most of the work in contracting, in all sectors. The agencies working in the contracting sector tend to treat it as volume work, so aim to place as many contractors with as many clients as they can, because that is what drives their business models and generates the revenues and profits.

So bear this in mind and be cautious when dealing with appeals from agents who may appear to be on your side, or claim they want to help you. All they really want is your signature on the contract and the hefty commission that comes with it. As we will show in chapter 5, you should always be fair to the agent, but never fall into the trap of believing that the agent is your friend.

A good agency, and there are many, won't beat around the bush with you. They will ask if they can send your CV out to a given client. They probably won't know very much about the nature of the work; they simply can't because they deal with all sorts of contracts and technologies. They may try to make sure you have the right profile, and you should help them to do so. But be cautious: agencies that claim to do more than these few simple steps may not, unless there is strong evidence to the contrary, be being totally honest with you.

Recruitment is generally a high volume 'bums on seats' game. Some agencies will try and justify higher margins to their clients based on them doing extra-special candidate selection and the like. This is questionable; most agencies do the same.

That's not to say agents don't work hard for their money. The truth is they work very hard to close deals. They have to make plenty of calls and line up loads of interviews for candidates before someone says yes. And that's just for starters.

Many contractors don't understand how hard agents work, and think they just do CV matching. That's true to a certain extent, but the hard work is creating the opportunities with a steady stream of clients and making it all happen.

So, whilst they may not be your best friends or always have your best interests at heart, there's every reason to be professional, friendly and fair with agents when dealing with them. After all, agencies are providing you with a cheap commission-only outsourced sales force – that's not to be taken lightly.

3.2.4 Going direct to the client

It is highly unusual for contractors to deal direct with clients when securing a contract, apart from at the interview stage. That said, contractors who are many years into their contracting career may find themselves dealing direct with clients, because it suits their relationship and the contractor is sufficiently in demand that they can dictate terms.

However, clients generally use agencies because they want to distance the client company from the contractor, so that there is no possibility of there being the slightest suggestion the contractor is an employee. Clients do not want a contractor claiming they are an employee and claiming employment rights, which is something both clients and contractors want to avoid.

In addition, clients use recruitment agencies to find candidates that match their requirements because that is what agencies do – they match people with work opportunities. A client, who may be a busy project manager, does not want to sit down at a computer, post adverts, wait for the responses and then sift through them to try and identify likely candidates. Especially as, along the way, they'll probably also be contacted by salespeople from trade magazines and other job sites trying to sell them recruitment advertising space, as well as by recruitment agencies selling their services.

A rule of thumb is not to sign anything before an agency sets you up with an interview, because that will allow you flexibility if offered the opportunity to go direct as a result of your own networking and not the agent's. The client will have an agreement with the agency which prevents them from taking you on direct if the agent has introduced you.

3.2.5 Attending interviews

This, like every part of the transition process, is crucial. If you do not perform at this stage then you will not win the contract. We cover interview techniques in chapter 5 and advanced interviewing and sales techniques in chapter 10, but the key points are also given below.

Preparation for the interview is hugely important. Find out why the client needs you, research the background of the client company, check you understand and have the skills they are looking for, and prepare your own list of questions.

The basic do's and don'ts for contractor interviews are the same as when interviewing for permanent employment. Dress properly, take an umbrella if it is raining, make sure you know where you are going, and if you are driving make sure you can park.

Never be late. This, unless you have called ahead with a very good excuse, will almost certainly lose you the contract. Know the names and titles of the interviewers – the agency should be able to tell you these.

The interviewer(s) will be looking for a number of attributes during the interview. They will want to know if you are articulate and a good communicator; are you going to get on with the team; is the chemistry there? When talking about the technical aspects of the contract, the interviewer will be able to tell very quickly if you have a good grasp of the subject.

Be sure to ask your questions when invited, or during the interview, if appropriate. These will demonstrate to the interviewer that you have thought about the contract, prepared and hopefully asked intelligent questions to better communicate your expertise and suitability for the position. Remember, they're not looking for an employee to train up into the position; they will expect you to have the skills, experience and expertise to be up and running from day one.

The client may offer you the contract at the interview. Alternatively, after the interview, the agent will normally phone to find out how it went. That is an opportunity for you to discuss how the interview went and also, if you decided that the contract does not suit you, to tell the agent. Agents can sometimes be very useful in these circumstances, by giving you the client's feedback. Listen carefully, as this feedback could well help you refine your CV and improve your interview technique.

3.2.6 Dealing with contracts and IR35 issues

Great news – you have been offered your first contract! There may be some attempts at haggling over the rates by your agent but you will be offered a contract at an agreed rate for a particular starting date.

The contract from the agent arrives in the post or by email. It looks fine, as most contracts are fairly standard, and so you prepare to sign it. But wait! What about IR35?

As we have explained, IR35 is the tax legislation that means HMRC can tax some contractors as though they are employees of their clients. This could reduce your take-home pay by as much as 25%. So it is essential to be clear on the IR35 implications before you sign any contract.

There are many factors that can lead to a contractor being found 'within IR35' by HMRC, and we explain these in detail in chapter 9. The wording in a contractor's contract with their agency and end user client can be one of these factors.

So, at this stage it is worth using some of the funds you have set aside for professional fees to ask a solicitor or specialist IR35 consultancy to review the contract. This can amount to a maximum of £200, and frequently much less, but if the review throws up any issues, it could end up saving you tens of thousands.

3.2.7 Getting payment structures into place

Once you've landed a contract, how do you bill for it? A lot depends on what choice you've made for the legal organisation of your company – whether you have opted for your own limited company or decided to work through an umbrella company. Chapter 6 discusses these options and how to set up your preferred trading entity in more detail.

But you should understand at this point that you will have great difficulty working as a self-employed person in your own right because clients don't want the risk. Agencies and clients will want to deal with your own limited company or with your 'umbrella company', which is a limited company that treats you as an employee – legally grouping many contractors under its 'umbrella.'

Contractors can generally make the most money by working through a limited company. This involves picking up some basic legal knowledge and undertaking some administrative steps, but it's nothing too daunting and there are step-by-step guides later in this book.

You will also need to open a company bank account if you are trading through your own limited company. This is a fairly straightforward process and is explained in chapter 6. If you are working through an umbrella company, you would use their bank account to get paid, and they will then pay you.

However, if you have a poor credit history or County Court Judgements on record, getting a business bank account could be very difficult. Added to this, typically no client or agency will pay into a personal bank account – they want a business bank account.

3.2.8 Starting your first contract

You are almost at the end of the transition phase from being a permanent employee to becoming a contractor. All that remains is for you to undertake your first contract and, of course, get paid.

Starting a contract is not the same as starting a new permanent job. You are not joining the client company as a member of the 'extended corporate family'; you are there to do a very specific series of tasks for which you expect to be handsomely rewarded in cash. There are no company socials, no benefits and you shouldn't even use the subsidised staff canteen – these might seem petty points, but as we'll explain later in this book, IR35 makes them important to be aware of.

However, starting your first contract is the start of something new and exciting and you will become part of the wider contracting community. Remember that when working for your client, you are not only the operations person expected to deliver on the contract, you are also the account manager for your client, so the relationship is very different from that between a manager and an employee.

3.2.9 Getting paid

When you are contracting, you will need to complete timesheets and raise invoices so that you can get paid.

Most agencies will provide standard timesheets that you complete on a daily basis, entering the number of hours that you have worked that day. You would normally sign and submit the timesheet for countersignature by the client at the end of each week. Increasingly this happens electronically – you complete the form on-screen and the project manager clicks a button to authorise payment.

If you are running your own limited company, you need to prepare your own invoices and submit them to the agency or direct to the client, if there is no agency. Invoices are required to have specific information about the work, the client and your company, which is explained in chapter 5. If you're contracting through an umbrella company, you'll usually be asked to mail, email or fax timesheets, so that they can prepare an invoice.

Payment times vary and most agencies have strict deadlines, so be sure to submit any paperwork in good time, particularly if cash is tight in the first few months of your first contract.

If you are working through an agent, or some umbrella companies, you should not have to wait for the client to pay the agency before you get paid. If your agency does this, then something is not right, and you should take a look at chapter 9 for a solution.

As a new contractor you'll undoubtedly enjoy regularly checking out your bank account balance and looking through your statements; it's a real pleasure seeing just how much more you are now earning. Enjoy it!

4.

Marketing yourself — your curriculum vitae (CV)

4.1 Introduction to CV writing

Your curriculum vitae, or CV, has one purpose: to get an agent or client interested in speaking to you on the telephone with a view to lining up an interview for a new contract. It is the key marketing document you will use to get shortlisted for a possible contract and start increasing your income.

The crucial decision about whether or not you get shortlisted for an interview is made entirely on the basis of these pages, to which the reader at the agency or client will devote perhaps 20 seconds for the first make-or-break reading.

As a result, to ensure a successful career as a contractor, your CV deserves a lot of thought. That's because it is possible to be really good at what you do, and really experienced at it, but then to get passed over time and again because your CV wasn't eye catching enough and did not do the job of getting you noticed.

Even if you are more comfortable writing computer code or engineering specifications, it is worth your investment in time to write a good CV to ensure a successful contracting career. It is possible to pay a professional CV writer to write a CV for you, but you need to ensure they have a track record in writing high impact CVs that got their clients work, and that they are not just a typing service. You should expect to pay more than £100 for a good CV.

Many people find writing about themselves really tough, particularly understanding what is going to get that agent or client to pick up the phone. So this chapter will guide you through all the key steps to do just that.

The following sections detail what makes a CV that will get you an interview; a CV that will put you in front of the decision makers who can then make their own judgments about your technical skills and expertise.

Remember the key steps in the process are:

- Get noticed by an agent using your CV
- Get an interview using your CV (and possibly also a quick phone conversation)
- Get the contract offer by performing well at interview.

4.2 How CVs are used

To fully appreciate how CVs are used by agencies and clients, you need to understand the CV filtering process. For example there might be 200 CVs on the agent's or client's desk for one contract. These CVs need to be filtered down to around ten, which the agent or client will then go over in detail. The process generally works like this:

Step 1 – The five-second look at each of the first 200 CVs
Straight into the bin goes:

- Anything longer than four pages – this is too long and the agent or client can't be bothered to read it
- Any CV without a profile or list of skills on the front page. There's no time to search for them
- Any CV that is a big essay with sentences, not broken into bite-sized chunks and without bullet points. These CVs are just too much hassle to read.

So, this might leave the client or agent with around 100 CVs for the next stage.

Step 2 — The ten-second scan of the front page of the next 100 CVs
Agents or clients put CVs straight into the bin if:

- The profile and skills on front page do not match the contract's requirement.

Clients or agents are then left with probably around 40 CVs for some more serious consideration.

Step 3 — The 'potentials' pile of 40 CVs for more consideration

- In a nutshell, at this crucial stage, only these types of CVs stay in: Those where the profile and skills on front page exactly match the contract's requirements.

At the risk of stating the obvious, a simple principle to adopt is not to apply for any contract where the skills and experience listed on your CV do not specifically match the client's or agent's requirements. This principle does sound obvious, but many contractors are tempted to scatter their vague CVs out to the four winds, "just in case" one gets them an interview. It won't!

This approach can also be counterproductive, because you are wasting clients' and agents' time – you need to be targeting your CV to a client's specific requirements.

You are also wasting your time, which could be more profitably spent producing that one CV on which you have highlighted your specific expertise that makes you right for the contract. But remember a subtle point, although you should never include falsehoods on a CV, you can and should emphasise those elements of your skills and experience that suit the particular contract you are applying for.

Remember your experience is like a box of chocolates to a client – there are lots of goodies but you need to present the ones the client wants rather than leaving them to have a rummage around to see if there is anything that takes their fancy.

Step 4 — The 'strong possibilities' pile of the last 10 CVs
There are now 10 CVs left and the agent or client will now feel brave enough to look beyond the first page to find some or all of the non-technical qualities they will be looking for, that:

- You have recent experience using the skills you claim to have on the front of your CV
- You have staying power and a good contracting record, eg past contracts that have been renewed. Lots of small contracts and no renewals can raise warning flags for potential clients
- Your experience was gained with credible firms – preferably blue chip
- You have a good academic background, although in many sectors this is a bonus and not mandatory for many roles, if you have the right experience.

If you meet the criteria at this point you will probably be called by the agent for a reality check to ensure you can speak and sound vaguely like the person described on the CV you sent in. The agent will be looking for around four to six potential candidates who sound like they know what they are talking about.

Try and sound interested; if you don't or indicate you have a number of promising opportunities at this stage the agent won't bother with you.

The interview stage then filters out a range of undesirable personality types and those who have made what look to be overinflated claims on their CV. Make sure you are not one of them!

A key point to remember is that, in the eyes of the agent or potential client, it really doesn't matter how many letters you have after your name, they don't make you God's gift to British industry. Far from it, in fact – the agent or client has boxes to tick, so target your application accordingly.

Been there, done that!

Bad CVs generally mean no interview

Dave says: One of my team recommended someone and they sent their CV over. It was terrible, with ten pages of life history and, under normal circumstances, it would have been binned. But because he was highly recommended, I took the time to go through all those pages and interviewed him anyway. It turned out he was great and I hired him. So, whilst your track record and reputation is incredibly important, so too is your CV and it is doubly important that you get this across to the reader.

4.3 CVs, sales and marketing

A CV is the contractor's primary sales and marketing tool, and without a carefully crafted CV a contractor simply won't get any work. You will fail the tests of how a CV is used and be forced to consider returning to full time permanent employment with its lower pay and lack of flexibility.

Contractors provide a service, in the same way any knowledge-based business does, such as a management consultancy or professional practice. Management consultants have glossy brochures, fancy direct mail campaigns and flash websites to wow clients into hiring them.

A CV is no different. It is your brochure, website, door-to-door flyers, advertising campaign, etc all rolled into one. It tells prospective clients who want to part with their cash for services like yours what features and benefits they will receive from choosing you over and above all the other service providers.

CVs, although a contractor's key marketing and sales tool, are only one component of the contractor's arsenal. The interview is also a vital stage of the sales and marketing process and interview techniques are a fundamental skill for contractors to master; they are covered in more detail in chapter 5.

Mastering the CV creation process is important for contractors who want to get that next contract, or the best contracts. The important items to include are:

- Your profile
- Your relevant skills
- Your relevant achievements
- Previous relevant clients, with skills employed, and achievements.

Even with impressive skill sets and decades of relevant experience, if contractors don't understand how to market and sell themselves, they will not win the best contracts.

Having a winning CV is one of the keys to what makes a successful contractor. And having a first rate profile is what makes a winning CV, because for most agents it's the only thing they read. Or not, if your profile is poor.

4.4 Writing a high impact CV

To create the best impression possible – so that the client or agent thinks, 'Wow, this person is perfect!' – you need to understand how to structure your CV for maximum impact.

Treat your CV as a work in progress of which you have more than one version. Using it effectively is a learning curve and, after writing your first collection of high impact targeted CVs for your first tranche of contracts, you will then know better how to target your CVs for subsequent contracts, which should be much more lucrative.

As detailed in the previous section, during the filtering process you only have a few seconds of the agent's or client's time to make an impact – or it's the bin. If a contractor's CV does not scream at the reader 'I'm perfect for the job', then the CV has failed.

A high-impact targeted CV communicates on the front page that the candidate, you, is perfect for the position that needs to be filled.

4.4.1 Front page

You only have one sheet of A4 to make that few-seconds' impact. If you start listing all the studies you completed 20 years ago, and the fact that you love squash and have a clean driving licence, your impact will be minimal and your CV will be one of the first rejected.

As an example, here is a list of unhelpful and unfocused information that wastes space on the front page, and wastes the time of the client or agent:

- A list of schools you attended with examinations, grades, addresses. Who cares! It's better to demonstrate that you have the list of skills they are after
- A list of hobbies. Who cares! Tell them what you have achieved by applying the skills you have
- Your work history. Who cares! Tell them what benefits your clients have gained from your work. Why should they hire you?

So now that you've removed the worthless information, just what should be on the front page of your CV? Well, first of all, why are you the right person for this job? You need to show that you:

- Have the skills they are looking for
- That you have successfully applied those skills for other clients
- That you have provided business value to those clients while using those skills.

There are essentially four sections to the front page of a high-impact CV:

- Your name, address and contact details – three lines
- A profile of you – four lines
- Your list of skills or expertise – about ten bullet points
- Your list of achievements – about five bullet points.

Here is an example:

Joe Bloggs
Tel: 01234 5677889 Mobile: 07123 456789
Email: joebloggs@pleasespamme.com
10 Bloggs House, London E12 4LP

PROFILE

Highly proficient SENIOR ANALYST PROGRAMMER with 10 years experience building financial risk applications for major blue chip clients using OO, C++, Oracle, UML, ADO. Full life cycle knowledge, including RUP, SSADM, and PRINCE methodologies. Now seeking next rewarding opportunity to make a successful impact in a customer focused team.

EXPERTISE

- C++ (8 years)
- Oracle (version xyx, 9 years)
- OO, Rational Rose, UML, OCL
- Design Patterns, Design By Contract
- SSADM, RAD, DSDM, XP, SCRUM
- Meets tight and demanding deadlines under pressure

(and so on – you need about ten bullet points here).

ACHIEVEMENTS

- Successfully re-engineered existing risk analysis application, cutting down the run time from 30 minutes to 10 seconds. This enabled fund managers to risk analyse figures in real time, resulting in the company being more competitive in the marketplace, increasing revenues by 50%
- Trained and mentored junior developers in OO techniques, resulting in significant productivity rate increases and less time to market. Increase in speed of development enabled IT to become 50% more responsive to clients' demands for change and enhancements
- Automated manual reconciliation of system data with market data, resulting in task being completed with 100% accuracy in one minute, as opposed to three hours.

Box 4.1 Sample first page

The emphasis in these introductory sections should be on your 'features and benefits' and their value to the client; that is to say, how has the client saved money, or become more efficient resulting in cost savings and, as the example in box 4.1 illustrates, it is possible to very clearly define how the contractor can add real value to a client's operation.

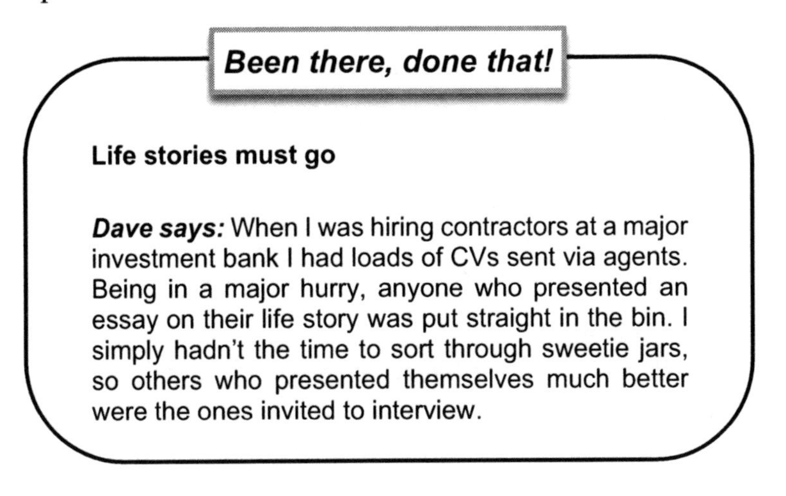

Your features and benefits and their value means:

- I have these skills
- Someone has paid me for them
- They generated tangible, positive results.

Profile

The profile is a very short (four-line maximum) summary that states three main points:

- What you are – your job title
- Your experience and what you have done.
- What you are now looking for.

It is placed at the top of the front page of your CV below your name.

For example:

> Experienced **DEVELOPMENT TEAM LEADER** with 10 years experience training and leading development teams to build Object Orientated Internet/Intranet applications using C#.NET, ASP.NET, SQL SERVER. Now seeking next challenging and rewarding position in a customer focused organisation.

Motivation for a well targeted profile

When the agent or client reads your profile the ideal reaction you want is: 'Wow! This person looks perfect. I'll carry on reading the rest of the CV and probably invite them for interview.'

A poorly targeted profile, on the other hand, might invoke responses of, 'Oh, this person is one of those, and we don't need one of those', or, 'This person is a generalist, and we're looking for a specialist.' Your profile should be adapted to match each application you make to optimise your chances of being selected for interview.

Your title

Use **BOLD UPPER CASE LETTERS** for your title. It will have more visual priority over the rest of the front page and ensure it gets read. Use the exact same words for your title as you find in the application. If the requirement is for a 'Software Engineer', then you are a '**SOFTWARE ENGINEER**'. If the requirement is for a 'Senior Developer' then you are now a '**SENIOR DEVELOPER**'.

You do not have to use the same title that you had at your last permanent role. You are now your own boss, so you now call the shots on your title, as long as you are being accurate.

With regard to the IT market, since it is not a profession, such as accounting or law, anyone can call themselves what they like without any formal qualifications. This results in many differences in what people expect certain job titles to mean. Provided you are confident you can do the job, you can be as flexible as you like with your job title.

You can also rename previous positions you've had in other companies (permanent or contract) to adapt to the position you are now applying for. You will want your job titles to look like you are progressing through your career.

One word of warning: never try and trade up your skills. For example, 'Senior developer now looking for a team leader position'. It will never work in the contract world. They will simply hire a team leader. Trading up works in the permanent market, because they get you cheaper than contractors in return for training you and offering you career growth. The agency and client are looking for the 'finished article' – that is now what contracting is about.

In your 'now seeking…' sentence you simply need to state exactly what they want to hear, rather than what you want or aspire to.
For example, there is little point in saying, 'Looking to transfer my expertise to the banking sector'. This would be something you want, not what you can offer. The client is unlikely to have a requirement to pay contract rates to cross train someone for their position!

Contractors are hired because they have the skills the client wants and can hit the ground running. Contractors are never hired to be trained by the client, and neither does the client want the impression that the candidate wants to work for them to learn new skills and add them to their CV.

It is all about the client, and what you can do for them, not about what the client can do for you and your contracting career.

This is totally different from job seeking in the permanent sector, where there is a two way exchange. In contracting it is all one way; you get paid big money for what you can do for the client, not what the client can do for you.

Expertise
This section of a CV needs about 10 bullet points that prove that you are the most qualified and effective person for the contract. A classic approach that will gain the notice of the agent or client is to highlight in bold the words that match the advertisement.

It is also important to ensure that you show a broad range of skills, rather than devoting too many lines of the CV to one area. You can put multiple skills from the same area on one line.

Make sure you remember to add personal qualities, like 'Meets tight and demanding deadlines under pressure'. A hugely qualified specialist is of no value to a client if they cannot demonstrate they can perform.

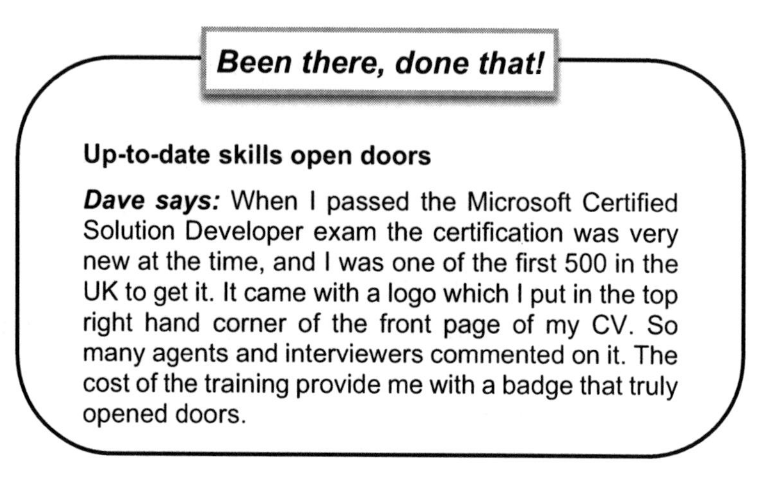
Been there, done that!

Up-to-date skills open doors

Dave says: When I passed the Microsoft Certified Solution Developer exam the certification was very new at the time, and I was one of the first 500 in the UK to get it. It came with a logo which I put in the top right hand corner of the front page of my CV. So many agents and interviewers commented on it. The cost of the training provide me with a badge that truly opened doors.

Achievements
Achievements are about measurable benefits you provided to your clients that justified why you were awarded the contract in the first place. They are things you did that saved time, made things easier, saved money, made more money, and so on.

One of the common mistakes when writing a CV is to write the achievements as a set of skills that you have acquired and then to focus on how you benefited from them, rather than on the benefits you generated for the client.

You really have to dig deep and think about what business benefits you added by applying your skills, and how those projects added value to the client's business, be it in terms of time saving or profitability. Something tangible is important.

To develop the right content for your CV based on your past projects, think about organisations' objectives and how you have helped your clients (or former employers) achieve them.

Remember, all clients or organisations generally want to achieve some or all of the following, to:

- Make more profits
- Sell more products or services
- Become more efficient
- Get more customers
- Beat the competition
- Improve customer satisfaction
- Enter new markets
- Improve quality.

So bear these in mind and then use the following set formula for writing down your achievements:

- Which set of skills you used
- Who it helped
- A quantifiable measure of how it helped.

Here's a list of classic items that are not achievements:

- "I trained somebody"
- "I built something"
- "I learned X, Y, and Z".

These are not achievements. They are list of 'stuff that you did'. It does not explain what benefit you created for the client who paid you money and what value you brought to that client.

Another example of an achievement that is starting to get there, but not quite is:

- Developed a spreadsheet that helped save ten staff some time and make money.

That is not quite specific enough. A better example of presenting the above might be:

- Developed and implemented a bespoke spreadsheet application for the client's traders, which reduced the time to calculate financial forecasts from three hours to fifteen seconds. This not only saved time, but enabled the traders to become more responsive to market change, and resulted in a measurable increase in profit of 12% over two months.

Keep a list of around ten achievements in a separate document and then just pick out the four or five most relevant to the position you are applying for.

Achievements – so what!?

The 'so what!?' test is probably the most important test you need to pass in order to secure that contract. CVs are full of statements that fail the 'so what!?' test, so analyse your achievement in the context of the contract you are applying for. Are you: a) Impressed, b) Mildly impressed, or c) Thinking, 'so what!?

Example 1 – So what!?
Achievement: "Mentored other team members"
Response: So what!?
You trained some staff, and then what? The client spent money for you to train staff and what benefit did it achieve for them?

Example 2 – So what!?
Achievement: "Made document retrieval faster"
Response: So what!?
How much faster? How much did you spend, and how much did you save? What was the measurable benefit to the business?

Example 3 – Slightly better
Achievement: "Mentored team members, which improved their skills"
Response: Better than before, but this does not hugely excite.
So, you used your training skills to train some people, which resulted in them getting improved skills, and then what? How did they apply those new skills and what was the result?

Example 4 – Right on the nail
Achievement: "Used expert knowledge of project management to deliver application ahead of schedule and under budget. This resulted in obtaining a first mover advantage over competitors and subsequent capture of 70% of market share."
Response: Very impressed. Can you come and do this for me? Please.

The lesson from the 'so what!?' test is to recognise what achievements have created benefits for the client. When listing achievements, ask 'so what?' for each one – would these stand out from a CV and catch the attention of an agent or potential client?

4.4.2 Second page

The second page of the CV is about providing reassurance. The primary task has been achieved – the agent or client has actually turned the page. At this stage they are looking to see that:

- You've worked for the right organisations, preferably in the same industry
- Contracts you've worked on have been renewed – you have staying power

- You've successfully applied the skills mentioned on the front page.

The second page of the CV is all about reinforcing the impression you have given of yourself on the front page as being perfect for the contract.

Work experience

The second page is also where you list your work experience. No need for essays; the best approach is to use short bullet points. This section explains the things you did and what skills you used. You should also add some examples of added value. Box 4.2 illustrates an example of a contract experience.

www.mlhsbc.co.uk - Merrill Lynch HSBC
Development Team Leader - Retail Banking
Feb 2007 - July 2008 (18 months, 3 renewals)

- Managed team of five developers for the design and development of retail banking functionality
- Responsible for implementation of end-to-end requirements: from software requirements, design and development, UAT and release
- An eight-tiered architecture, built using Object Orientation. A web front end with a number of distinct tiers written in .NET linking to a back end mainframe.

And so on...

Box 4.2 Work experience example

Some key factors also include explicitly listing the number of months the contract lasted and the number of renewals. This tells the reader that you are reliable and that people value your work. It also means the reader does not have to struggle with working out contract lengths themselves. They can scan down the page and see you have lots of long contracts and renewals, which is another tick in their box. Keep the information brief yet informative – no one wants to read essays. Highlight the key information in bold text so it stands out when scanned quickly.

Education, training and hobbies

Page two is also where you list your education, training, and hobbies. Keep this information compact. Some agents and clients like to see you have the right academic background for the contract; others like the 'Married, 2 children' information because agents and clients think it implies stability.

However, it is not necessary to list every GCSE, with grades, and your interest in Carniolan beekeeping. The focus should be on the practical and tangible. If you have 10 years commercial experience, your education is somewhat irrelevant.

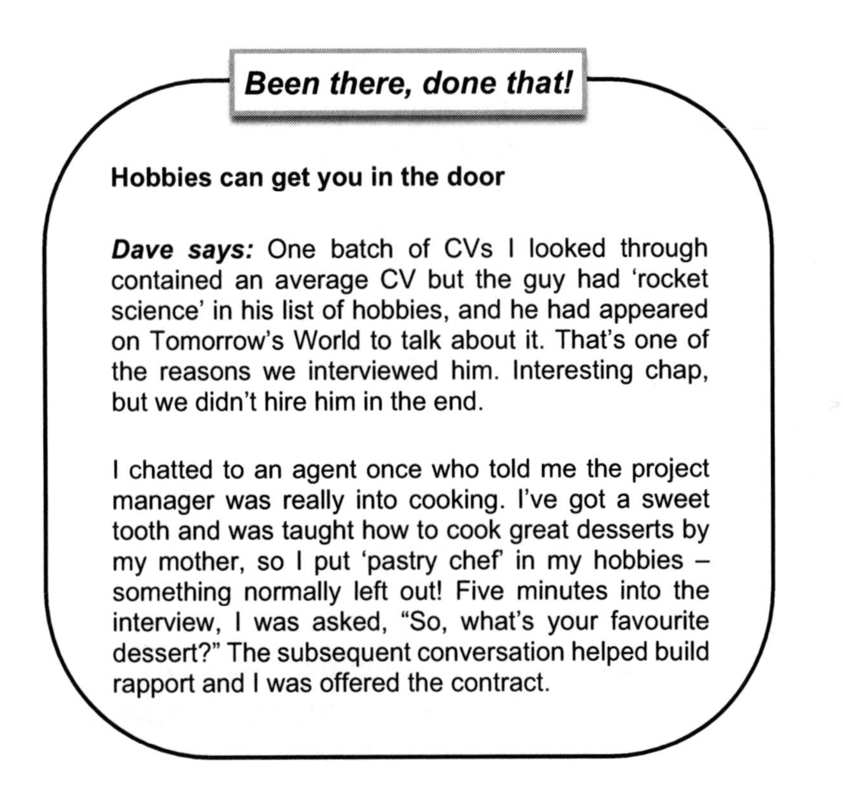

Been there, done that!

Hobbies can get you in the door

Dave says: One batch of CVs I looked through contained an average CV but the guy had 'rocket science' in his list of hobbies, and he had appeared on Tomorrow's World to talk about it. That's one of the reasons we interviewed him. Interesting chap, but we didn't hire him in the end.

I chatted to an agent once who told me the project manager was really into cooking. I've got a sweet tooth and was taught how to cook great desserts by my mother, so I put 'pastry chef' in my hobbies – something normally left out! Five minutes into the interview, I was asked, "So, what's your favourite dessert?" The subsequent conversation helped build rapport and I was offered the contract.

4.5 Targeting CVs – you can have more than one

The next step after creating the generic content for your high impact CV is to tailor that content so that it perfectly matches the role that you are applying for.

Say you have worked in circuses for several years, and you regularly perform on the trapeze, alternating your act with a lion-taming show. If the advert for the contract says they are looking for a trapeze artist, then you edit the CV to make it look as though you are the best trapeze artist in the entire country. If the client is looking for a lion tamer, then the same rules apply.

So you effectively have two CVs that focus separately on your most relevant experience for that role. Only if the advertisement is for someone with general circus skills should you give equal weight to both areas of expertise.

Contractors need to emphasise the strengths and experience gained from previous positions and demonstrate they have *key transferable skills* that can be applied in the new position. So, if you are going for a trapeze artist position for which you have three years experience, but have done five solid years of lion taming, it would be best to play down the lion taming experience and focus more on your trapeze experience. This is often referred to as putting your best foot forward.

The best way to show the targeting approach is to demonstrate how a CV can be developed to match the needs of a particular contract's role.

Overall, the CV in Box 4.3 has many virtues and does not suffer from some of the common mistakes made by contractors when writing their CV. However, it can be enhanced to provide significantly more impact.

Let us take look at each section in turn to see how each could be improved.

Mr John Smith

99 High Street, Anywhere Town, Sussex AB1 9XY

T: +44 (0) 1323 44444 M: +44 (0) 7321 321321 E: john@johncedricsmithonline.com

PROFILE

I am a versatile and energetic problem solver and manager. I have experience in facilities management, project management, staff management, system design and software development. With fifteen years experience in Information Technology I am looking to take my expertise into an organisation requiring a manager focusing on end user requirements.

EXPERTISE

Microsoft Office	Microsoft Windows	UNIX implementation and administration
Systems Analysis	Systems Design	Network Design & Implementation
Business Analysis	Macro Programming	InfoBASIC
Staff Management	Change management	Perl Account Management
Studying for Security+	Report Writing for technicians and end users	

ABC SOFTWARE COMPANY

1994 – Present

ABC Software Company provides software and facilities management services to Lloyd's insurance brokers and commodity traders. During my eight years with the company I have had significant exposure to both the facilities and software sides of both client areas.

Director of Facilities Management
Grew department to generate half the company's annual revenue.
Expanded department to service twelve clients over twenty sites.
Grew department from one to eleven staff.
Provided technical consultative services to clients at board level.
Translated client requirements into technical specifications.
Provided lateral thinking solutions for all company clients.
Provided account management for client sites.
Managed budgets and growth in line with company expectations.
Provided day to day technical assistance to staff.
Associate Director
Created the facilities management department.
Provided account management for a variety of company clients.
Specialist project work relating to software systems integration.
Analyst/Programmer
Systems design for insurance and commodity trading packages.
Software development for insurance and commodity trading packages.

XYZ COMPUTERS LTD

1989 – 1994

XYZ Computers Ltd provides subscription and advertising management software to the magazine publishing industry. During my time at the company I had a customer based role, spending much time on site making bespoke changes to software systems. The systems programming role developed as the company undertook a project to convert the bureau system from a legacy mainframe platform to an open UNIX base.

Systems Programmer

UNIX systems programmer on an application conversion project.

Created job and print managing systems familiar to VMS operators.

Automated the conversion of legacy JCL script to UNIX shell script.

Created a JCL script generator for UNIX.

Programmer

Specified and coded changes to the standard subscription packages.

Specified and coded bespoke modules as defined by clients.

Liaised with clients at board level regarding change requirements.

INTERNATIONAL COMMUNICATIONS ASSOCIATION (ICA)

1987 – 1989

ICA provided communications services to journalists prior to the prevalence of the internet. Specialising in transmission of news stories to and from disparate systems, a great deal of integration and analysis work was required. Specialist work included a pilot project to transmit press releases from the United States Information Agency to major news outlets in Israel via the United States Embassy in Tel Aviv.

Communications Consultant

Designed and coded bespoke messaging software.

Liaised with news providers to integrate with their systems.

Managed communications systems to ensure prompt delivery of news

EDUCATION

BSc (Hons) Upper Second, Open University; Computing Subjects & Change Management 1996

3 GCE A Levels, Trinity School; Physics, Maths, Electronics 1986

Currently studying for the CompTIA Security+ Qualification

PERSONAL

Date of birth :	21 August 1969	Nationality :	British
Marital status :	Divorced	Driving licence :	Full, Clean
Dependents :	One	Languages :	English, German

REFERENCES

Professional and personal references are available on demand.

Box 4.3 What could be improved on this CV?

Here is the original profile:

I am a versatile and energetic problem solver and manager. I have experience in facilities management, project management, staff management, system design and software development. With fifteen years experience in Information Technology I am looking to take my expertise into an organisation requiring a manager focusing on end user requirements.

This profile does not quite leap out at the reader. It is not targeted to a specific opportunity and describes a range of skills that can be offered and invites the reader to select one or more of these skills. However, it is very rare that an agency or client places an advert for an all-in-one 'Facilities Manager, Project Manager, Staff Manager, System Designer, Software Developer', so the objective is to target what the client or agency wants to hear in relation to the specific contract they are advertising.

Take the hypothetical case of a vacancy for a project manager. In the advertised vacancy it will probably define experience required and industry sector. The CV has to communicate this information in just a few seconds, because that is how long it will take to find its way into the bin if high impact communication is not successfully achieved.

So, a revised profile could be the following:

Versatile and very successful **PROJECT MANAGER** with a wealth of technical and commercial skills acquired across a wide range of demanding roles, with over 10 years experience in the insurance and commodities sector. Now seeking next challenging and rewarding opportunity to demonstrate substantial abilities and make an effective contribution in a successful, end user focused team.

The use of the pronoun 'I' has been dropped and then the information in the brief has been targeted with the particular position in mind, using words and phrases that matched the contract description. The contract seeker's main skill that is relevant to the role is emphasised with bold upper case letters and words that match those given in the advertisement.

Now, let's look at the next area on this all-important front page.

Microsoft Office	Microsoft Windows	UNIX implementation and administration
Systems Analysis	Systems Design	Network Design & Implementation
Business Analysis	Macro Programming	Studying for Security+
Staff Management	Change management	Perl Account Management
InfoBASIC	Report Writing for technicians and end users	

Box 4.4 Original expertise to compare and contrast.

As written, this **expertise** section reads more like a list of courses and training that have been attended and does not effectively describe all the skills that will match the job title of 'Project Manager' in the profile. Note that courses and training would be better placed in a section on the second page.

The expertise should describe a list of skills you have that are directly relevant to the contract to which you are applying. It should also have a combination of skills, both technical and personal.

- Powerful **project planning** and implementation skills – delivery focused.
- Skilled with MS Office, Windows and UNIX implementation and administration.
- **Full project life cycle** – configuration management and change management.
- Track record of academic achievement and career development – fluent in German.
- Effective communication and negotiation techniques – skilled in **account management**.
- Systems design and software development skills for insurance and commodity trading.
- Reliably **meets demanding deadlines** and targets working under pressure.

Box 4.5 Updated expertise

...and so on. Using around 10 bullet points would be ideal here.

Notice that we have used bullet points for more readability. And for the items that are most relevant we have put them in bold to make them stand out during the kind of five- to ten-second scan a client or agent might make.

If, for example, we were looking to target a systems designer role rather than a project manager one, we would amend the profile and expertise list to suit. The golden rule is always telling the client or agent what they want to hear, without being untruthful, and not going into unnecessary detail about your life story and work history.

The next section to add to the high impact front page in this sample CV highlights your **achievements**. This is completely missing from the original CV and is probably the most important section of the front page. It shows you have used your skills and expertise to deliver some value to those whom you have worked for. It also shows you think commercially, not just in terms of tasks to be completed.

There are some clues in the work history and we can use some of these to develop a couple of achievements, like this:

ACHIEVEMENTS

- Played lead role in successful initiative to rapidly expand client base to twelve clients across twenty sites and generate half of company's annual revenues.
- Used extensive technical skills and experience to develop bespoke software packages that gained the company a competitive edge in the insurance and commodities markets.

On page two of the original CV, the career history section also requires some work. The original section says:

XYZ COMPUTERS LTD
1989 – 1994

XYZ Computers Ltd provides subscription and advertising management software to the magazine publishing industry. During my time at the company I had a customer based role, spending much time on site making bespoke changes to software systems. The systems programming role developed as the company undertook a project to convert the bureau system from a legacy mainframe platform to an open UNIX base.

Systems Programmer

UNIX systems programmer on an application conversion project.
Created job and print managing systems familiar to VMS operators.
Automated the conversion of legacy JCL script to UNIX shell script.
Created a JCL script generator for UNIX.

Programmer

Specified and coded changes to the standard subscription packages.
Specified and coded bespoke modules as defined by clients.

Liaised with clients at board level regarding change requirements.

Although appearing quite effective, some potential improvements could include removing the use of 'I', as with the rest of the CV and using more bullet points.

The education section of the original CV is well written. It lists higher education qualifications and 'A' levels without giving detailed information about schools and colleges and years attended. However, if contractors have gone to schools with a high personal branding value, e.g. public schools like Eton and Harrow, or state schools like Hockerill Anglo-European College or Colchester Royal Grammar School, then there may be occasions when it is worth including this information.

Training and development can be an important section and the original CV does not have one. It would be the place to list all the courses and training relevant to the contract position being advertised.

The interests/personal section is fine, although it might be worth swapping 'divorced' to single and working on the formatting to improve readability.

John Smith's CV has been totally transformed to reflect a different skill set.

PROFILE
High calibre **BUSINESS ANALYST** with 7 years experience in business and systems analysis. Heavy emphasis on business process modelling using OO techniques, UML, and case tools. Full life cycle experience. Now seeking next rewarding and challenging opportunity in a successful customer focused team.

EXPERTISE
- Powerful **project planning** and implementation skills – delivery focused.
- Skilled with MS Office, Windows and UNIX implementation and administration.
- **Full project life cycle** – configuration management and change management.
- Track record of academic achievement and career development – fluent in German.
- Effective communication and negotiation techniques – skilled in **account management**.
- Systems design and software development skills for insurance and commodity trading.
- Reliably **meets demanding deadlines** and targets working under pressure.

ACHIEVEMENTS
- Played lead role in successful initiative to rapidly expand client base to twelve clients across twenty sites and generate half of company's annual revenues.
- Used extensive technical skills and experience to develop bespoke software packages that gained the company a competitive edge in the insurance and commodities markets.

And so on.....

Box 4.6 John Smith's front page

4.6 Common mistakes

Getting to the interview stages involves impressing a potential employer with your CV. But who gets the job offer?

The fact is that the contractor who gets the job offer is not always the best contractor available for the job. They are the best person available at knowing how to get offered a job.

To reiterate the key point about the contract search process, to get a job offer you need to get an interview, and to get the interview you need a good CV. Generally the people with the best written and most focused, tailormade CVs will get interviewed.

And very often the best available people fall at the first hurdle, with their CVs being put straight into the bin or onto the 'rejects' pile, because they don't make it clear to the reader that they are perfect for the contract on offer.

To avoid being the best contractor that cannot get any work, here are some things to avoid when compiling your CV:

Far too long: If a CV is more than three pages long then everything on the third page and beyond is unlikely to be read. If the agent filtering the CVs has 200 to read, contractors have a short window to impress. So keep your CV to a maximum of three pages, preferably two.

Detail: Avoid too much detail which overlaps with the purpose of the other CV sections. The number of years and a list of your primary skills are sufficient.

Remember, the purposes of the sections are:

Profile: What your primary skills are and what you are looking for.
Expertise: List of your skills, which closely matches the client's requirements
Achievements: Backs up the expertise list, showing how you create value.
Career history: Shows that you've 'been there and done that'.

Too many sentences: Often sentences on a CV contain too many words and the reader misses the key points. So it's better to write well spaced bullet points where the most relevant information is highlighted in bold.

For example, which of the following is quicker to read?

This:

On this project we made use of the.NET Framework and utilised all the main namespaces. We used an intercepting filter pattern which we hooked into ASP.NET to implement user level functional security for the 5000 users. Model View Controller was used to connect the pages to the middle tier, which was written in C#.

Or this:

- ASP.NET, C#, **.NET Framework**.
- 5,000 users. **Functional security**.
- **Design Patterns**: Intercepting Filter, Model View Controller.

Avoid irrelevant information: You may have some aspects of your career that you are quite rightly very proud of but, unfortunately, have nothing to do with the client requirements. Leave them off the CV or mention them in a way that highlights how they might be relevant.

For example: If you are a SENIOR GAMES PROGRAMMER applying for a position in a bank, it would be sensible to change your title to 'SENIOR DEVELOPER'.

Another example: If you have worked for software houses, but are applying to work in an organisation that might have something against the 'software house type mentality', then it would be sensible to leave out 'X years experience working in software houses'. However, if the client was a software house, then of course you would leave it in and highlight it.

The same applies to mentioning skills that have become redundant. You might have been the most highly rewarded coal miner in the country, but if no one wants coal miners anymore, don't mention it.

No profile: If your CV does not have a profile that says precisely what you are and what you're good at, then the client or agent is going to have to guess by reading your CV. And because they do not have time to read the whole thing, your CV will probably go into the bin. Make sure have a profile on your CV, and ensure it is tailored to the position. Here is an example for a senior lion tamer position for a global circus:

> Enthusiastic **LION TAMER** with 10 years experience gained with leading global circuses. Extensive experience teaching and mentoring junior tamers, developing the skills of cubs and adult lions, and attracting audiences with daring new tricks. Now seeking rewarding and challenging position with major circus.

The key element of this profile is the professional title that appears in bold so it stands out. This is what you asked for, and this is what I am!

No expertise section: Without a summary of your skills the reader needs to read the whole CV and pick out the skills themselves. This is a real headache and will guarantee your CV is put either in the bin or at the bottom of the pile. If an agent or client has 200 CVs to read for one contract, they only need to find ten good candidates from their initial scan of CVs. Make sure yours gets chosen by showing clearly you have the specific skills and expertise required for that particular contract.

No achievements section: This key section, which demonstrates to the client that you are commercially focused, rather than someone who just 'does stuff' regardless of the outcome, is the section often missed out on contractors' CVs. So having a good achievements section is likely to put you above the rest who do not.

Achievements state the measurable benefits you provided to your clients that justified your existence. They are things you did that saved time, saved money, made more money, won more business and so on.

Not targeted to the role: Each time you send your CV out it should be targeted directly to the position you are going for. You may be the best soil nailing geotechnical engineer in Europe, but if that is not what the client wants, then do not call yourself one of those. Find out as much as you can about the role before you send your CV. If the client wants an experienced oil and gas engineer, make sure your profile includes the phrase, '**EXPERIENCED OIL AND GAS ENGINEER**'.

Education details on the front page: Don't waste the valuable 'real estate' on the front page by cluttering it up with details of your education. For example, if you have 10 years relevant experience, that is what to highlight on page one. If you have only been working for a couple of years, then it might be worth mentioning education in the expertise and achievement section, but still put the main details in a section on the second page.

Too much detail about your education: If you have 10 years experience, then no one cares that you got a B in religious studies 14 years ago. List your A levels, GCSEs, NVQs, etc as a one line summary, but keep your degree on a separate line. For example:

> 2:1 in lion taming from Circus University, Nutsville.
> 2 A levels, 9 GCSEs

One exception is if you are a graduate looking for a position and you have little or no experience. If you have studied courses that are relevant to the role and can show some transferable skills then it is worth going into detail. For example, if you were applying for a lion taming role which involved helping train others and feeding the animals, then it would be worth going into more detail:

2:1 in lion taming from Circus University, Nutsville
Tamed eight lions over course of three years
Taught and mentored lion taming for last two years
Studied the diets, health and mating habits of lions.

Once again the key elements of the role have been highlighted in bold.

Too much use of 'I'

Too much use of the word 'I' can appear self indulgent and does not give the appearance of a professional approach. Remove it entirely from your CV, and instead use action words like 'designed', 'improved', 'completed', 'created' and 'initiated'.

In summary

Writing a CV well involves getting inside the head of the people who are going to read it. The front page should convince the reader in no uncertain terms that you are the best person for the role.

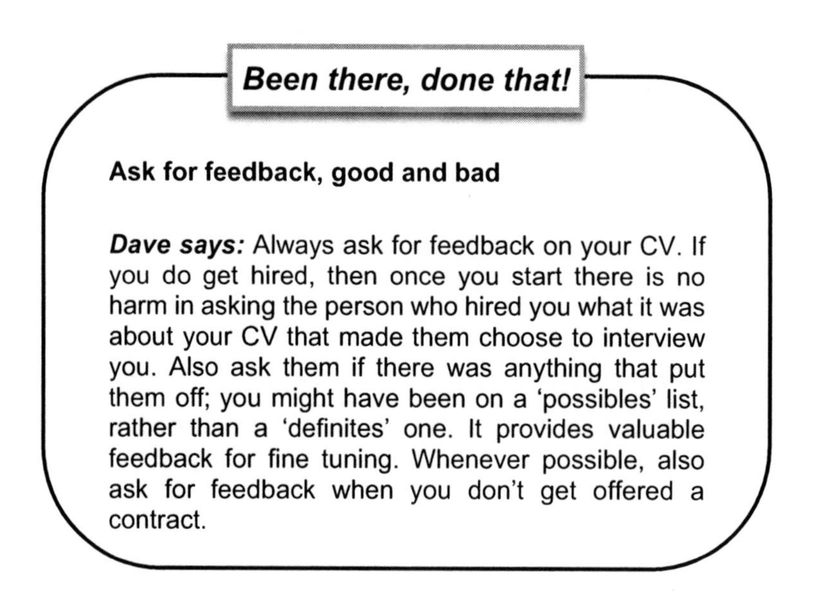

Been there, done that!

Ask for feedback, good and bad

Dave says: Always ask for feedback on your CV. If you do get hired, then once you start there is no harm in asking the person who hired you what it was about your CV that made them choose to interview you. Also ask them if there was anything that put them off; you might have been on a 'possibles' list, rather than a 'definites' one. It provides valuable feedback for fine tuning. Whenever possible, also ask for feedback when you don't get offered a contract.

5.

Finding and securing a contract

5.1 Overview

There is no better way to start contracting than to get that first contract. If your skills are what they should be and, most importantly, you get the preparation and approach right, this won't be a difficult thing to do.

Of course, there are some crucial administrative matters that need to be taken care of – like making sure you get paid! – but we'll deal with those later. First, let's sort out what you need to know to get that first contract. Because there's no better confirmation of having made the right career choice.

Finding and securing a contract is a process with a series of steps that result in paid work. However, you should remember that searching for a contract is different to looking for permanent employment; very different.

Not understanding the game and how it is played will mean fewer contracts, and that could lead to long periods when you are not working and not getting paid, which defeats the object of contracting. The key is getting just right the balance between time off and times when you want to be contracting and minimising downtime.

It could also mean working for a daily or hourly rate that is lower than the market rate for the job. Doing that is likely to mean that your recruitment agent will be charging the market rate to the client, and thereby getting a higher share of what you earn than they should. In other words, they'll be pocketing 'your' money!

Playing a good game will ensure that you spend little time in-between contracts, and that you are always earning the market rate or higher.

Contractors can in theory deal direct with clients or go via recruitment agencies. The fact is that, as highlighted in the last chapter, most clients prefer to deal through an agency and, as a result, most contracts in most sectors are only available through agencies.

That is not to say a first time contractor cannot find a contract direct with a client; it is certainly possible. But in practice it means more paperwork for the contractor, as covered below in section 5.5. However given the volume of contracts available through agencies versus those available direct, the likelihood is that your first contract will be via an agency.

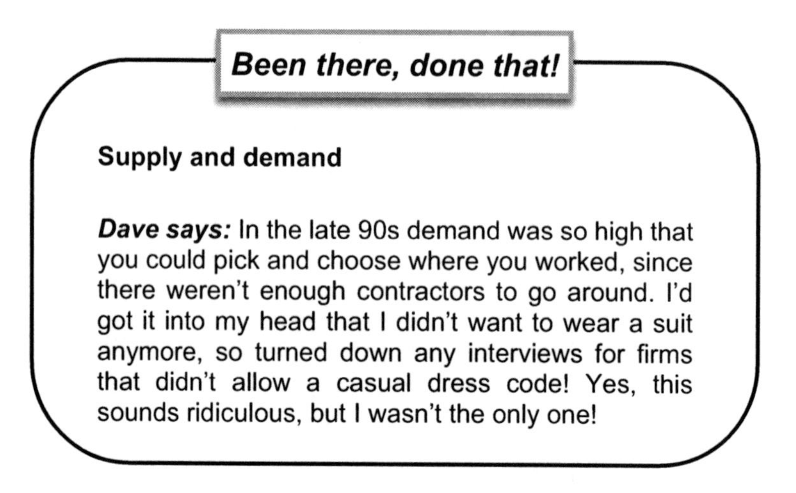

5.2 Using job boards

Job boards are a vital tool in the contract search, linking you, the contract seeker, with the recruitment agency or client. With the exception of those contracts won through networking or by word of mouth, which are frequently not advertised at all, virtually every contract is advertised on the internet somewhere.

At the time of writing, the main job boards for the majority of contracting sectors include:

- Jobserve
- CWJobs
- Jobsite
- Monster.

In addition to these major job boards, there are various specialist sites generally dedicated to particular sectors, such as IT or engineering, and some drill down even further, focusing specifically on, for example web development or oilfield engineering. Plus there are many others covering other sectors like marketing, finance and medicine, among others.

The first stage of the process is to register with those job boards likely to provide the right sort of contracts. The right job boards should be identified during your market research stage (chapters 2 and 3) when making the transition between permanent employment and contracting.

Been there, done that!

Making yourself a target

Dave says: Posting your CV on job boards is a great way to get your name out in the market. Many recruitment agents will start sourcing for their positions by mining those CV databases before they put adverts out.

The only problem is that for first timers it can attract a whole bunch of telephone traffic from agencies who will want to fill the position you are vacating at your current firm. This can result in a lot of wasted telephone calls from agents asking, 'So who was your boss at XYZ'.

If you suspect they are phishing for leads then ask them about the role they are looking to fill. If they are vague and then get back to asking about your old boss then you can be sure they are indeed phishing. Just tell them that if they secure you an interview you'll be happy to give that information out.

The same thing happens when you move from contract to contract. As soon as you put your 'hello I'm looking' flag up agents will call you to find out why you are leaving and what your boss's name is.

Been there, done that!

Was I gullible

Dave says: I secured my first contract very quickly, by being introduced to the owner of a blue chip recruitment firm, so I never had the telephone hassle. So I didn't learn the telephone tactics and motivations of agents until the end of my first contract.

Being a newbie I'd spend hours chatting to agents telling them who my ex bosses were until eventually my ex-bosses told me to stop passing their information onto agents! It wasn't until someone told me what they were doing that the penny dropped. Man, was I gullible!

Work the job boards hard, particularly by using tools like key word searches and automated alerts. Clients and agencies do not always get the copy and information 100% right in their contract posts, so keep any searches wide enough to capture contracts where the job descriptions and skills required might have 'gone astray'. It is better to spend time deleting contracts not relevant than missing out on contracts that would be perfect for you.

With most contracts being advertised by recruitment agencies, agencies are naturally huge users of job boards and frequently post contract opportunities across many sites, including the four named above. Check that you are not looking at the same contract opportunity if you see something interesting on two or more job boards.

Job boards present an important route into the recruitment agencies, and give you opportunities to send in highly targeted CVs (see chapter 4) in direct response to contract opportunities.

5.3 Working with agencies

Most successful contractors have worked with recruitment agencies during their career. Many will never contract direct for a client and always work through agencies. Agencies, or agents, are a vital element of the contracting process, performing a variety of tasks, some of which are not obvious to the contractor but are nonetheless hugely important to the entire sector. However, working with agencies is not always a smooth ride.

5.3.1 The agent is not working for you

Agencies do not work *for* contractors and do not always provide a top quality service. They may take your CV and then you won't hear anything from them again, despite the fact that they promised you work right away. An agency could forget to renew your contract on time. They may try to change the conditions of your contract when you renew, or even in the middle of the contract, so that they earn more money.

The key to all this is to remember that the agent is not working on your behalf. When you start out contracting you will be approached by agents who will assure you that they have only your best interests at heart. They will spend a long time on the telephone asking all about you, and taking all sorts of professional detail to, they say, find just the right slot for you.

But in fact the agent generally has little interest in you personally. Agencies earn commission on your fees from the client company. This is expressed in the form of a 'margin' – in other words, the agency takes a percentage of the total fee that the client pays for your services. The agency has a separate contract with the end-client that regulates all the agency business. This contract does not particularly concern you (although it can be important later should tax issues arise which are covered in chapter 8, when we talk about IR35).

Ultimately, the agent is there to fill a slot for the client and collect your fees for you. The agent earns more money as more slots get filled. In other words, the agent is similar to a salesman working on commission – do not expect more from them than that. They have their own needs and priorities, just like everybody else. However, don't forget that the agency is effectively your commission-only sales force, and so you really should respect them for the essential role they perform in this regard.

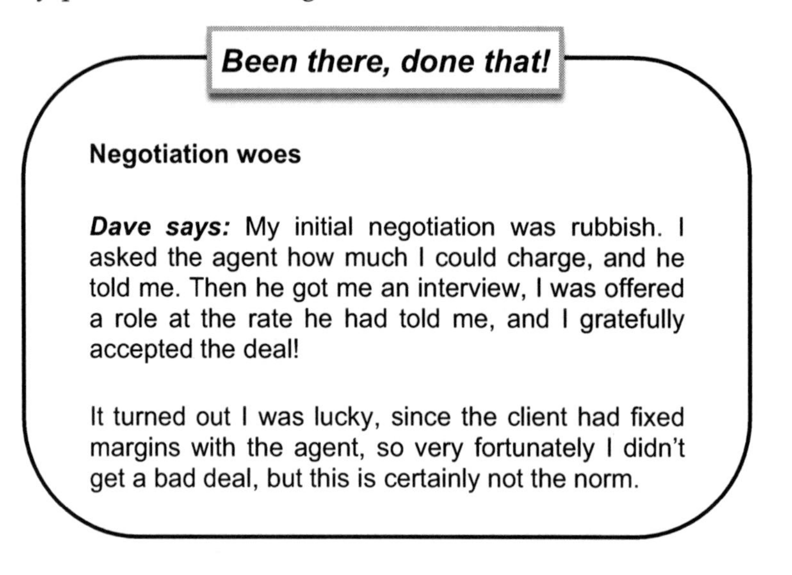

Once you fit the slot and start work on a contract, you have made a sale for the agent, and that is what the agent primarily cares about. If you can renew your contract, then the agent will pay attention to you while you negotiate the renewal. Or, if you have the skills to fill another slot on the agent's books, you are of interest for as long as that lasts.

After that, all that you mean to the agent is a pile of paperwork.

5.3.2 Treat your agent fairly

But that doesn't mean you should avoid agents, because if you use them right they are likely to be the key to you having a long, happy and profitable contracting career. So it's worth putting in the effort early on to understand where the agent is coming from; that way you will save yourself a lot of time, stress and bother.

Provide the agent with the details needed to fill the slot; be polite to the agent while you are both negotiating an agreement; and always be fair and reasonable with the agent.

But do not expect the agent to do more than the business requires: the agent won't help you with your problems, and, in general, will be on the side of the client rather than the contractor. And in business terms that's probably as it should be, because, after all, it is the client who is paying the bills.

Keep an eye on the agent. Make sure you get paid on time. Make sure your renewal goes through as agreed. Read the contracts you receive from an agent carefully, and have them reviewed if they appear to wildly contradict the contract law outlined in chapter 7.

5.3.3 Finally, the agent calls

If you've followed the CV guidance in chapter 4 and your CV has found its way to the top of the pile, the agent will give you a call and ask you about arranging an interview with the client. You may be about to make a deal. So what do you, the contractor, charge for your services?

Chapter 3 details how to go about setting a rate. But if you're not certain about what to charge, at this stage, just tell the agent that you charge the 'market rate' and wait for an offer.

The agent may offer you a low rate, which will allow for a nice healthy margin for them, but you can negotiate this up a bit. After all, the agent is finding you work, and deserves to be fairly rewarded for that service. Of course, if your particular skill set is in high demand, push for as much as you think you have a right to. Experience in doing these negotiations will soon help you to get the range right.

When you are first negotiating with the agent over money, try to be vague and non-committal, because the agent wants to hear: a) that you are perfect for the role; and b) that you are inexperienced enough to let them get away with enjoying a higher margin by passing on less to you of what the client is prepared to pay.

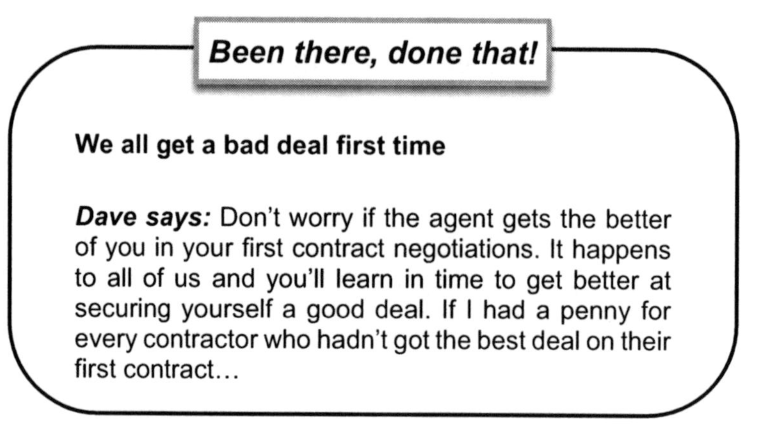

So, during conversations, sound really keen about the position, give the impression that you will fit in perfectly, but be vague on rate. You want to get them to say a figure first. So, you will say 'market rate' and they will keep asking you what that is.

You then throw it back to them and ask them what they think they can get you in the door for. They may come in low and you can say that it sounds about right for the role, but you could suggest this figure as part of a range, e.g. £400 to £500 per day. Then when you get the offer you can simply open negotiations at the top end and stick to your range. If you ask for more, you really need to qualify the request by saying something like "I've been offered more elsewhere and if you match it I'll take this one."

After an interview you might get a call like, 'They like you, but can only afford XYZ'. This is probably just the agent trying to increase their margin, and they might be playing two contractors off against each other. You'll need to stand your ground here, and balance your negotiation with any other offer you might have. You can help your negotiations by trying to establish the strength of your position at the interview stage by asking at the end:

- Do you have any reservations about hiring me?
- Do you have other candidates to see?
- Have you seen anyone else, and were they any good?
- Are you happy with the rate I am quoting you?

Been there, done that!

Stuffed... for a year

Dave says: On one contract I had to interview and hire other contractors and was given a list of agencies to call. Agents quoted the final rate to me for this one chap at £45 an hour – pretty much the same the rest of us were being charged at.

When he turned up on site we found out he was getting paid only £30 an hour, meaning the agency was taking a huge margin. This was his own fault for poor negotiation, but nonetheless a really bad deal for him. The firm tried to sort it out, but the agency wouldn't budge, and he was stuck on that rate for a year.

I learnt from this, and in the future when I hired contractors I told them what they should be charging, much to the annoyance of the agents. Having upset contractors on your team is much worse than having an upset agent whose wages you pay!

Many managers won't work out you are trying to work out how keen they are in order to establish your bargaining position and will be open and honest about things.

So the key is to be vague with the agent and ensure you get yourself an interview, because once you get the offer you have miles more bargaining power. Agents aren't keen on contractors doing this, in the same way contractors aren't keen on the agents getting the better end of a deal, but it is all par for the course. It is simply business and, as a contractor, you are in business for yourself, so you should not feel guilty about it.

The most important thing to remember about negotiation is that everyone needs to feel they are getting a good deal. If one party feels hard done by then the long term arrangement won't be satisfactory to all.

5.3.4 Agency opt-out regulations

In 2003, the Department of Trade and Industry, now the Department of Business, Enterprise and Regulatory Reform (BERR) adopted a code called "Conduct of Employment Agencies and Employment Business Regulations".

Guidance from BERR says these were intended to govern the conduct of the private recruitment industry and establish a framework of minimum standards that work seekers and hirers are entitled to expect.

The regulations are intended to protect equal rights for all temporary and agency workers, and they are especially concerned with 'fly-by-night' agencies and 'gangmasters.' The average contractor is not too concerned with those kinds of issues, but the regulations apply equally to contractor 'agency workers' as well.

In practice, compliance with the conduct of employment regulations means that agencies have to behave very much like employers. For example, they have to verify much of the personal information and career references of the contractors.

Many contractors and agencies alike find the regulations cumbersome and unnecessary. Contractors have many contracts over their career and providing documentation for a new agency about every contract is a burden. And for the agency, which then has to check all the records and references, it would be costly and time consuming. In fact, it is just not practical in the fast moving contract industry, where contractors are generally as far away from being 'vulnerable workers' as it is possible to get!

Agency workers do have the opportunity to opt out of the regulations, and this provides contractors, if confident of their ability to manage their agency, a way to avoid the costly and time-consuming requirements.

Another key factor for contractors when considering their standing under the regulations is their 'IR35 status'. Opting in suggests that the contractor is in some way under the 'control' of the agency, an issue covered in detail in chapter 8. But on the other hand, opting in can make the transition from contracting back to permanent work easier; you can work for the client without the client having to pay a large finder's fee to the agency, although few contractors make this change.

However, beware – you have the right to opt in and the agency is legally not allowed to encourage you to opt out. But you may find yourself not getting interviews if you have chosen to opt in. Not surprisingly, there are very few contractors who do opt in.

So is there ever a downside to 'opting out' of the code of regulations? Essentially, contractors need to be their own business managers. They should check that the terms proposed by an agency are both reasonable and acceptable. Basically, they should behave like business people looking after the best interests of their business.

5.4 Basic sales – the contract search process

As a contractor, you are in business for yourself. Whether working through a limited company or an umbrella company, or contracting directly with a client or through an agent, the responsibility to generate new business (i.e. keep finding new contracts) lies with you.

This is why developing sales and marketing skills is so important for every contractor. The CV, covered in chapter 4, is the contractor's marketing literature, customised according to the target market and matching the product, i.e. the contractor, with the market, i.e. the contract.

Sales is the process of keeping a constant stream of contract leads coming through. The larger the sales hopper, the more potential contracts you can apply for, and the more chance there is of winning a contract. Let that hopper run dry and no more contracts will appear.

So the contract search process is no different from how marketing and sales professionals sell products and services throughout industry and commerce. A simplified summary is:

- Lead generation – the contracting equivalent would be finding contracts using job boards and agencies
- Sales proposal – a contractor sending a tailored CV that effectively lays out a solution to the client's project issues and needs
- Closing the deal – this is when a contractor, after interview, has convinced the client that they are the right person for the role, negotiated a good fee and won the contract.

Finding your first contract might appear to be administrative hell, but it gets to be far easier, quicker and, at times, even enjoyable. However it is vital to keep on top of the 'sales' process. Chapter 3 listed a series of daily activities that will drive the contract search process, and these should be followed to ensure success:

- Chase agencies you have sent applications or CVs to by telephone and email
- Keep searching job boards and other sources of contracts
- Maintain a steady stream of applications
- Network, by maintaining social and more formal links with contacts in your industry.

You decrease your chances of securing a contract considerably if all you do is send off emails to agents and wait for the phone to ring. Making contract applications is not like tennis, where you wait for the agent to hit the ball back. You need to keep hitting plenty of balls over the net until they notice you. And you also need to chase the agent to ensure they pick your ball up!

If you are only one of a few who are applying for the position then they might phone you. If they have plenty of applications then your email might not even get read. Other seasoned contractors will be phoning the agents shortly after sending them emails to ensure they get their CV to the top of the pile for review. If you don't also do this you are one step behind the competition. So you need to chase them by phone.

Most good agents are goal-driven and work hard, so they can be difficult to get hold of. Even if you leave a message requesting that they call you back they are unlikely to do so. Whilst this might appear rude, it isn't intentionally done to upset contractors. It is just the way the industry works. Agents would rather spend more time chasing new business than speaking to every contractor who applies for a position. Therefore, if they don't call back then ring them again.

Making lots of telephone calls to chase business can be time consuming. It is therefore important to make optimum use of your time, and that means filtering out time-wasting activities.

It is advisable to keep notes of when you have tried to speak to agents about positions so that you develop a good sense of when to cut your losses and move on to the next position. Check out chapter 10 for more tips on how to make the sales process really work in your favour.

5.5 Contracting direct

Contracting direct with the client can have advantages as, for example, there is no middleman such as an agency to take a cut of your contract fee. This could work for the client, because you might be slightly cheaper, and it might work for you because you might get slightly more than if contracting through an agency.

However, the chances of a new contractor securing an immediate contract direct with a client are slim. But contracts can come from anywhere, and there might be opportunities to apply direct, particularly in some sectors and for those with certain skill sets – like highly specialised contractors with a small number of potential clients.

A major difference between contracting direct and contracting through an agent is that the contractor is entirely responsible for arranging their own contract between the client and the contractor's limited company.

Getting started

The first place to start is winning a contract. The process is similar to that described already, but obviously involves considering contracts that are being advertised by end-user clients rather than agencies.

Start with market research and work through the job boards and other sources of trade information. For example, if you spot an article in a trade magazine that a major mechanical and electrical engineering firm has started a major job and is already complaining of skills shortages, this may be a good lead. But beware of inefficient use of your time.

It is also worth considering creating the infrastructure to start contracting sooner rather than later. This could mean incorporating a limited company and opening a company bank account or investigating an umbrella company before a contract has been found. As contracts can start within a week (or even sooner!) of the client agreeing the deal, a contractor might have to move fast finding experts to create and check contracts made direct with the client, advising on IR35 status and so on.

Pitfalls of going direct

When contracting direct chasing payment can be a pain, particularly if you contract with a large organisation that thinks it's fine to pay in 60 days, or more. When you contract via an agent they typically pay you before they get paid, by 'factoring out' their invoices. You could do this yourself if you contract direct, but it does mean time and money spent on chasing payment when you could be doing something more productive and profitable.

Just because you go direct doesn't automatically mean you will earn more. The client has spent more time and resources finding you rather than outsourcing it to an agent. So they will be looking to get that back. Also, bear in mind the extra time you might spend trying to find a contract, whilst not getting paid.

The cost of your own sales, in downtime when you are not earning, is unlikely to be more than the extra money you might get paid by going direct. So going direct is certainly not the road to significantly increased riches.

Even if you find your own contracts through networking, many firms will still insist you bill via their agency, which will take a cut, as this insulates them from legal issues and helps their administration.

5.6 Interviews

The agent has made the call and you have made it to the interview stage with the end user client. Or you may have found a contract direct. So you now need to ensure you maximise your chances of being offered the position by effectively preparing for and conducting the interview.

Without effective preparation, it is almost guaranteed that you will not get offered the contract. The prospective client, frequently accompanied by a colleague from the human resources department, will instantly spot lack of preparation and think, "Will this person's slack approach to preparation affect any work they might do for us? Yes, probably."

Preparation does not have to be difficult or overly time consuming and, in fact, can often prove interesting and even enjoyable on a professional level. Do it right and it will easily become part of the natural cycle of your interviews for new contracts.

5.6.1 The Basics – Where, when and with whom?

Ensure you know the interview location and leave plenty of time to account for delays in travel. Arriving at an interview late means you already start the interview from behind the rest of the candidates. It gives the impression that you can't organise yourself and plan. Better to be an hour early than a minute late. You can always grab a coffee and go through your notes. It also reduces the panic that could set in if you arrive in a hurry and aren't relaxed.

If you are driving then ensure in advance that you will be able to park, that the car has petrol in it, and that you have change in your pocket for parking meters. On the morning before you set off check the road traffic reports. Take an umbrella in case it rains. You don't want to turn up soaked from head to toe. And make sure you look the part. In many cases this will mean a nice suit or smart trousers/skirt and jacket, with a plain shirt and tie – traditional business wear, in other words.

If you're being interviewed for a consumer brand that appears to be relaxed and laid-back, don't make the mistake of thinking that they have a relaxed approach to their work, too – they will almost certainly want to see that you have a professional attitude and that this is reflected in how you dress for an interview.

Don't carry your documents in a plastic bag; neatly folded in an envelope is fine, whilst even better would be to have a smart briefcase or a corporate-looking handbag or folder.

Make sure you know the name of the person or people you are meeting and their job title(s). If the name(s) appears difficult to pronounce then ensure you check first with your agent or the client's HR manager who arranged the interview, so that you get it right. If the person you are meeting has a name that doesn't instantly make their gender obvious, find out from the agent whether they are male or female. This avoids you making mistakes, like assuming they are the secretary to the person you are meeting when in actual fact they are the person you are meeting.

Keep details on you in case you have trouble finding the place and need to make a phone call to confirm them. Also, if you are late then you can phone in advance to warn them. If you are working through an agent, you can always question them about any special dress codes or instructions.

5.6.2 Motivation – What the client will be looking for

It is important to try and examine and understand the needs and motivations of the client, so that you can work out why they might need you as a contractor to solve a problem for them. This understanding should help drive the rest of the interview preparation.

An event has occurred which has necessitated the need of the client to hire a contractor. They advertise and filter candidates down to those they wish to interview. These are some of the things they will be looking for in an interview:

- Is this person skilled for the position? Can they achieve what we need them to?
- Do I feel they have a good grasp of their subject matter?
- Do they follow the industry and keep up with the latest advancements?
- Can this person work on their own and use their initiative?

- Is this a nice person to get on with or do I think they are arrogant with a self inflated ego and delusions of grandeur?
- Do I like them?
- Will they fit into our corporate culture?
- Is this person going to make me look stupid, or support me and help me to look good?
- Are they presentable?
- Do they suffer from personal hygiene problems?
- Can they communicate with other human beings?
- Do they perhaps know a little bit more than other candidates, which could help give the company an edge?
- Do they understand my problems and what would be required of them?
- Do they give an indication of laziness or are they prepared to get stuck in?
- Do I feel they are trying to solve my problems or just trying to get a contract?
- Are they a positive person who will motivate those around them or a merchant of doom that will bring everyone down?
- Are they a good listener?
- Are they more focused on telling me how great they are than on trying to understand how they can fulfil the needs of the contract?
- Are they commercially aware? Will they bring that awareness to the contract, helping us achieve our commercial goals by creatively using their skills, rather than just sticking rigidly to the specifications and doing what they're told to and no more?
- Do they know anything about our company? Or the challenges and opportunities facing our sector?

Knowing these are the kind of questions the interviewer will be looking to answer, use them to drive the preparation.

Step 1: Find out why they need you

They will need you for perhaps one of the following common reasons:

- The client is spending too much money and feel that by spending more money on you, you will make things more efficient
- Someone else has left the job and they need to be replaced
- They need you to do a bespoke piece of work due to legislation they need to adhere to, or because they don't have the skills in-house
- They need you to train some of their staff with the niche skills you offer.

Press your agent to find out what the real reason is. In addition, use other contacts to find out. You might know someone else who works there. If you cannot find this out then it will be the first thing you will need to ascertain at the start of the interview. Without knowing the answer to this basic question, it is pretty much impossible to tailor your responses to meet their requirements.

Step 2: Learn about the company

This is to ensure you tick the interviewing client's box for 'at least they did their homework and found out a bit about the company'. At the start of the interview you will most certainly be asked 'Do you know much about the company?'. You will not look convincing if you say no. You need something prepared.

An answer that will normally suffice would be something along the generalised form of 'Yes, I researched your company last week. [tells them you made an effort]. I understand you have 20,000 thousand employees over 40 countries. It was interesting to read recently in the news about XYZ. This might make an impact on the share price, which looks to be holding up well. Do you own shares in the company? [Notice how it finishes on a question to keep the flow of conversation going].

In addition, if you know you are going there to interview for a contract that is to solve a specific problem for them, find out about it. Go to their website if they have one, or trawl the internet to find out what you can.

This type of information is very useful background:

- How many employees
- When the company was formed and who started it
- The company mission statement and unique selling proposition (USP)
- Offices locations, both national and international
- Expansion rate of the company
- Annual turnover
- Current share price, and how it has done over time
- Recent press statements.

Step 3: Write down the skills required for the contract
Make a short list of what you think the requirements are. Use the motivation of what they are looking for in an interview to drive this part. An example of an IT contractor's list might be something like this:

- .NET Development – 5 years experience – I comfortably qualify
- Replace an existing team member – so some maintenance involved. Wonder why they are leaving?
- Good communication skills – so I will be speaking to end users
- Small project – so should have done deployments, maintenance, testing and so on over the whole life cycle
- Can work on my own – so probably need to be commercially aware. Cost versus benefits and so on.

Notice that this example has mainly focused on the technical skills. Keep in mind all the other non-technical ones though, as these will be needed to drive the motivation behind your list of questions.

Step 4: Your list of questions
This is a key element of the process. There is nothing wrong with physically getting out your list of questions when you are at the interview and using them. It shows you have prepared and made an effort.

It is better to commit them to memory as they will then not look as wooden when asked. Even if you do remember the whole lot, still get out your piece of paper at the end to show them that you did do some preparation.

Your list of questions should follow these guidelines:

- The questions you ask must promote discussion about topics where you can demonstrate you have all the skills required for the job
- Your questions must address all of the aspects the interviewer is looking for
- Your questions should also demonstrate that you know just that little bit more than is required. A bit like 'bonus features' for them if they take you on. But take care not to over-do it, as you don't want them to think your core skills lie elsewhere.

Step 5: The day of the interview
Before you leave the house, do a quick search on the internet to get latest share prices, and any mention of the company in the news. Having fresh up to date information on the company will give you extra points when they ask the inevitable first question.

Step 6: Waiting in reception
Get your notes out. Brush up on the company facts. Try and commit your questions to memory. If you see one, grab a copy of any magazine published by the company and try and read something about recent press statements and company news – the sort of topics that can generate good, relevant conversation during the interview.

Been there, done that!

Research pays

Dave says: I remember once attending an interview with a client that provides breakdown and recovery services to drivers. I was waiting outside the guy's office and picked up an internal magazine that talked about a new laptop they had purpose-made for their drivers, because existing ones couldn't cope with the wet. When I mentioned this in my response to 'what do you know about us' the guy was seriously impressed and said that was news that had only just come out. I got offered the position.

Another good trick is to take a look around the walls of the offices and see if you can spot any award certificates, like ISO 9001, Investors in People and so on. They can be useful in your opening conversation or for answering the first question.

Step 7: Your opening conversation

You meet, shake hands and then you are led to the room where the interview is taking place. Chances are you are probably met by the person who is interviewing you. It is a good idea to have an opening conversation prepared for the walk between reception and the room. It removes the awkward silence and gets you off to a good start. Some examples might include:

"So, how long have you been working for XYZ Ltd?"

"I noticed you had an award for XYZ. You must be proud of that."

You will tend to find the interviewer will ask the inevitable 'Did you have any trouble getting here? or 'Did you find us OK?' Always answer 'No problem.' Then continue: 'So, tell me, how long have you been working for XYZ Ltd?', or another one of your prepared questions. Don't start going into how you got here, which route you took and so on. It is boring and they really don't care. Switch it round and get them talking about themselves and the company. Take an interest from the start.

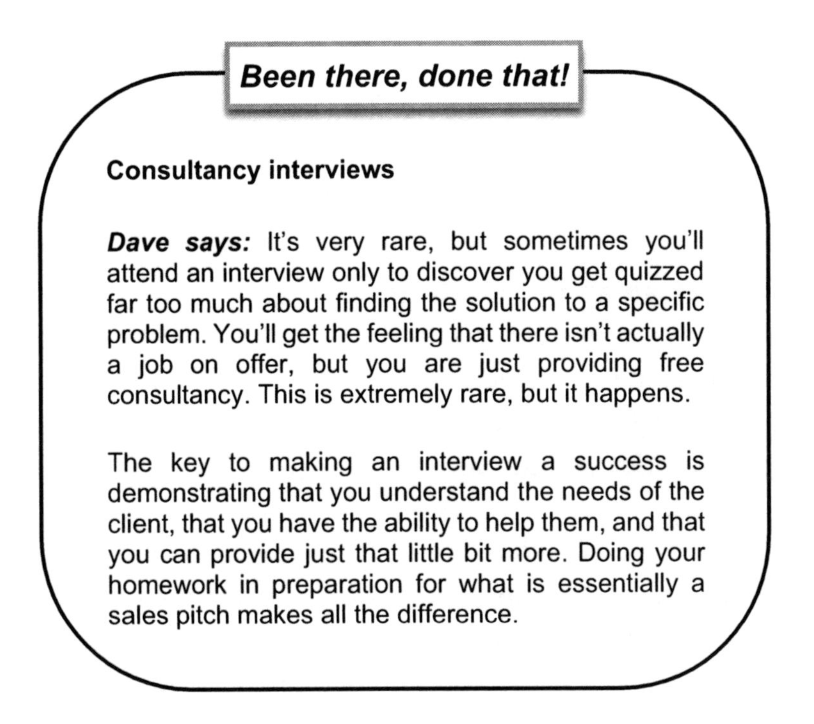

Been there, done that!

Consultancy interviews

Dave says: It's very rare, but sometimes you'll attend an interview only to discover you get quizzed far too much about finding the solution to a specific problem. You'll get the feeling that there isn't actually a job on offer, but you are just providing free consultancy. This is extremely rare, but it happens.

The key to making an interview a success is demonstrating that you understand the needs of the client, that you have the ability to help them, and that you can provide just that little bit more. Doing your homework in preparation for what is essentially a sales pitch makes all the difference.

5.6.3 After the interview

After your interview the agent will normally phone you to see how it went. They will naturally want to know if they are close to finalising a deal themselves. The agent will also try to gauge both the strength of the client's interest in you and the strength of your interest in the position.

If you weren't interested in the position, then tell the agent outright to avoid wasting their time, but make sure you tell them why. It will normally be because the position was not as originally described to you, which will be useful feedback for the agent. It helps to maintain a good relationship with the agent who may call you again for a more relevant role.

If you are very interested in the position, then try not to sound overly keen, as it could result in the agent thinking that they can increase their margin by lowering your rate, knowing that you are likely to accept.

It is not uncommon for an agent to later offer you the position with the story "...the client liked you, and wants to hire you but they can only pay XYZ." Try not to get caught out with this common technique, by sticking to your guns over the rate.

5.6.4 Where can an interview go wrong?

Other than failing to treat the interview like a sales meeting, which is the number one common mistake, there are some other common mistakes that can also guarantee the client won't be calling you or your agent to offer you the contract:

Wrongly focused on what the contract does for you rather than how you can help the client: Never discuss why the role would be good for you and what you would get out of it. The client does not care. They are solely interested in whether they can trust you to do the job on time and to budget. Clients pay you top money to help them solve their problems, not yours.

Failure to address their problems: You fail to understand the problems they want solved and summarise how your relevant experience will be of benefit to them in solving their problems. It is down to you to convince them you can meet their needs, not for them to establish this from general stuff you say.

Not being absolutely honest (in other words, telling lies): Sometimes candidates pretend they know something rather than admitting that they don't. You will be caught out and no one hires a 'blagger' as they are far too risky. The client wants to know that at the end of the day they can trust you to either get something done, or put your hand up and ask for help.

Been there, done that!

Bow out early

Dave says: Some projects that clients want you to do are truly awful and you won't be interested, and neither will many other contractors.

I once attended an interview for an internet start-up that wanted me to 'look after' their current system, which was riddled with software defects, and apply patches to it whilst another team built the replacement. Hardly attractive, so I cut the interview short and wished them the best of luck finding someone.

If you attend an interview and the project has been over-sold to you, then feel free to say so and stop the interview in a polite way. There's no point you all wasting any more time.

In my contracting career I attended three interviews like this. They all had the same thing in common – they wanted contractors to come in and maintain their legacy system. Contractors don't really do this – they live on the cutting edge.

Inability to listen/failure to answer the question: Sometimes candidates, particularly technical types, can 'go off on one' and get carried away by drilling down into some detailed technical area when it is not required and/or doesn't answer the question they've been asked.

Interrupting too much: This is interpreted as, and is, just plain rude. Wait for the other person to finish speaking. Make notes whilst they are speaking if you are worried you will forget your points by the time they have finished. Be aware that your eagerness may be mistaken for bad manners.

Talking too much: Some people simply too talk much – don't be one of them. Ensure the conversation is evenly balanced. If they speak for 90% of the time you won't get your points across and will fail to impress them. If you speak 90% of the time, they will think you talk too much and are a poor listener.

Lack of preparation: Lack of preparation means you know nothing about the company and don't have a list of relevant questions to ask that will get everything across that will help you sell yourself. Make sure you at least know the basics about the company and never assume you already have that knowledge – chances are you'll simply end up looking foolish when you discover, for example, that the CEO you're referring to was forced out by shareholders two months ago! You should also create a set of open questions that provoke conversations about topics that you know a lot about.

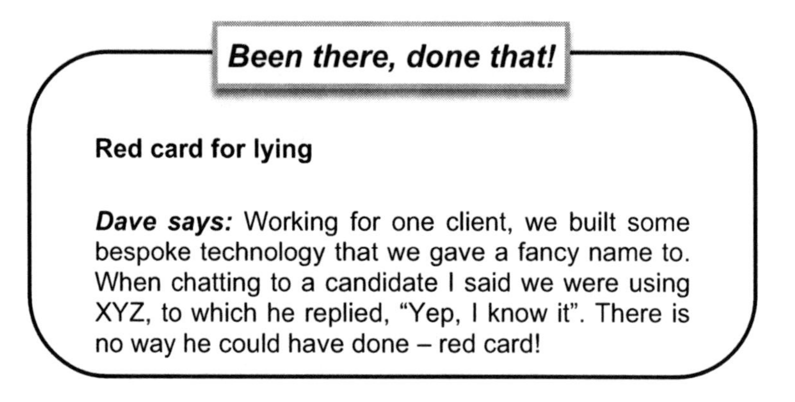

Poor timing: Too much focus on one issue means you fail to shine in other areas, and can get to the end of the interview without having properly sold yourself.

Poorly targeted answers: Align your responses to be appropriate for the interviewer. If they are non-technical then don't bore them with deep technical information they know nothing about. They won't be impressed. Use familiar buzzwords and describe the benefits in terms of how your skills will make sure you meet deadlines and how your approach to the project will help improve their business.

Lack of commercial awareness: If you fail to show you understand business and the concept of cost versus benefit, then the interviewers will be worried that you will spend too much time building something they don't want. Do demonstrate your commercial acumen.

Discussion of money: It is just the wrong place to do this and makes you look like a novice. Do this with the agent or, if contracting direct, with the client's HR people after you've successfully completed the interview. Never discuss money with your prospective project manager or other people that might be interviewing you.

That said, there is nothing wrong by finishing with, 'Are you comfortable with the rate I've quoted?'. This is useful to know as sometimes the agent may try and negotiate you down on a rate by saying the client cannot afford you.

Know it all: Don't give the impression you know everything. No one likes an ego – they wreck teams, cause mayhem and ultimately don't complete the contract as it should be, preferring to complete it in the way they 'know' is best.

Lack of interest: Lack of knowledge about the company, the sector and the project will show you are not that bothered. Do some homework about the company.

Boring: No one likes working with someone who is dull. Use your sense of humour, within reason, and relax and be yourself.

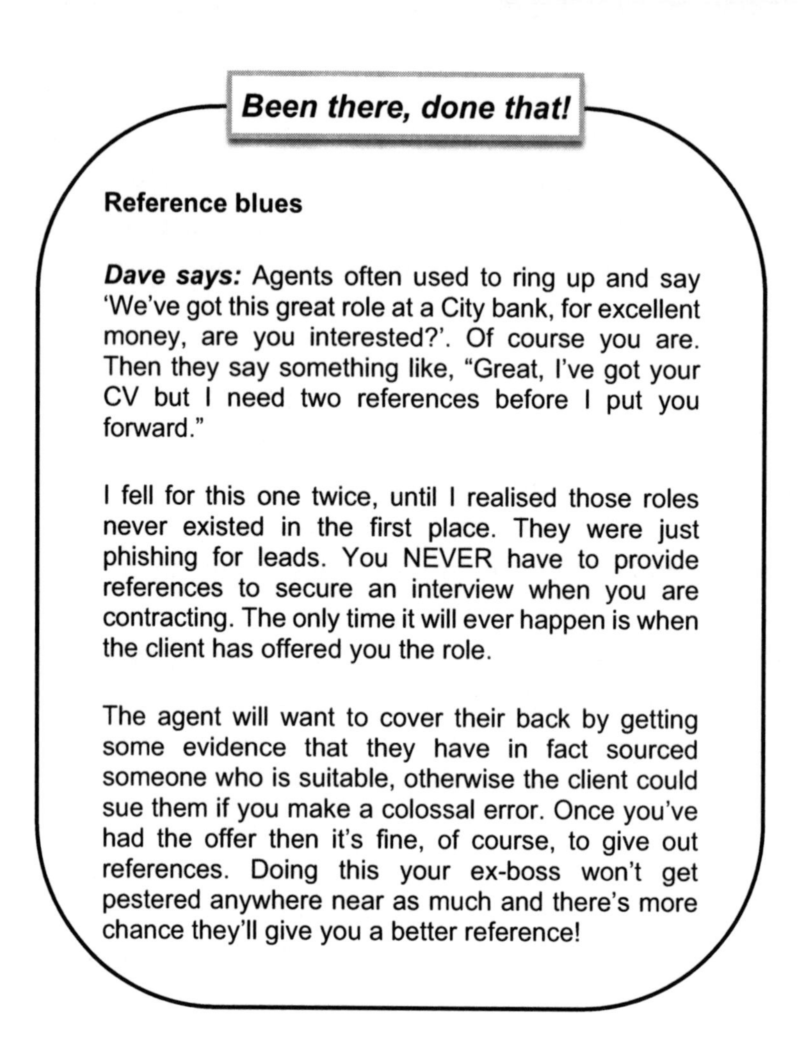

5.7 Negotiation

Assuming the interview was a success, you are now in a good position to negotiate the rate you want with your soon-to-be agent. You have either had a go-ahead from the client, or a lot of encouragement. That means you now tell the agency you want a rate that is at the top end of the range you previously discussed, or maybe a little bit more if you have been offered more elsewhere.

The agency is so close to signing a deal that they will almost certainly accommodate a slightly reduced margin if it means closing the deal, getting a reasonable margin and being able to move on to the next deal. If you decide to walk away now, the agent risks annoying the client, losing money and possibly losing out to another agency.

What happens if the agency refuses or says they want to think about it? The course of action is to play the game and just let them dither. They will usually come back to you soon enough. Again though, the important thing here is that everyone is happy with the deal that gets struck.

But you do need to consider whether or not you want to lose the deal altogether. For each deal you refuse you are likely to spend a certain amount of time out of work, unless you have a few on the table at once. You earn nothing when you're not working, so you need to decide if the extra money is worth it for you to say 'no'.

When the agency calls back, agree to the deal if you want to, and then ask the agency to send on the contract as soon as possible – you will want to review this before going any further. Chapter 7 will help you to know what to consider at this point.

5.8 Contract Offer

The agent will be keen to get you to sign the contract immediately to finalise the deal and secure their revenue stream. However, before signing, it is important you get your contract checked by a qualified lawyer, and preferably a specialist in contractor affairs and IR35.

This is to ensure the terms are fair, and most importantly to establish your IR35 position, which was introduced in chapter 3 and is covered in more detail in chapter 8. Failure to invest a little time and money at this stage could potentially cost you huge sums in the future, as has been found out by contractors investigated by HMRC who have been found not to have got the paperwork right from the start.

Been there, done that!

Get it checked

Dave says: I started contracting before IR35 even existed, and in those days contractors rarely got their contracts checked by lawyers. Provided there were no crazy clauses about working silly hours for nothing, we tended just to sign them. The contracting landscape is very different now, though, and a legal review is essential if you plan on staying outside IR35.

If you've never used a lawyer before, don't baulk at the process or the cost – it is not difficult and neither is it too expensive. Remember, you should be earning a lot more as a contractor and using a lawyer should be seen as buying you peace of mind and ultimately saving you money.

The contract will require the name of the company who the agency will be doing business with – either your own limited company or an umbrella company, both of which are dealt with in future chapters.

After negotiating and agreeing the contract it is simply a case of liaising with the agent to sign it. Most will be keen for this to happen as soon as possible to close the deal, although some will send them via post for your signature and return.

5.9 Starting the contract

Starting a contract is not the same as starting a new job when in permanent employment. The client is expecting the contractor to hit the ground running, with no gentle introduction to colleagues, lunches on the first day, silver business card holders or staff induction programmes. Work starts immediately.

As with the interview, do your preparation before you arrive on the first day. Chances are, the location of the interview will be the client's site and the person who conducted the interview will be the project manager. But don't assume this – check beforehand.

The client's site, which should always be referred to as such, is not your permanent place of work. If you're working through your own limited company which has a home office, that is your principal place of work.

Why is this important? Because as a contractor you can enjoy travel and subsistence allowances, which will reduce the amount of tax you pay. The client's site is not your place of work so you can claim travel to and from this location, plus subsistence costs like lunches when working on site (but not in the staff canteen! – see chapter 8 to find out why).

Know what time and date you are due to start the contract. As most contracts start very quickly, this is an easier mistake to make than you would imagine, and if a major project is being launched the day you are supposed to start, with project team briefings arranged for many contractors and client employees, arriving a day late will not be popular, and is technically a breach of contract (remember, you are no longer a permanent employee, but a company/contractor providing a service).

Get to know your colleagues and your way around quickly, and get used to doing this. Establishing and maintaining good working relationships is essential not just for the current contract, but also as a source of future contracts. If you are both good at what you do and great to work with people will remember you.

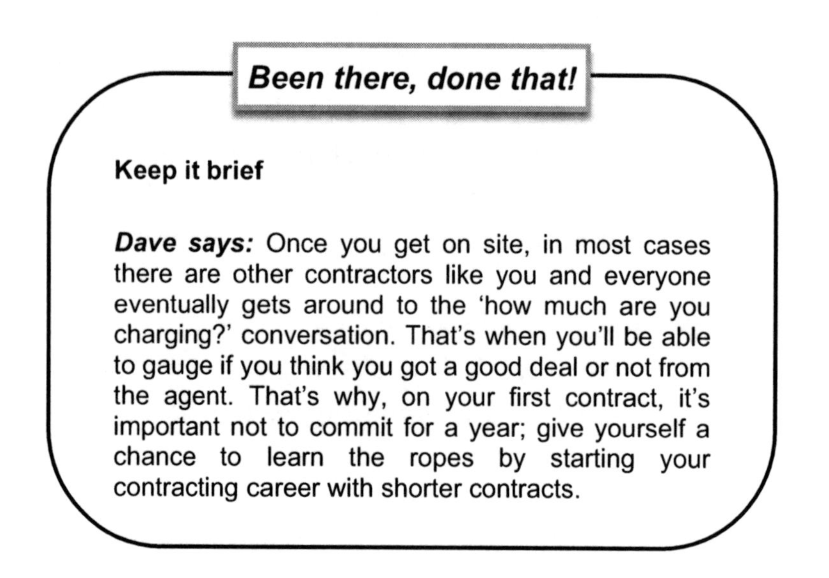

5.10 Getting paid

One of the main drivers for becoming a contractor is of course to earn more money. This requires you having a payment mechanism in place so that the agency, or the client if you are contracting direct, can actually pay you.

Depending on the nature of the contract and whether it is inside or outside of IR35, you will need to decide on a trading option (covered in chapter 6) and then deal with the admin associated with this option. Most contractors either work through their own limited company or an umbrella company, and there will be different payment methods for each.

You need to find out from the agent how their payment mechanism works. Most contractors are paid weekly or monthly and the process is generally:

- The contractor works their hours during the week, completes a weekly timesheet and submits this for sign-off by the client's representative, usually the project manager

- The copy of the signed-off timesheet is sent to the agent or umbrella company by the contractor
- The agent or umbrella company does the sums – typically hourly rate times hours worked – and invoices the client accordingly (in the agent's case the hourly rate will be higher to allow for their margin)
- The contractor working for an agent through their own limited company directly invoices the agent for their fees; contractors working through an umbrella company get paid their PAYE 'salary' by their umbrella company 'employer'.

The above process has been simplified and there are complications regarding Value Added Tax (VAT), travel and subsistence costs and other issues, all of which are covered in later chapters in more detail. It is important for contractors to keep on top of their paperwork. It is worth the effort as the financial rewards can be considerable.

6.

How to set up and run your business

6.1 Introduction

Now you have got you first contract, you will need to create the correct trading vehicle and supporting administration to ensure that you can get paid and are working within the law.

The UK has a variety of ways a contractor can do business, and section 6.2 covers these. However, in practice, most contractors will be either working through their own limited company or through an umbrella company.

A limited company carries a certain burden of administration and duties and responsibilities; they are after all separate legal entities in their own right and the contractor is responsible for ensuring that they are run in accordance with UK law.

However, the major advantage of a limited company is that a contractor can earn much more money through entirely legal tax efficient procedures and, should they desire, be able to make significant provision for retirement or semi-retirement.

Umbrella companies remove most of the administrative burden and much of the responsibility but the opportunity to earn and save is low compared to a limited company.

There is a threshold at which the costs of running a limited company are higher than the tax benefits. This is approximately £25 per hour, although the exact amount will depend on your personal circumstances. If you are paid less than this amount, an umbrella company may be the best option.

It is also important to understand that the nature of the contract with the client may dictate the most efficient way to trade. If the contractor is outside IR35 (covered in chapter 8), then it is generally much more effective to work through a limited company. If the contractor is caught by IR35, which means the taxman will treat them as an employee regardless of how they trade, it may be more advantageous for some contractors to use umbrella companies — if they're being taxed as employees, why should they have the burden of a limited company without the financial benefits? Let someone else take the strain.

The final and most important factor that dictates trading options for contractors – and limits most to either limited or umbrella companies – is that clients and agents tend to insist on them. Most simply will not work with sole traders and will insist on having the additional layer of the limited company or umbrella company between them and the contractor, so that there can be little or no doubt in the taxman's mind that the contractor is not a permanent employee of the client.

6.2 Your trading options

6.2.1 Limited company

For any contractors, including those new to contracting, a limited company is the ideal solution to maximise all those benefits that led them into contracting in the first place: more net income, flexibility, a better lifestyle, provision for their future, ring-fenced personal and business assets – the list goes on. However, there is an administrative burden of running a limited company that other trading options do not have, or have less of.

A limited company is a separate legal trading entity from the contractor. This means that the company can enter into agreements that are separate from the contractor, like bank loans or lease hire agreements and, most importantly, contracts.

Incorporation of a limited company is a quick and cost-effective process (see section 6.3.1), which usually results in the contractor becoming a director and shareholder of the company. Some contractors have spouses, family members or business colleagues as co-directors and/or shareholders, although in some cases these can lead to complications we'll discuss later.

Once the limited company is formed and a bank account is opened, the contractor can issue invoices for contracts and start trading. It's as quick and easy as that. However, if you have a poor credit record and County Court Judgements (CCJs) then you may find it very difficult to open a business bank account, which would rule out a limited company as your trading option.

The major difference between a permanent employee being paid a salary once a month, with National Insurance Contributions (NICs) and Pay As You Earn (PAYE) income tax deducted at source, and limited scope to claim for expenses and a contractor being paid through their own limited company can be summed up in one word: dividends.

Shareholders in a limited company receive some or all of their income via dividends instead of salary. Dividends do attract income tax, but this is calculated some time after the dividends have been paid. And, importantly, dividends do not attract NICs.

Also, because a contractor's legitimate expenses are deductible from their limited company, this can add considerably to their net earnings, mainly by reducing the overall amount on which they have to pay tax. Not only that, but as most contractors will have gross billings in a year that exceed the value added tax (VAT) threshold, they can also save significant sums on purchases, by being able to reclaim the VAT.

On balance, the limited company route is one of the best for maximising earnings. And although the administration can be a nuisance, even this can be considerably reduced by using accountants and other service providers, whose charges are generally a relatively small percentage of the additional income being earned by the contractor.

6.2.2 Umbrella company

An umbrella company is, in simple terms, a way for the contractor to "outsource" their payroll to the umbrella company so that they effectively become a PAYE employee. If caught within IR35, and therefore not able to benefit from limited company status, rather than having the cost and bother of setting up a limited company, a contractor can simply work via an umbrella company, or 'brolly'.

The umbrella company itself is a perfectly legitimate limited company, with the usual associated shareholders, directors, articles of association and so on. Using this solution, the contractor would not be a director nor have the responsibilities associated with running a limited company. The umbrella company provider would take care of all accountancy and taxation matters, and also deal with most of the administration matters.

The contractor simply completes a timesheet and forwards it to the umbrella company, which then invoices the agent or client. Following payment by the agent to the umbrella company, a payment is made by the umbrella company to the contractor, just as if they were a permanent employee.

Umbrella companies usually have a management team responsible for matters relating to the company and accounts and so on, and a client services team who liaise with contractors on a day to day basis. In this context, the contractor is the client and pays a fee to the umbrella company for the umbrella's services, usually a fixed fee per month.

Since the Managed Service Company Legislation was introduced in the 2007 Budget (see section 6.2.5) there is only one viable choice for an umbrella company, which is the PAYE Umbrella.

A PAYE Umbrella treats all your income as salary. This means you pay the employer's NICs, employees NICs and PAYE on all your income. It is also possible to benefit from tax relief on travel and subsistence expenses when working through an umbrella company, plus VAT savings if the umbrella allows the purchase of capital equipment such as computers.

6.2.3 Partnerships and LLPs

Contractors will almost certainly find that there is no particular advantage in choosing a partnership or Limited Liability Partnership (LLP) instead of a limited company as the main vehicle for their businesses.

LLPs were originally created for professionals like accountants and lawyers who wanted to group their companies into large associations of partners. The big accounting firms still use this form of business so that they can share profits, but keep expenses and problems separate.

The advantage of LLPs is that the partners can split all income between them as dividends. You can also do this in a limited company, but the recordkeeping obligations for LLPs are far less complex.

Similar to a partnership, a LLP consists of two or more persons who agree to share a business. They are obliged to register their partnership with Companies House, just like a limited company. The partnership then becomes a company that can do almost everything a limited company can do: own property, sign contracts, incur debts and so on. Liability is limited to the money that the partners invested in the business and any personal guarantees they have given to raise finance.

The difference between a LLP and a limited company is that the LLP cannot issue shares, or hold share capital, nor does it have company directors. The rules that govern how shareholders interact with company assets don't apply to LLPs.

There are a number of disadvantages that LLPs suffer. Because those in the LLP enjoy limited liability, the protection of those dealing with an LLP requires that the LLP maintain accounting records, and that it prepares and delivers audited annual accounts to Company House. The exemptions available to limited companies, for example with respect to the delivery of abbreviated accounts and exemption from audit, also apply to LLPs.

What is different here for LLPs is that they cannot keep anything secret; all financial information must be disclosed, whereas a limited company runs its finances according to its own requirements. This is not a problem for a major accounting firm, but could be one for a small business.

Then there is a certain amount of legal uncertainty related to running a LLP. The LLP is a relatively new structure in British law, and both HMRC and the courts may not react predictably to it. So unless you have a very good reason for wanting to form a LLP, it's probably best avoided.

6.2.4 Sole Trader

Sole traders are probably the oldest trading option known to humankind, where someone has a skill or product to sell – be they stone tools or financial services – and they conduct a transaction directly with the buyer.

Trading as a sole trader can be highly tax efficient, particularly for a tradesperson working from home, as a significant amount of costs can be put through the sole trader's business, reducing their overall income tax and NICs.

There is also the greatly reduced regulatory and administrative burden. Tax paperwork for sole traders is much simpler and there is virtually no regulatory burden outside of tax legislation.

To many contractors, the option of trading as a sole trader must be very attractive. There is, however, one major barrier to contractors wanting to work on contracts as sole traders – they won't get any contracts!

It's very simple; no agencies or clients will sign a contract with a sole trader. Because there is no intermediary, such as a limited company, umbrella company or partnership, the risks of the contractor being considered by HMRC to be an employee with full employment rights is too great for any client.

The other major reason why agencies and clients will not contract directly with a sole trader is because if the contractor does not pay their full tax and NICs, the agency or client is liable to HMRC for these costs.

6.2.5 Managed Service Companies – avoid!

A Managed Service Company (MSC) provides contractors with a composite company solution to manage their invoicing and accounting. This typically means that twenty contractors become non-director shareholders and the company is managed by the organisation running the scheme, usually called the scheme provider, which manages all the administration, invoicing, accountancy and so on.

The contractors are then paid a low salary plus dividends in addition to claiming various expenses allowable under the corporate structure. This method of payment provides many financial benefits, since it avoids large amounts of NICs and income tax that would otherwise be payable if the contractor was paid entirely by salary.

But contractors should avoid any company which offers to manage their limited company for them, or which suggests putting them into a limited company it shares with others. Why?

Well, MSCs were once a widely-used trading option for contractors, but have been virtually regulated out of existence by the MSC legislation introduced in 2007. So be in no doubt: if you get involved with this kind of company, you run the very real risk of extensive tax liabilities later on.

The law requires that if a contractor works through a limited company, they run it themselves. Contractors can hire an accountant, or a lawyer, but they only give the contractor advice. Professional advisers don't actually make decisions for the contractor and they don't collect contractors' fees.

The best advice is to stay away from any company that offers such services: don't even go there!

6.2.6 Using an offshore company

Using offshore arrangements has been one of the many popular trading options contractors have used to maximise their earnings and minimise their tax payments.

Some offshore options still exist for contractors, but HMRC has clamped down heavily on most, using a range of powers that allow the taxman simply to request contractors' banking details from the banks and so target them for investigation.

If considering an offshore option, such as an Employee Benefits Trust, ensure you conduct your due diligence into the scheme and satisfy yourself that you won't get into trouble with HMRC.

6.3 Setting up and running a limited company

Creating and running a limited company may seem like a daunting task for new contractors, but as long as the process is understood, you are organised and you use the right professional advice at the right time, it does not have to be onerous. In fact, the setting up can be remarkably quick, inexpensive and easy.

6.3.1 Choosing an accountant

Whilst some contractors attempt to manage their accounting and tax affairs themselves, this is not the most efficient way of doing things and could result in all sorts of problems if mistakes are made.

So, when answering the question, 'do I need an accountant?', the answer is almost certainly 'yes'. And not just any old accountant from your local high street. Ideally, you should select an accountant that has a track record of managing contractors' affairs and has professional qualifications from a recognised accounting body.

The size of the firm will also have an impact on the service you receive. If you prefer a more personal service at partner level with the same individual, a smaller firm may suit your needs better than one of the national or international firms.

As with many service providers, those that come with a personal recommendation from a friend or colleague generally work out well; similarly, asking others for advice will help you find out which accountants to avoid.

For a comprehensive and specialist service, you should expect to be paying £60-£150 per month, at the time of writing. Check carefully what is included in the price – some offer cheaper options and then charge extra for completing personal tax returns and other paperwork. You should also be aware of what other services might be charged as 'extras'; what to you might seem like a quick conversation for a bit of friendly advice, might be charged to you by your accountant as professional consultancy services.

If you feel you are not getting the service you should from your accountant, then it is not a problem to change. There will be a certain amount of disruption but it will fairly quickly settle back into a routine again.

6.3.2 Registering a company

The limited company is an organisation that is called a 'moral person' in law: this means that it has its own identity and does business under its own name. It makes or loses money, can acquire debt and pay taxes all by itself, just like a physical person.

Understanding this is important, because it explains why the legal formation of a limited company works the way it does. Just as a baby is registered in the birth rolls when it is born, a company is registered in the official list of companies when you start it. This list is kept by Companies House.

Choose a name for your company, decide where it is based, and decide who's going to be part of it. Try choosing a general name that does not have your name, which may have IR35 implications, and allows some latitude if you branch out in the future.

Let's look at a typical example: "World's Greatest Contractors Ltd." which is being set up by the imaginary contractors John and Joan Dunn. John and Joan will both work for the company, and so they issue £100 worth of ordinary shares that they divide between them, with each owning 50%.

In this division of ordinary shares, dividends paid out will have to be proportional to the shareholding division, but only for ordinary shares. In other words, in the example, each gets 50% of dividend income, but this would not be the case if a preferential share division is used.

They could also include any other shareholders in the company that they might choose to have, so long as the total amount of shares is divided proportionately to the capital (the total number of shares).

John and Joan are also not obliged to issue ordinary shares: there are many different types of shares, for example preference shares, which are linked to specific rules related to the company's operations. If you seek a structure of this kind, you should probably take advice from a professional, as it has tax implications and could significantly affect your earnings if you get it wrong.

Once you've made all the decisions above, you have a choice of options for filing the company:

- Online at Companies House and, for a fee of about £20 at the time of writing, set up your company. The online forms will guide you through the setup process. Companies House will check to confirm that the name you've chosen is not in use, and it will ask you to appoint a company director and a company secretary
- Use a company formation agent, who will go through a very similar process but may be in a position to recommend alternative structures you may not have thought of. Naturally, their fees will be considerably more than £20, typically £50 to £100+
- Use an accountant, who will quite often bundle incorporation into a range of services, such as recommending different share types for tax purposes and supplying standard documents, with correspondingly higher fees.

In our example, Joan takes the company directorship and John becomes the company secretary, although one person could take on both roles. Being a director has certain legal responsibilities, which are important and covered in section 6.3.12.

If you chose to file at Companies House yourself, you will also need to file a Memorandum of Association. This is a document that tells everyone why you've set up the company and how you plan to run it. This document can have significant legal importance in tax disputes and any legal proceedings; for example, tax inspectors and courts would look closely at this in an IR35 case.

A company formation agent or accountant would typically prepare and submit the documentation for you as part of their fee, and it is generally prudent to use their services.

A key document to arise from this process is the Certificate of Incorporation that includes your new company number. This is required for a number of purposes including, importantly, for setting up the business bank account and registering with an agency.

6.3.3 Getting a business bank account

Choosing and setting-up a bank account for your limited company should be fairly straightforward, as long as you have an established and good banking record in the UK. Your company's money needs to be traceable throughout every stage of the transaction and clearly separated from your own personal finances.

The types of activity going through your account will be:

- Receiving money from clients or agents for your work
- Paying your own salary
- Paying dividends
- Paying monthly NICs and PAYE taxes, plus annual Corporation Tax
- Claiming for personal expenses incurred
- Direct debits for items like mobile phones and internet connections
- Paying for other business expenses, such as accountant's fees
- Payments to the company credit card
- VAT payments (if you are registered).

There is no such thing as a special 'contractor's bank account'; instead, you are looking for a straightforward business banking account.

When you set this up, you will need a copy of your company's Certificate of Incorporation and will be asked to sign mandates and provide specimen signatures. In addition you may also be required to present yourself at a local branch to identify yourself, with a passport, utility bills and similar, to satisfy the requirements of money laundering legislation.

Some aspects to consider when choosing a provider are:

Online banking (and telephone banking): Most contractors find that they want to access banking services outside traditional banking hours, so this can be a good option. Making payments online or over the phone saves having to write and post cheques, and payments rarely go astray. Access to real-time balances and statements are extremely useful, particularly when reconciling items for your VAT return, or checking that a client has actually paid you. Be sure to check if there are any fees for using internet banking.

Charges or interest: All banks for small business are required by law to either offer interest rates on the account or free banking. Given the small number of transactions and the fact that you will always have money in the account, the interest rate option might be better. Bear in mind that you will have tax money saved in the account, which is not due until nine months after your year end. Some banks also offer a high interest business account in addition to a standard business account. If you belong to a business organisation or professional body, check to find out whether they have negotiated any deals for free banking. For example, Federation of Small Businesses (FSB) members get free business banking through The Co-operative Bank, and access to a guaranteed interest account for large amounts, like their tax savings.

Credit card: A company credit card can be handy for keeping all company credit card purchases in one place. If the bank does not provide one, though, you can always use a dedicated personal one, and then claim expenses at a later date. But it is generally best to, whenever possible, totally separate your personal and business spending.

Interest: Some accounts pay interest on balances and, if you are likely to at times have large amounts in the account, you should 'shop around' for the best interest rates, just as you would for personal savings.

Existing bank: If your current bank offers a business bank account with all the features you are looking for, this might be the 'less hassle' way to open your account. Bear in mind, however, that you might not want your bank to know about your future contracting career if, for example, they are about to offer you a mortgage based on your previous earnings as a permanent employee.

As with all financial services, it is always best to shop around, negotiate and examine the small print before you take the plunge.

6.3.4 Getting insurance

New contractors need to consider two broad areas of insurance for contracting through their limited company:

- Company insurances – professional indemnity and 'business insurance'
- Income protection insurances.

Income protection insurances are covered in chapter 12, so in this section the focus will be on company insurances, of which there are generally two types that contractors must have in place when they start contracting: Professional Indemnity (PI) insurance and 'Business insurance'.

Professional indemnity (PI) insurance

When working as a full time permanent employee, should you make an error on a client's system or when specifying materials for an infrastructure project, you are not personally liable for the implications of that error, and the costs that might be incurred if the client chose to sue your employer for damages. Your employer's company, or the legal entity that entered into the contract, is liable, as might be the directors of that business, if the error was severe and harmful. Of course, the error might cost you your job, but not millions of pounds.

However, when working as a contractor through your own limited company, your company is liable, and as you are a director and shareholder in the company, the client may come after you for damages.

Professional indemnity insurance is designed for when a client decides to take action over an error or perceived error. It provides defence fees and possibly a payout to the client if professional negligence is proved.

You may consider this a small risk, and that it is therefore not necessary to have PI insurance. But the bottom line is that pretty much all agents and clients will require that, as part of your contract, you hold a current professional indemnity cover up to a certain value. So PI insurance is not only a safety net from writ-happy clients, but also an essential sales tool you must have to be a contractor.

PI insurance is readily available for contractors at reasonable prices from a wide range of insurance brokers. It is worth shopping around and also asking colleagues and contacts, especially if they have had cause to use their insurance. Also check with any professional or business bodies you belong to, as they might have negotiated good deals on behalf of their membership.

Policy prices vary according to a number of factors, including:

- The level of cover you require
- The annual turnover, or forecast turnover, of your limited company
- The number of employees in your company
- Your track record and level of expertise
- The types of projects you work on and clients you work for.

'Business insurance'

'Business insurance' is a catch-all term used to describe a basket of other essential or recommended insurances for contractors who are working on client contracts through their own limited company. They can include:

- Public liability, to protect your company against claims by a third party – agents and clients will insist you have this up to a minimum level
- Employers' liability, which is a legal requirement if your business has any employees, including you and co-directors, such as a spouse or business partner
- Portable equipment/business equipment, as domestic contents insurance will not pay out for damage and loss of business assets, such as computers and other equipment you have bought for your company
- Legal expenses, to cover legal actions or investigation by HMRC
- Business interruption, which would compensate for loss of earnings in the case of a fire or flood preventing you from working
- Buildings, if you have your own dedicated business premises.

There are a wide range of options available to suit the needs of most contractors and the cost of each policy will depend on the nature and level required.

6.3.5 Running the company – the administration

When contracting through your own limited company, there are always ongoing administration tasks to complete; but these should not be onerous, as long as you keep on top of them. Many contractors employ their spouse or partner to manage this side of the business, which also enables them to be paid a salary.

But ultimately you are in charge. Any accountants or other professional advisers you might hire will only be as good as the information you provide them with. The GIGO principle applies – garbage in, garbage out. So provide accurate and timely records to your accountant and they will more than justify their fees. And the same is true of legal advisers when checking contracts.

IR35 issues

IR35 is a fundamental issue that you will need to get to grips with at the very start of your contracting career, during the course of your contracts if things change, and every time you accept a contract. The effort you put into understanding IR35 and its implications, for example by reading chapter 8, will more than repay itself both in terms of cash – taking home as much of your gross earnings as you legally can – and in terms of peace of mind – knowing the tax inspector won't come a-callin'!

You may need to seek specialist legal advice for the various contracts you undertake in order to ensure that the way you are being paid is valid and will stand up to scrutiny on an IR35 inspection. Such advice is not at all expensive in terms of the extra earnings you will enjoy by being legally outside IR35, and the cost is certainly tiny for the peace of mind it will buy.

Client and contract files

Create and maintain a file for each client and each separate contract, even if you are contracting through an agency. In each file include:

- Original signed and dated contracts
- Any correspondence between you and the agent and you and the client, including, if appropriate, notes of telephone conversations
- Copies of invoices (for the sake of convenience)
- Copies of timesheets.

If you are investigated by HMRC and are being defended by an IR35 specialist, they will want all this information as soon as possible. Creating and maintaining these files from the start saves you time, and quite possibly large sums of money at a later stage. But don't worry, if you follow the advice in this book you are unlikely to get investigated by HMRC; and even if you are, you will have all the information at your disposal to prove that you are contracting and getting paid legally.

Invoicing Your Client/Agent

You will need to invoice your agent, or the client's accounts department, each week or month. To do so, your invoice must be accompanied by a timesheet that has been approved by your client.

You will need to ensure it is forwarded to them within their prescribed deadline to avoid delays in payment. Keep copies on file, make sure you get paid on time, and have a system in place to chase for payments as soon as they become overdue.

Each invoice you raise must include your company's details. The following should be included:

- Company name
- Company address
- Company telephone number and email address.
- Company number
- Company VAT registration number (if relevant).

Each of your invoices must have a unique invoice number and be sequential. Although called a number, it can include letters. A common method is to prefix invoices with letters that indicate the client.

For example, if you provided services for IBM and the BBC, for IBM you could use IBM001 and IBM002, and so on. For the BBC you could use BBC001 and BBC002. Using three placements for the numbers will ensure they also sort in order and HMRC requires numbers to be sequential for each client.

Dates are also extremely important, especially when it comes to chasing payments. You should include the following dates:

- Today's date: the date the invoice was raised
- Due date: the date by which payment should be made. Normally 30 days after the invoice date.

The client details should include the name and address of the agency, or client if contracting directly.

In the fees part of the invoice, include:

- A description of the services provided
- The net amount due
- The VAT amount, if you are VAT registered
- The gross/total amount due.

For example:

20 Days @ £500 per day
Amount: £10,000
VAT: £1,500 at current rate of 15%
Total: £11,500

You will have agreed the payment terms with the agent or client at the time you negotiated the contract. It is very important to include the payment terms on the invoice, as these will support your case in the event of any dispute. Also specify how you would like to receive the money. For example:

Payment should be made within 30 days by cheque or money transfer. Cheques should be made payable to 'My Company Ltd'.
Money transfers should be sent to:
The Contractors Bank
Sort Code: 01-01-01
Account Number: 012345678
Reference: Use invoice number

Most agencies and clients do not pay via cheque and choose money transfer. Cheques can be inconvenient if you can't get to a branch during opening hours because, for instance, the client's site is an oil drilling platform in the North Sea; they also have a habit of 'getting lost in the post', which is a very convenient excuse for clients who want to hold on to their money (your money!) for a few more days. If you wish only to be paid by money transfer, then use the following:

Payment should be made within 30 days by money transfer only to the following account:
The Contractors Bank
Sort Code: 01-01-01
Account Number: 012345678
Reference: Use invoice number

Example invoices and templates can be downloaded from www.contractorcalculator.co.uk.

Your agency or client will specify how they would like to receive the invoice. Some clients will request a paper copy, others prefer an electronic invoice. If you are permitted to submit your invoice via email then it is useful to convert the invoice into PDF format so that it cannot be altered.

Most agencies and clients require a timesheet to be signed and a copy included with the invoice. Ensure you take a copy of the timesheet for your own records before sending it in.

Recording Transactions

You will also need a system to record all your company's transactions, principally:

- Payments
- Invoices
- Expenses.

A simple spreadsheet will do, although you can work from the company bank account when calculating the quarter's income and expenditure for forwarding to the accountant. When setting this up, ask your accountant if they would prefer to receive the information in a particular format, as doing so will probably save them time and you money. They will plug individual transactions into their software to make their calculations.

Some accountants have a recommended software package, while others will suggest a spreadsheet that you will keep yourself and forward to them once a month, quarter or even year, when they prepare your accounts. It is worthwhile preparing and maintaining a spreadsheet that records the expenses you pay out of your own pocket and subsequently claim back from the business.

Payroll Matters

As company director you normally take a salary from the company, whether or not you are working under IR35. You will need to arrange for payslips to be prepared and ensure that the necessary taxes are paid at the right time.

Most accountants include a full payroll service as part of their package to contractors, which will avoid the need for you to be involved in the detailed calculations. Alternatively, there are companies that specialise just in payroll. If you really want to do it yourself, which is unlikely to be an efficient use of your time, HMRC runs free workshops to help small businesses, and government-funded organisations like Business Link can help too.

If you use your accountant or a payroll company, they will send you a payslip once a month and you will have to send a cheque to HMRC, or pay online when you are told to. Following the end of the tax year, it will be necessary to file an employer's annual return (form P35), together with forms P14, P60 and P11D if you have taken any expenses or benefits in kind from the company during the year.

There is nothing stopping you doing this yourself, if you wish to. But your accountant would normally deal with these so that your involvement is simply providing all the necessary information and approving the documents before they are submitted to HMRC.

Dividend Planning

If you are working outside the scope of IR35, then the bulk of your income from the company will be taken by way of dividends, reducing your tax liabilities. It is vital that the necessary documents (board minutes and dividend counterfoils) are prepared at the time you take each dividend, but these are short documents that take a very short time to prepare.

Real problems can arise if the necessary procedures are not followed. In addition, you will need to ensure that your dividend drawings are not in excess of the company's profits after corporation tax – this could leave you with unexpected tax bills. It is generally prudent to check with your accountant how much you can withdraw as dividends before acting.

Accounts
The company will need to submit accounts to the Inspector of Taxes and Companies House once each year. Penalties arise for late filing, so it is important that you ensure that the documents are prepared in due time. Your accountant will normally prepare these for you, which you then approve for forwarding.

You need to supply your accountant with all the information and records so they can prepare the accounts on your behalf. Supply these as soon as you can, because it will avoid your accountant having to rush your work because it is being done at the same time as all the other people who have left it until the last minute.

Finally, make sure you do check your accounts before approving them – accountants can make mistakes and, in the eyes of HMRC, any errors are yours, not your accountants.

Company secretarial matters
Companies House will issue a company return once every year, which you will need to complete and forward to Companies House, together with their annual fee. Or you can file the annual return online, which is very quick and costs less. Various other forms will have to be submitted to Companies House if the circumstances of the directors or company change, even for such seemingly unconnected matters like you moving home.

Most accountants will take on the administration element of company secretarial duties for an additional fee, although you are still required to check and sign all documents yourself.

Personal tax return
As a company director it will usually be necessary for you to file a personal tax return under self-assessment. Your accountant can prepare this for you, and with some accountants the service is included, while others may charge you extra.

VAT Return

Assuming you are VAT registered, which you almost certainly will be, you will need to complete a VAT return every quarter and send the return with a cheque to HMRC for the balance of VAT left over after purchases. Your accountant could do this for you for an additional fee, but it's a very simple task.

6.3.6 Value Added Tax – VAT

Value Added Tax (VAT) is levied on most business transactions and on many goods and some services. Some services, such as insurance, and some types of education, training and loans are deemed to be 'exempt'. However, in nearly all cases, services offered by contractors will attract VAT, both because of the nature of the service – for example, IT and engineering services are not exempt – and because most contractors' companies have a turnover that means registration is compulsory.

It is compulsory to register for VAT if your turnover reaches the VAT registration threshold limit, which tends to change on an annual basis, but usually means if you forecast your contracting gross income that you bill through your company to be above around £67,000, you will have to register anyway. Companies over the limit which fail to register can be fined.

Businesses with turnovers of less than the limit can also register if they wish. Many do so for cost efficiency reasons, or because they feel a VAT registration makes their company appear more established.

To make the most of your cash-flow and reduce start-up costs, it's a good idea to apply for VAT registration when you are forming your company. It might not be compulsory at that stage, but most contractors want to apply for "voluntary registration" in order to recover input VAT on start-up expenses, like computer costs, professional fees and other business-related costs on which VAT is charged. There are two types of VAT:

Output VAT: This is added to your company invoices. You charge the agent or client £1,000 plus VAT at 15% (the current rate) so your total invoice is for £1,150. Output VAT = £150

Input VAT: This is paid on purchases the company makes. If you pay your accountant £500 they will charge you VAT at 15%, so their total invoice will be £575. Input VAT = £75

Every quarter the difference between the amount of input VAT collected and output VAT paid is then paid to HMRC as part of the quarterly VAT return.

As VAT is generally paid to HMRC on a quarterly basis, your company gains a cash-flow advantage and you can even earn interest on this money. Another advantage of registering is to avoid anybody dealing with your company knowing, without checking with Companies House, that your turnover is below £67k per annum.

Although most contractors would agree that VAT registration is an overall benefit to their company, there are disadvantages, the most obvious of which is that you will need to prepare VAT returns and ensure that your accounting records provide the required information for disclosure on the VAT returns. This means keeping accurate, detailed records and VAT receipts and invoices for all transactions in the return. But you should be doing that in any case.

There are some unusual cases where it is best to delay VAT registration for as long as possible. If, for example, your client was not VAT registered themselves, as in the case of a financial services company, they would not thank you for adding 'unnecessary' VAT to your invoices, as they could not recover that money themselves.

One final downside is that, as a VAT registered trader, you will also be subject to periodic VAT inspections, usually once every six years. But it's not difficult to do everything right, and so these inspections should not be a concern to you.

Contractors have the choice of three schemes through which they can operate their VAT returns to HMRC:

Cash Accounting: To qualify for this scheme, your company's estimated annual turnover must be less than £1.35 million per year (at the time of writing). You only account for VAT actually received from your clients and paid to your suppliers for goods and services. This scheme is the most appropriate for most contractors.

Flat Rate VAT Scheme: You pay a fixed rate of VAT based on your company's revenue and depending on the sector you work in. You cannot claim VAT back, but this might work better depending on how much you spend on VAT-rated goods and services. Seeking advice from an accountant would be valuable to determine if the flat rate scheme is appropriate for you.

Annual Accounting: You make a single annual return and payment is normally made in nine equal instalments, with a tenth balancing payment to settle the liability and balance the books. The maximum turnover limit for this scheme is £1.35 million per year (at the time of writing). Few contractors actually use this scheme in practice and it is probably better to ensure that your books/VAT accounting is fully up to date on a quarterly basis, rather than be faced with an entire year to account for as the annual return deadline approaches. Investing time in understanding how to make VAT work for you is well worth it.

6.3.7 Expenses

Efficient recording and processing of expenses can significantly reduce a contractor's tax bill, and thus boost their net income. In addition, understanding what is allowable and making full use of those allowances can significantly reduce a contractor's personal outgoings. So time invested in understanding the rules surrounding expenses is likely to be time well spent.

Every legitimate business expense is deductible against your final tax bill. This means that allowable expenses become part of the overhead of your company. The higher the overhead, the less profit the business makes and the lower will be your company's corporation tax bill.

This may sound back to front – after all, surely you want to have as much profit as possible to maximise your net income? Well, yes, but it's a balancing act: by understanding and applying the full range of allowances available to you and your business you can shift costs around from your personal net income (you buy a sandwich for lunch when working at a client's site) to the company's gross income (the company buys your lunch when you're working at a client's site).

According to HMRC, expenses are deductible if incurred wholly, necessarily and exclusively in the performance of duties. Technically speaking, this means if you buy a laptop which is exclusively for your work, it can be deducted. And technically speaking, if it is used as a family computer evenings and weekends, it is in theory not deductible. Or only that proportion that is used for work may be deductible. You work it out!

When starting out in contracting, you will find that you will almost certainly incur up-front costs simply setting up the business. These are formation and pre-trading expenses and many will be paid out of your own pocket because your company has no client and therefore no cash; it may not even have a bank account. But this is not a problem, as the taxman reasonably says that these expenses can still be claimed, as long as they are legitimate. They should ideally be claimed all in one go and as soon as the company has the cash to pay you for them.

After formation and for as long as you are contracting through your own limited company, you will incur ongoing expenses. These should be claimed on an ongoing basis, weekly, monthly or as appropriate. Most contractors process expenses every three months in the same cycle as completing their VAT return.

Formation and pre-trading expenses you can claim

Your formation expenses are the costs you incurred to register your company. You will probably have a bill for at least one of the following:

- Registering the company with Companies House directly by yourself
- Using a formation agent
- Using an accountant.

This bill could be between anything from about £20 to many hundreds, and is deductible.

Pre-trading expenditure you can claim

Any valid expenses you can claim whilst contracting that are incurred in anticipation of your trading can be claimed, as if they have been incurred on the first day of trading. These might include:

- Travel
- Printing of stationery
- Reference materials and books (like this one)
- Professional and trade body subscriptions
- Advertising
- Website production and hosting fees
- Legal fees (such as for contract drafting or review)
- Equipment and other capital costs. All associated equipment can be charged to the company if the equipment can be

justified for use in the company's trade. These would include things like computer hardware and software, office furniture, telephones, a PDA (personal digital assistant), and so on. They can also be sold from your personal ownership to the company.

- Business insurances, such as Professional Indemnity and Public Liability
- Office costs, for example rent
- Any costs associated with setting up an office for the company, such as desks, office chairs and filing cabinets.

On the day the company starts trading, usually when you issue your first invoice in expectation of your first payment, you can present your limited company with an expenses form detailing all the above costs.

It is unlikely that the full amount can be reclaimed in one go, but you can transfer the amount in tranches as long as you make a careful note of what each payment from your company account into your personal account is for.

Ongoing expenses you can claim

These expenses are incurred as part of the ongoing operations of the business and should be claimed on a regular basis.

- Travel expenses, such as rail, bus, taxi and air fares
- Motor expenses (mileage claims, if the car is personally owned)
- Accommodation and subsistence
- Telephone and mobile phone calls and subscriptions, when used for business, of course
- Certain books, magazines, subscriptions and courses – where directly related to business and your contract work.

These above expenses are likely to be paid for out of your own pocket and reclaimed using an expenses form. Wherever possible separate your personal and business spending; therefore, it is best to pay for these expenses using a company credit card or cheque.

Other expenses that are paid for directly by the company include:

- Your gross salary
- Your spouse's or partner's salary, which must be actually paid to that person for a real job, and should be at a realistic level for the actual duties performed
- Salaries for other employees or, more likely, payments to other contractors you hire as substitutes or to handle specialist areas of a contract you are working on
- Bank charges and interest charges on your company bank account
- Pension scheme – where paid by the company to a scheme approved by HMRC
- Business insurances – professional indemnity, business contents and other business-related insurances
- Corporation tax, employer's national insurance contributions and VAT, if your company is VAT registered
- Professional fees, such as for accountants and solicitors
- Marketing expenses, including advertising, company flyers and updating your website
- Office expenses and stationery (it is generally possible to get a company account with most large stationers that can be paid monthly in arrears)
- Computer costs, including hardware, software licenses and peripherals.

Expenses you incur for running a home office can also be claimed, if you spend at least some of your time working from home. HMRC will allow you to claim a proportion of your household costs as a deductible expense if the right criteria are met. These criteria include:

- If an area of the home is used exclusively for business purposes and is in use during specific hours of the day. The room used must look like an office, so have for example, a PC workstation, desk, chair and filing cabinets. Using a laptop at the kitchen table won't qualify
- A reasonable claim relating to the business. The time spent should be realistic, for example from nine in the morning until five thirty in the evening. Also, the area used should not be a disproportionately large area of the domestic living space.

If you meet these criteria, then the types of household expenses that can be claimed include:

- Utilities, such as gas, electricity and water and waste, or fuel oil depending on your heating system
- Insurance – if there is no separate business policy, a proportion of the household policy can be allowed
- Council tax – a proportion of the total bill can be claimed
- Mortgage interest – A proportion of the mortgage interest is allowable, but capital repayments are excluded
- Rent – A proportion of the rent of a home is allowable if a part of the property qualifies as being used for business purposes
- Repairs and maintenance – A proportion of the total cost of general repairs and maintenance can be claimed; this would include roof repairs, for example, but not decorating a room that is not used for business purposes.

So how does it work? Well, you basically calculate the proportion of the house space used and the time spent using that area of the house as an office, then apply that multiple to the household expenses. Your accountant will be able to help you make sure you get this calculation correct. HMRC pay special attention to what they consider "excessive" claims for 'use of home as office' so it's important to get things right and avoid waving a red flag that results in a tax investigation.

At the time of writing, HMRC has not extensively tested these rules, so you are strongly advised to pass any claims to your accountant for checking.

How to claim expenses

When running your own company and paying out of your own pocket for contracting expenses, especially cash expenses, it really pays to have a simple system to ensure that not only are you are keeping statutory accounting records for tax and VAT purposes, but that you are also claiming everything you are entitled to.

Many contractors are used to the expenses systems that big companies have for their employees. Usually, the company has a standard expenses form that employees fill in each month, and then the next month the money they have paid out on behalf of the company is paid back to them alongside their salary.

When you are contracting through your own limited company you must always keep a clear record of any expenses you wish to claim. These records do not need to be complex, as long as they keep to the rules laid down by HMRC. And the good thing about having a system in place is that it can act as a reminder to you to claim everything that is allowable by the taxman.

It is very important to get receipts for every business related purchase. Where it might not be possible to provide a receipt – say, for example, your train ticket gets swallowed by the ticket barrier – the expense can still be claimed, but careful note must be made of exact amounts, times and reasons for travel. This is because it might be necessary to prove to the HMRC at a later date that you were on that train, or had bought that snack from a street vendor.

If you are planning on claiming VAT on expenses, then you must get a VAT receipt for each specific expense for any costs that are VAT rated. Most suppliers, such as petrol stations or sandwich shops, will provide a receipt that includes the necessary information. If using your local stationers to buy printer ink and you get an old fashioned till receipt without the details make sure you ask for a separate VAT receipts. For example, train tickets do not have VAT added, but motoring expenses do.

You can claim expenses from your own limited company at any time. It could be daily, weekly, monthly, quarterly or even annually. Many contractors claim expenses quarterly, as this matches the cycle of their company's VAT returns.

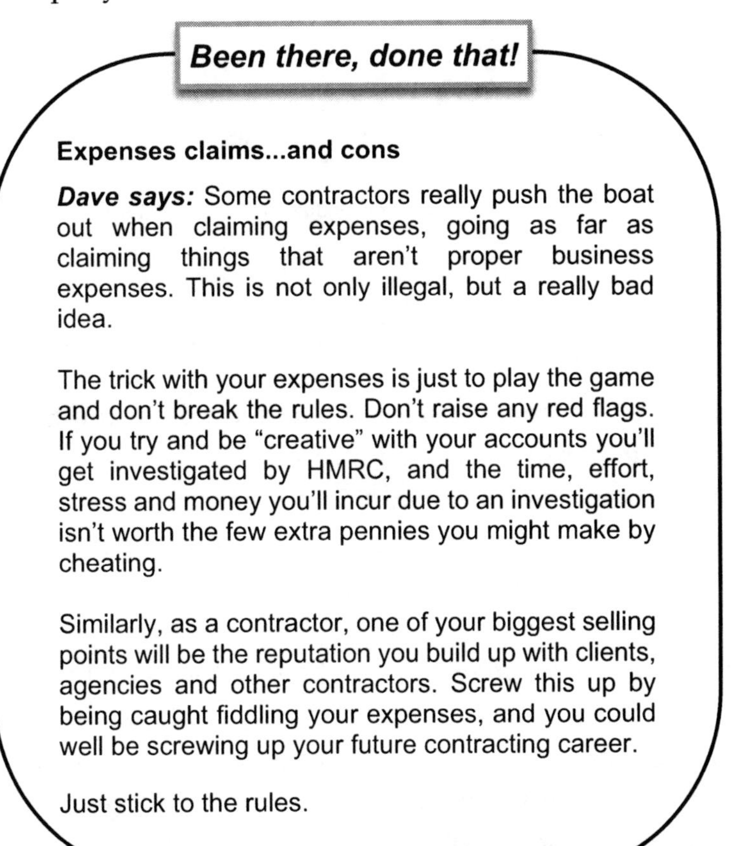
Been there, done that!

Expenses claims...and cons

Dave says: Some contractors really push the boat out when claiming expenses, going as far as claiming things that aren't proper business expenses. This is not only illegal, but a really bad idea.

The trick with your expenses is just to play the game and don't break the rules. Don't raise any red flags. If you try and be "creative" with your accounts you'll get investigated by HMRC, and the time, effort, stress and money you'll incur due to an investigation isn't worth the few extra pennies you might make by cheating.

Similarly, as a contractor, one of your biggest selling points will be the reputation you build up with clients, agencies and other contractors. Screw this up by being caught fiddling your expenses, and you could well be screwing up your future contracting career.

Just stick to the rules.

Cash flow may also determine when you claim expenses. If client invoices, billed monthly, are outstanding and there is not enough cash in the business to pay you, then there is little point making a claim at that time. However, the paperwork could be submitted and the expenses accrued, or delayed, until there is enough cash in the company bank account.

Although expenses forms can vary, especially if you use forms supplied by your accountant, there is always some key information required:

- Date of the expense
- Nature of the expense
- Amount of expense.

A basic expenses form can be created in Excel, and look something like this:

Date	Details	Amount (£)
1st Jan 2008	Train fare to client X at client's site in Basingstoke	£22.80
23rd Jan 2008	Mono printer cartridge	£27.49
10th Feb 2008	Stationery - 100 x stamps	£32.00
Total		£82.29

- The first column contains the date on the receipt, or the date of the expense if there is no receipt
- The second column contains a sentence about the nature of the expense; "Trip to client X's site in Basingstoke"
- The third column contains the amount of the expense.

Your expenses forms may have to have a fourth column for VAT. You need to check with your accountants about how best to manage your VAT claims, at least initially until you get into the swing of things. Obviously this only applies if you are VAT-registered, which you almost certainly will be.

At the time of writing the standard VAT rate is 15%. So to calculate the VAT of most VAT-rated goods and services, divide the price you paid by 115, and then multiply that figure by 15 to give the VAT. Fortunately, most receipts provide this calculation for you, or you can request a VAT receipt for most purchases, such as fuel. Not all goods and services are VAT rated, so make sure you only claim what you can.

Total the amounts, print the expenses form, attach the receipts and at the end of the expenses period, transfer exactly that amount of money from your company's business bank account to your personal account, or write yourself a business cheque. Then make sure you file the paperwork somewhere safe or send it to your accountant for record keeping.

6.3.8 Taxation

If you are typical of most contractors outside IR35 working through your own limited company, you will at some point during the year have to be aware of, manage, calculate and pay the following taxes:

- Value Added Tax (VAT)
- Corporation tax
- Income tax
- National Insurance Contributions (NICs)
- Capital Gains Tax (CGT).

VAT has been listed first because, if you process your VAT quarterly, you are managing it yourself on an ongoing basis and it is purely through your limited company. The other taxes tend to be calculated by your accountant, or sometimes HMRC, on your behalf. Some of these taxes will be paid through your limited company and some you will pay personally.

Taxes paid through your limited company

Corporation Tax: All limited companies are subject to Corporation Tax at varying rates, usually between 21% and 29.75% (at the time of writing). These rates tend to be changed on a generally annual basis, with announcements typically made in the Chancellor's Budget. Probably the majority of contracting companies will pay at the lowest rate, which at the time of writing is applied to companies with profits of up to £300,000.

If your contract is not caught by IR35, then you will most likely take the traditional route of a low salary combined with high dividends. Since dividends can only be paid from company profits, you will need to pay corporation tax at the prevailing rate on your net company profit. This is discussed in more detail in section 6.3.8.

Your accountant will prepare and submit a company tax return on your behalf, based on the financial record you have provided and after you have checked and signed the return. Corporation Tax is payable nine months after your company year end.

Employer's National Insurance Contributions (NICs): This is a company cost based on the amount of your gross salary at the rate of 12.8% (at the time of writing). If your contract is not caught by IR35, then the best advice would be to take a lower salary, potentially avoiding Employer's National Insurance Contributions altogether. No National Insurance Contributions are chargeable on company dividends. Employer's National Insurance is paid monthly. However, if you do take a salary that is high enough to qualify for NIC payments, you are more likely to receive a full state pension on retirement.

VAT: VAT is covered in detail in section 6.3.6.

Taxes you pay personally

Income tax: If you are working in an IR35-caught contract, your entire income from the company will be subject to Pay As You Earn (PAYE) income tax and will be deducted at source; this is also the case if you are working through an umbrella company. If your contract is not caught by IR35, then only a very small amount of your income tax liability, if any, will be deducted through PAYE, assuming you are taking a low salary and high dividends.

On IR35 exempt contracts, you will receive dividends, on which there will be tax credits covering your basic rate tax liability. If your taxable income is less than the higher rate threshold, then you will not have any further income tax liability. Any income in excess of the higher rate tax threshold means you will pay more tax on it (at 25% of the net dividend at the time of writing). Income tax is paid monthly through PAYE and calculated annually if you take the low salary-high dividend approach.

Employee's National Insurance Contributions (NICs): If your contract is caught by IR35, then you will have to pay Employee's National Insurance Contributions on your salary (not dividends), at varying rates.

If your contract is not caught by IR35, then you will pay very little, if any, Employee's National Insurance Contributions, since the bulk of your income will be taken through dividends, which do not attract National Insurance Contributions of any kind. Employee's National Insurance Contributions are paid monthly.

Capital Gains Tax: You may be subject to Capital Gains Tax when you close your company and make a capital distribution to yourself as shareholder. Exemptions and reliefs are available through which it may be possible to reduce your tax bill.

Of course if you do have other assets and incomes, such as property, shares and other financial assets, there are various other taxes, payments, duties and methods by which HMRC will tax you. This scenario definitely requires specialist accounting and financial expertise from your accountant.

6.3.9 Salary and dividend

Tax efficiency is one of the popular reasons contractors choose to start a career in contracting. Despite various tax and related legislation over the past couple of decades, you can still trade perfectly within the law in a highly tax efficient manner.

If your contract is outside IR35 (see chapter 8), then the best strategy to adopt to maximise net earnings is the low salary-high dividend approach.

You do not start paying income tax on a salary until you have reached the basic rate, which creeps up most years and is currently £6,035. That means you can pay yourself, and potentially your spouse or partner, £503 per month each without attracting income tax and with minimal employee National Insurance Contributions.

If you then take most of the remaining profits after salaries, costs and corporation tax as a dividend, you do not pay any NICs on this sum, and then income tax according to the prevailing lower and upper rates.

Should you have other shareholders in the business, their shares, assuming they are ordinary shares, will also accrue dividends pro rata according to their percentage holding/s.

This is a highly tax efficient and entirely legal method of disbursing funds through the company into net income, as you also receive a dividend tax credit, which is designed so profits are not taxed twice through corporation tax and income tax. The tax credit is 10% of the gross dividend. What you actually receive from the company is the net dividend.

For example:

The company pays a net dividend of £9k.
[This is equal to 90% of the gross dividend of £10k.]

Tax credit is £1k
[10% of the gross dividend].

If you are a basic rate tax payer, you pay 10% of the gross dividend in tax. This is considered already paid via the tax credit, hence no more tax to pay.

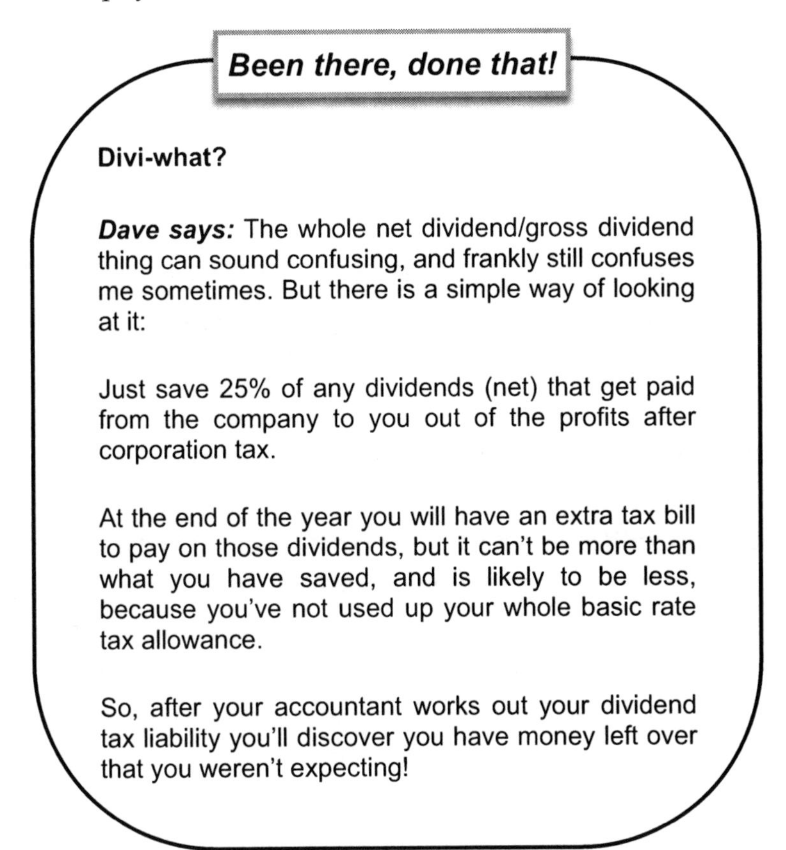

If you are a higher rate tax payer, you would be charged tax at the rate of 32.5% of the gross dividend in tax, i.e. £3,250. From this liability would be deducted the tax credit of £1k, so your net higher rate tax liability is £2,250, which is equivalent to 25% of your net dividend of £9k. As a rough guide you can expect to enter the higher rate tax band after earning approximately £25 per hour.

6.3.10 Personal taxation and Self Assessment

As a director of your own limited company, you will be required to complete a Self-Assessment form and annual personal tax return to "self assess" the amount of income tax and capital gains tax you must pay each year. This is in addition to your responsibilities for completing any corporation tax paperwork.

The tax year in the UK runs from 6th April to the 5th April the following year. The final deadline for filing your tax return online with HMRC is 31st January following the end of the tax year. Paper returns and online returns asking HMRC to complete the calculations have deadlines that are now much earlier: 31st October for the former and 30th December for the latter. These dates are correct at the time of writing, but you should always check in case there have been changes.

If you fail to file your tax return by HMRC's deadlines you will be fined £100. Further penalties may arise for persistent late or non filing. In practice, though, your accountant will complete the return and calculations of tax due and file your personal tax return on your behalf, after you have checked and signed it. Easy!

Working outside IR35 through your own limited company, you will only be paying income tax on your small salary as you go along. This can take a bit of getting used to and it is essential to get into the discipline of putting aside a proportion of your net income to allow for your tax liabilities. The nice thing is you will be earning interest on the amount, rather than it already being in the government's coffers.

In addition, after your first year, HMRC will start asking for 'payments on account'. They now know what you should expect to be earning so have some basis for calculating what to ask you for. You can ask your accountant to dispute the figure if, for example, you know your income may drop because, say, you plan to have a month's holiday between contracts.

However, regularly stashing away money is a good habit. It means you are more likely to have a pleasant surprise when the tax bill becomes due, because you have 'over-provisioned' for tax. If your earnings fall into the higher tax bracket, then saving 25% of your dividend should be more than sufficient, although as with all tax planning you should run this by your accountant.

6.3.11 HMRC investigations

If you do things right, and contract by the rules, there is no reason to fear an HMRC investigation. Nevertheless, if you or your limited company learn that an investigation is underway, it is prudent to take professional advice before talking to or corresponding with HMRC.

The reason is not to hide anything, but because the UK's taxation authorities have an extremely broad investigative remit, with tremendous powers – in many cases, unlike other areas of UK law, you can be found guilty until you can prove your innocence. That is why care should be taken when disclosing information to a tax inspector, because even seemingly innocent statements you make informally or 'off the record' can be used against you in a court of law. Take care.

HMRC has IT systems that work very effectively – probably because they were largely built by IT contractors – which means that all the information they gather on you, and others doing similar work to you, is captured and cross referenced in a series of sophisticated databases.

The tax authorities have the luxury of being able to look back through six years of your records, which means that they can come after you for what they perceive to be unpaid tax from many years ago. This can add up to quite a sum, especially when interest and penalties are added.

HMRC investigations can become costly, time consuming and very stressful for you, even if you know you are entirely innocent. But there are ways you can minimise the risk of an investigation. And the best defence against an investigation is to prevent one happening in the first place.

There is a wide range of insurance policies specially designed to provide contractors with expert assistance in the event that they come under investigation. Most investigation insurance will cover the costs of the defence, even if it goes to court, but check carefully what your policy covers.

HMRC looks for particular features of companies when targeting them for inspections, and some of the more common clues they look for are covered below.

IR35: Factors leading to an IR35/payroll inspection include:

- Ticking the box on your Employer's Annual Return (form P35) that some or all of your income may fall within IR35
- Paying a small salary/large dividend
- Having a company name which is obviously that of a contractor's company. If you look and sound like a contractor, this inevitably leads to questions about your IR35 status.

If you claim you are outside IR35 you will be asked to justify your reasons. You should ensure that you have a very good justification and strong argument for your decision. Chapter 8 covers IR35 extensively.

Changes in share structure: Factors that could trigger an investigation are:

- Major changes in a company's shareholding structures, including dividend waivers
- Any shareholders that are non productive or aren't working in the business
- Any shareholders that are not resident in the UK.

HMRC may well ask you for a commercial justification of the arrangements above.

Non-allowable expenses: HMRC is aware that many contractors may not know that certain expenses are not allowable. Examples include business entertaining, business clothing and private use of company assets. Expenses have been covered in section 6.3.6 – take heed, don't take advantage and if in doubt don't claim it as a company expense.

Travel expenses: If you submit high claims for travel you are likely to be asked by HMRC to provide both justification and documentary evidence. Claims without receipts for travel and subsistence should be avoided wherever possible.

Use of home as office: Any claims you make for expenses for "use of home as office" should be fully justifiable. HMRC is aware that contractors have previously made claims without any real justification.

Company car expenses: Company cars in a one-person contractor company are becoming highly unusual, as it is rarely a cost-effective option. If you do have a company car, you should fully account for the benefit-in-kind tax arising and also the Class 1A National Insurance.

HMRC cross checks the accounts of companies with cars to Class 1A/P11D forms and any under-declaration or non compliance is likely to be picked up and investigated.

P11D compliance: This is a key expenses form that has to be submitted at the end of the tax year by every contractor who is a director of their limited company and has expenses reimbursed by that company.

You should ensure that a form P11D is completed, making full disclosure of any benefits in kind and expenses reimbursed. HMRC do cross check expenses claimed in one-person companies to the director's form P11D, particularly if expense claims are high.

6.3.12 Directors' roles and responsibilities

As a director of a limited company, it is your responsibility to manage the company in accordance with the Articles of Association and company law. This sounds quite scary, but if you are organised, thorough and use professional help like accountants when necessary, nothing should go wrong.

Statutory documents

Your main personal responsibility is to ensure that statutory documents are delivered to the Registrar of Companies as and when required by the Companies Act. In particular, you are required to file:

- Accounts
- Annual Returns (form 363)
- Notice of change of directors and secretary, or in their particulars (for example a change of address)
- Notice of change of the company Registered Office (form 287).

Failure to file these documents correctly and on time could ultimately result in prosecution, a criminal conviction and a significant fine for each offence. But again, it's easy to do it right, particularly if you employ professional help, like an accountant.

Company accounts

As a director of a Private Limited Company, you will normally have a maximum of ten months from the accounting reference date in which to deliver your company's accounts to the Registrar of Companies. If you file the accounts late, then the minimum fine is £100, which rises up to a maximum of £1,000 if the accounts are more than one year late.

However your accountant should have all this under control as long as you provide them with the information they need in good time.

Corporation tax
In addition to filing the annual accounts with Companies House, you must also file them with HMRC, together with a corporation tax return (form CT600) and a corporation tax computation. The corporation tax and forms must be filed within nine months of the company's year-end, following a failure to do so a penalty of £100 is payable and interest may be charged on overdue tax.

Again, your accountant will manage this for you, and simply tell you where to send a cheque and how much.

Payroll, PAYE, NICs and IR35
As a company director, it is your responsibility to fully comply with all payroll regulations, including IR35 issues. This includes filing of the Employers Annual Return (form P35), forms P60, P14, P11D, P11D (b) and an IR35 calculation where appropriate. You are required to make PAYE and National Insurance payments in due time throughout the year by the due dates. In addition, if VAT registered, you will have a duty to complete VAT returns on time.

Professional assistance
Your accountants' responsibilities depend on the agreement you have with them, and they are of course ethically bound to carry out all duties and responsibilities for which they are instructed and paid, but most have a standard service that will incorporate all the above.

It is, however, your personal responsibility to ensure that the accounts and other statutory documents are done as required by law and by the due dates. You also have to supply a lot of the information to your accountants like all the financial records so they can complete the paperwork for you.

If necessary, you may need to chase them – don't just assume that they are getting on with the job. But if they're not, it's probably worth looking for another accountant.

6.3.13 Making the company dormant

You might decide to take a break from contracting, or perhaps use an umbrella company during a series of contracts that might be inside IR35. Of course, one option would be closing down your limited company, although this can be costly and time consuming.

If you believe you will need the company in the future then it might be better to make your company dormant. In order to do so, you must:

Prepare final trading accounts: Even if you cease trading halfway through your normal financial year, you must still use your usual accounting reference date. Companies House expects accounts made up to the usual financial year end, regardless of the date that the company actually ceased trading within the year.

Pay final Corporation Tax: Final trading accounts must be filed with the corporation tax inspector, as must your final corporation tax return (form CT600) with computation included. Once you have agreed and settled the final corporation tax assessment, you can then advise the corporation tax inspector that the company is now dormant.

Close payroll: You should close your company's payroll scheme by notifying the relevant Inspector of Taxes who deals with your PAYE that trading has now ceased and there are no employees. The Inspector of Taxes will then issue a final form P35 for the current tax year ending on the following 5 April. This form should be completed without delay and filed together with any associated P14s and P11Ds.

Close bank accounts: All interest bearing bank accounts should be closed and it may be worth closing any non interest bearing current accounts so you can avoid bank correspondence and statements being issued.

Terminate accountant/professional services: Advise your company accountant and let any other professional acting for your company know that any ongoing services and agreements are to be terminated while the company is dormant.

When you are working through your new umbrella company, or during a period of permanent employment, to maintain the company's dormant status there are still some tasks to complete:

Companies House: Even though your company is dormant, an Annual Return must be filed at Companies House together with the fee. You need to complete a Dormant Companies House form (DCA), made up to the usual accounting reference date.

Registered Address: Your company will need to maintain a registered office address, which can be either your home address or your accountant's office address.

Notice of change of directors and secretary or in their particulars: Even when your company is dormant, you still have a responsibility to advise Companies House if there are any changes in the company director's or secretary's circumstances by filing the appropriate change of director/secretary paperwork (form 288C), which can be downloaded from the Companies House website.

Cease Trading: It is vitally important to ensure that your company does not undertake even a single trading transaction, including receipt of bank interest or revenue generating transaction, during this period. Any such transactions occurring would require full trading accounts to be filed and the corporation tax return made to HMRC.

6.3.14 Closing down the company

You may have decided to close your company because you are thinking about returning to permanent work from contracting, or perhaps moving from a limited company to an umbrella solution on a permanent basis, and therefore do not want or need to keep the company dormant.

It is important to note that closing down your company incurs time and additional expense. It is only worth considering if you think you will never need to use it again and you do not feel it necessary to keep the company dormant.

Because it is costly and time consuming to open and close companies frequently, if you think you will be only be dipping into the contract market occasionally between periods of permanent employment, then an umbrella company is likely to be a better solution for you than your own limited company, even if you think you will be contracting outside of IR35.

If you are absolutely sure you want to close (or 'strike off') your limited company, then the following process applies. Many of these tasks must be completed promptly to avoid complications leading to further delays and costs:

Prepare final accounts: You should prepare your final trading accounts covering the period from the last annual accounts to the final date of trading. These must be submitted to HMRC, together with the corporation tax computation and Company Tax Return (form CT600). You should advise HMRC that these are the final trading accounts and that the company will shortly be dissolved.

HMRC will issue its final assessment and the final balance of corporation tax should be paid immediately, otherwise you run the risk of the Inspector of Taxes objecting to your company's striking off.

Close down the corporation tax scheme: Once you have settled your final corporation tax liability, you need to ask HMRC to close down the corporation tax scheme they have for the company.

Close payroll: Your Inspector of Taxes who deals with payroll should be advised that the company has ceased trading and will shortly be dissolved. They will issue you with a final Employers Annual Return (form P35), which you should complete immediately. You will then need to pay the final balance of PAYE income tax and NICs and then ask HMRC to close down your payroll scheme.

VAT registration: HMRC should be advised by you that the company has ceased trading and should be deregistered for VAT. They will issue a standard questionnaire that you need to complete and return. When HMRC receives your questionnaire it will issue a final VAT return. You should complete the return in the usual way and account for the final disposal of any fixed assets or trading stock, if appropriate (you might need to ask an accountant to help you with this.)

Application to Companies House: After your company has ceased trading for three months, you should complete and send Companies House form 652a together with your cheque for the current dissolution fee, which you'll find on the Companies House website. Companies House will then advertise your company in the London Gazette and, following a period of up to nine months, your company will be dissolved, when it officially ceases to exist.

You must ensure that on the date of dissolution there is no money in the company bank account or other assets held in the company's name, since bank accounts may be frozen and the sums transferred to the Treasury Solicitor acting for the Crown.

Final dividend: Finally, you need to calculate a final dividend, or capital distribution, for distribution to the shareholders. Shareholders are the lowest in the food chain for any final payments from the company, as final payments of corporation tax, VAT, PAYE and so on take precedence. You must pay your final dividend prior to the date of dissolution by Companies House.

If your company is experiencing financial difficulties or is insolvent when you want to close it down, you must talk to an accountant or insolvency practitioner, as this process is more complex.

6.3.15 Activity diary – regular tasks

To help you stay organised when you start running your limited company, it is sensible to put together a diary of those regular tasks you need to complete. Some tasks will vary according to the date of your financial year; others are set according to the tax year.

Variable diary dates

- Annual return (end of financial year on date of incorporation)
- Corporation tax self assessment return to HMRC (12 months after year end)
- Company accounts (10 months after year end)
- Changes in company and director particulars (as needed)
- VAT returns (quarterly).

Fixed diary dates

- 6 April — Official start of the tax year
- 19 May — Form P35 to HMRC
- 31 May — Issue P60 to employees
- 6 July — Forms P11D sent to HMRC
- 31 July — Income tax, second payment on account
- 31 October — Personal tax return (paper)
- 31 January — Personal tax return (electronic)
- 31 January — Income tax, first payment on account.

It is advisable to check with your accountant any lead times they need for the preparation of the above documents because, in some cases, it could be weeks or months ahead.

6.3.16 Changing accountants

You may reach a stage when your business is growing more complex than your original accountant is accustomed to handling. Or you may have had problems with the accountant's work, for example, they may have given you bad advice that led to problems with the taxman, or papers might have been filed late, leading you to be hit with penalties. Or you may wish to go outside IR35, and the accountant may try to convince you to stay within it for their own reasons.

Whatever drives you to it, there might come a time when you decide to change your accountant. Whatever your reason may be, there is a procedure that allows you to change accountants seamlessly. The professional accounting bodies, such as the Institute of Chartered Accountants, have set up a process that helps avoid disagreements and limits difficulties as much as possible.

There are two basic scenarios: either you and your accountant agree to part company, or you don't.

When you agree, your accountant may be sorry to see you go, but is obliged to allow you to change. In this case, ask your new accountant to contact the old one, and the necessary exchange of information and paperwork will take place. The professional accountancy bodies oblige members to provide documents without charge; nor should there be any charge for copies being made which the old accountant must keep.

When you disagree, your accountant still has to advise the new accountant about your affairs, but there are three areas in which problems may arise: non-payment, money-laundering, and matters about which the accountant would be responsible for reporting you to tax authorities. These are discussed below.

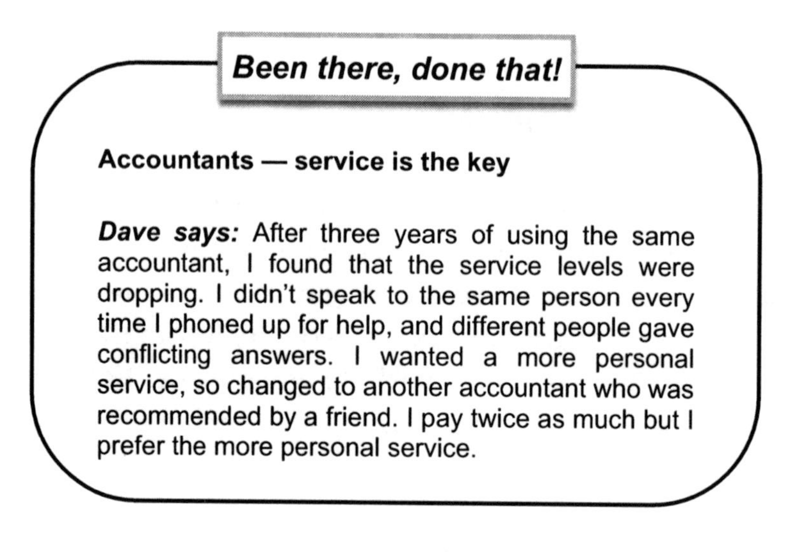

You and your accountant may not agree on fees owed. In this case, you should contact the accountant's professional body, which will arrange a fee arbitration. This is undoubtedly the fastest and fairest way for you to come to an agreement. Your original accountant may have the right to refuse to transfer information to the new accountant if fees are not paid, so the best way forward is arbitration.

Your original accountant may have other reasons for refusing to transfer your accounts to the new one. These would all involve unethical or illegal behaviour on your part. If your original accountant believes that you have committed fraud, for instance, you will have to permit the new accountant to discuss this with the original one. Should you believe this to be unfair, you will need to challenge the original accountant directly. You cannot ignore the allegation and move to a new accountant.

The same goes for accounting irregularities. If there are issues about your financial reporting, you have to settle them with the old accountant before moving on to the new one. But hopefully you've been running your business properly, and your change to a new accountant should be simple and a positive move forward for your business.

6.4 Trading through an umbrella company

Umbrella companies are designed to remove nearly all of the administration and company management associated with a limited company, which is why they are such a popular choice for contractors.

Naturally, there is a charge for such relative ease and convenience and, for those whose contracts are outside IR35, the real cost of using an umbrella company is in a considerably lower net income than they could otherwise earn by contracting through a limited company.

However, one of the principal features of life as a contractor is its flexibility, and different times or contracts may require different trading solutions. Switching between the two, or even sometimes running them concurrently, is certainly possible and sometimes advisable.

6.4.1 Choosing an umbrella scheme

The main advantages for using an umbrella company are:

- It means you avoid the hassle of running a limited company
- There is no need to be involved with running a spreadsheet, completing VAT returns, payroll matters, company accounts, taxation, director's responsibilities and so on
- For short term contractors, a main advantage is not having the costly process of forming a company and then arranging for it to be dissolved.

Types of scheme: The salary only scheme is the most common umbrella model on the market. Its distinctive features are that:

- It does not make any attempt to work outside the scope of IR35
- All your income is paid by salary only
- It allows for reasonable allowable expenses.

Contractors used to be able to use composite schemes that provided both dividend and salary payments, but the introduction of the Managed Services Company (MSC) legislation means these are no longer a viable option.

The market also offers alternative solutions involving foreign currency loans, offshore arrangements and other inventive methods of reducing the tax payable by contractors. These schemes are promoted on the basis that their payment methods give them an advantage over the standard/UK based umbrella company schemes. It is important to ensure that you are fully comfortable with the system being offered and to check very carefully the legality of any arrangement being offered and whether it is appropriate to your own circumstances.

Bear in mind also that legislation was introduced in the 2004 Budget making it a legal requirement for 'tax avoidance' schemes to be registered with HMRC. Suffice to say, some of these schemes present more of a risk.

Speed of processing transactions and payments: The most common complaint by contractors against their umbrella companies is that the speed of processing payments and quality of service is less than they had expected. So, before signing up with an umbrella company, it is advisable to check the following with potential providers:

- How quickly they will send an invoice to the agent following receipt of your timesheet
- How quickly they will they pay you when they receive the agency's money for your work

- Do they have any service guarantees and/or your money-back promises for service failures.

Monies held back: Some umbrella company providers make a point of holding back a proportion of your money. It is still your money, but it is there to cover holiday and sick pay, to cover periods between contracts, and even to cover bad debts arising from non-payment by your agency or client.

Other umbrella companies do not make any deductions whatsoever and simply pay out the full weekly/monthly amount of your agency payment. It is important to clarify in advance exactly when you will be paid and whether any monies will be retained for whatever reason.

Agency recommended umbrellas: Most agencies will recommend an umbrella company. These are usually judged on the quality of service the umbrella company offers both the agency and the contractor. The agency is looking for umbrella companies that offer hassle free options – hassle-free for the agency, primarily!

Some agencies have fixed policies (preferred supplier lists) for recommendations, whilst others have "commercial arrangements" with umbrellas, not necessarily based on the quality of service provided to the contractor. It is always a good idea to ask the agency why they recommend a particular umbrella company.

Expenses allowed: Some umbrella companies market their arrangement with HMRC for paying expenses without receipts, called a dispensation (see section 6.4.3). Reputable companies still insist contractors can justify legitimate expenses in the event they are investigated by HMRC.

HMRC takes a close interest in umbrella companies that have dispensations, particularly where expenses are paid without any justification or supporting vouchers – beware! Only ever claim legitimate expenses and always keep records and receipts; even if the umbrella company doesn't want to see them, the taxman might at some future time.

Fees charged: The marketing of fees by different umbrella companies varies considerably. At the time of writing, you should expect to pay between £25 and £30 per week for a high quality service. Some umbrella companies charge on a percentage basis, but will usually be prepared to negotiate if you are on a particularly high rate.

Experience and qualifications: Anybody can set themselves up as an umbrella company, without any experience or qualifications, so it is important to know exactly who you are trusting to handle your hard-earned money. Most of the quality umbrella schemes are run by qualified accountants, who will be able to offer personal and professional guarantees.

6.4.2 Joining an umbrella scheme

When joining an umbrella company for your first contract, or moving from a limited company arrangement, there is usually a process to work through. Having said that, you can usually be up and running with an umbrella within 24 hours, subject to some due diligence checks they will make.

Step 1: Inform your agent or client

You need to advise your agency or direct client of the name of the umbrella company you are using, so that they can prepare their contract with the umbrella company's name as "contractor".

Step 2: Contract preparation and signing

The contract will usually be sent directly to the umbrella company by the agent. The umbrella company will arrange for it to be signed by their director and forwarded onto you for checking/countersignature as required.

Step 3: Personal and bank details

The umbrella company will also have a standard application form for you to advise them of your name, address and bank details for transfers to your account.

Step 4: Tax details – P45

You will need to send the umbrella company your form P45 from your last employer.

If you do not have a form P45 they will issue you a form P46, which will enable them to obtain a tax code to operate on your salary.

Step 5: Umbrella contract

Some umbrella companies will ask you to sign their own standard contract between yourself as an individual employee/shareholder and themselves. This contract will specify the terms and conditions of the umbrella company service under which you agree to work and be paid.

Some contractors move from umbrella to umbrella in the hope of 'resetting' their expenses allowances or to escape a difficult contract. A reputable umbrella company will conduct due diligence on new contractors who join, so if you are attempting to escape problems you will almost certainly get found out.

6.4.3 Expenses and dispensations

A small minority of umbrella companies aggressively market their ability to maximise contractors' net pay, usually through ramping-up expenses claims that qualify for tax relief, such as travel and subsistence.

Most promote their dispensation from HMRC, which means they do not have to account for every single expenses transaction incurred by contractors up to a set amount. So, for example, the dispensation may state that contractors do not have to provide documentation for daily subsistence of up to £20.

What has happened is that many contractors automatically claim for the entire dispensation amount to maximise their tax relief and thus their net pay, even if they have not spent the money or cannot provide receipts. They have sometimes been encouraged to do so by their own umbrella companies, as part of their marketing and contractor retention strategy.

This problem has become so acute with a very small but vocal element of the umbrella market that, at the time of writing, the Treasury has undertaken a consultation on whether contractors working for umbrellas should be allowed to claim travel expenses at all.

It is a terrible idea for any contractor to falsely claim for expenses they have not incurred. Even if your umbrella company has a dispensation and encourages you to use it, HMRC can and does investigate specific individual contractors and ask them to validate their expenses.

The few extra quid you might 'earn' by falsifying your expenses will never compensate for the hassle in time, money and stress it will cause you if/when the taxman catches up with you.

6.4.4 Changing umbrella company

You can opt to change your umbrella company at any time, but to minimise the disruption it is best to do so between contracts. It may be that you are not happy with the level of fees or service from your current supplier, or you may switch to take advantage of a new contract.

You will have a contract of employment with your umbrella company and this will usually contain a notice period. Your first step is to write to your umbrella company giving formal notice. Reputable umbrella companies will not have exit fees or a need to hold back money. You should expect to receive a P45 fairly soon after you have left, unless there are outstanding invoices from your contract with the old umbrella company.

Contractors who hop from contract to contract and regularly change umbrella company will experience a time lag as their tax paperwork catches up; this is normal and the contractor's tax situation will 'net out' over time. It can take up to 12 weeks with a new umbrella company before your paperwork is in order and during that time you may be on an emergency tax code, paying more tax than you should. But don't worry – eventually this will correct itself.

However, if the contractor has not saved a sufficient level of fees for a 'rainy day', cash flow issues could arise.

When a contractor starts with a new umbrella, the umbrella is required to conduct a range of identity and due diligence checks. These include confirming the contractor's identity to conform with money laundering regulations, and also checking the tax and expenses history of the new contractor.

Contractors have been known to change umbrellas because they think they can 'reset' their expenses allowances, but this is not possible with a fully compliant umbrella company. In addition to the P45, which provides a snapshot of your tax and National Insurance Contributions (NICs) status, you will also be asked to supply your expenses history.

If you want to avoid the attention of HMRC, stay within the rules and inform your new umbrella company of your contracting history. You should also note that expenses incurred when working for previous umbrella companies are not allowable with your new umbrella, as they have technically been incurred with a former employer.

When you change umbrella company, you must also renew your contract with the agency or end-user client. Most agencies will issue a fresh contract with the new umbrella company without complaint.

It can be an end client that proves difficult and often does not understand why they should issue a new contract. So you should ensure you manage your clients' expectations when you are changing umbrella and clearly explain the situation to them.

The new contract with the agency or end-user client should be signed by a company officer of the umbrella company, as this is the legal entity entering into the deal. But some agencies require all parties to sign. In cases where, for example, intellectual property is an issue, the agency will want the contractor to sign as well as the umbrella company.

Contractors who are sometimes in the middle of one contract are offered another contract by a different agency or end-user client, perhaps with higher rates of pay, and are tempted to make the switch, changing umbrella company at the same time.

But you should think carefully about doing this, as the consequences could be severe if it is a breach of contract between the contractor and the umbrella, or the end-user client. You may find the agency or client pursues the umbrella, which in turn may seek to obtain redress from you.

6.5 Moving between trading vehicles

There could be very good business or personal reasons why you might want to move from one trading vehicle to another, and such reasons may outweigh the work required to make the transition. As long as the change is made with a good lead time and in an organised fashion, any disruption will be minimised.

6.5.1 Moving from a limited company to an umbrella

There are many potential reasons why you might want to move your contracting from your own limited company to an umbrella management company, and it is generally not an issue as long as you follow the correct process.

The 'hassle factor': Although most contractors find it easy to get into the habit of keeping up to date with their limited company obligations – especially if they use professional help – some might come to the decision that it's not for them. For example, they might simply get fed up with:

- The responsibility of being a director of their own limited company
- The discipline of regularly updating a spreadsheet or accounting system
- Responding to communications from accountants, HMRC, Companies House and so on
- Invoicing the agent every week
- Arranging insurances
- Running a company bank account
- Arranging for all documents and returns to be filed in good time to avoid late filing penalties.

By switching to an umbrella, some of these tasks disappear and others are completed by the umbrella company's operations team. But remember, you will still have to claim expenses, complete timesheets and send these to your umbrella company as a matter of routine. And you'll still have to keep proper records of your client, agency, contracting and tax affairs – there's no getting away from admin!

Existing legal, accounting or taxation problems: Your existing limited company may be encountering legal, accounting or taxation problems and you may not wish to place a new contract within that company. But don't feel that changing to an umbrella company will make those problems go away; in fact, it's unlikely to and could even make things worse, if only because you might be seen to be 'cutting and running'.

A reputable umbrella company will conduct its own due diligence on your background, so any skeletons will come to light, and you may have to make provisions for them with your new umbrella company.

IR35 issues: Many contractors go through periods when all their contracts are inside IR35. If this is happening beyond a financial year for your limited company, and is not likely to change in the foreseeable future, it might be time to cut your losses and make the switch. And if things do change, as long as you made your limited company dormant and did not dissolve it, then you can easily and inexpensively return to limited company status.

Self containment: An umbrella company may be ideal for short term situations or to keep the income and expenses of a particular contract 'self contained', outside of your usual limited company arrangement.

Overseas contracts: You may wish to accept a contract outside the UK, which could involve offshore arrangements that can be placed through a specialist offshore umbrella company.

Personal issues: There may be personal reasons why a new contract is kept outside the existing limited company, for example:

- Matrimonial or separation/divorce issues
- Agency contractual commitments
- Differing profit sharing arrangements between contracts. For example, where the existing limited company is owned by more than one shareholder but a new short term contract is to be entirely for the benefit of one contractor only.

Whatever the reason, there is generally a trading solution to be found by most contractors to suit their current conditions.

Practicalities: If you want to change from your own limited company to an umbrella company, you will need to consider the formal process of closing down the company or, alternatively, arranging to keep it on a dormant company basis.

Sections 6.3.13 and 6.3.14 go through both these processes in detail. It is generally accepted that, unless you have made a life-changing decision of some description, it is more efficient to keep your limited company dormant rather than close it down.

6.5.2 Moving from an umbrella to a limited company

As circumstances may point you towards contracting through an umbrella company from your limited company, so the reverse is true. You may have started contracting through an umbrella company and now want to continue your contracting career through your own limited company.

The potential reasons why you would wish to move from an umbrella company arrangement to that of having your own limited company could include the following:

- When you started life as a contractor, you were not sure if it would be a long term prospect, so decided to go for an umbrella company as a short term option. You have now decided that you like being a contractor, and having your own limited company seems a more appropriate solution for the future
- You wish to have a degree of control over your company affairs, to enable you to be more directly involved in expanding and developing your own limited company

- You are unhappy with the service of your existing umbrella company and feel you may avoid some of the problems if you take control yourself
- You are sensitive to umbrella company costs (they are usually more expensive than running your own limited company, since they do more work and take more responsibility). This is analogous to the difference between owning and renting a car.

Practicalities: Moving from an umbrella company to a limited company should be fairly painless, as long as you follow some simple steps.

Firstly, you will need to examine the existing contractual arrangements you have committed to with your existing umbrella company and your agency.

It will be difficult to transfer an existing running contract from an umbrella company to a new limited company, unless you have the co-operation of the umbrella company and the client and/or agency concerned. Difficult, but not impossible. Often it is the client who is the most awkward, as they have to sign a new contract which may involve a long-winded process with their HR or procurement teams. Some umbrella companies have a tie-in period with penalties or additional costs if you leave early – make sure you check your contract first.

There may be a 'closing down' process or dissolution procedure for leaving an umbrella company which is effectively giving notice as you would to any employer. You should ensure that the umbrella company pays you fully for all amounts owed and any retentions for holiday pay or contingencies, which they may have held back during the period of the contract.

Section 6.3 details all the stages of setting up and running your own limited company.

7.

Contracts and contract law

7.1 Introduction to law for contractors

A contractor, by definition, is reviewing and signing contracts on an ongoing basis, unlike a permanent employee who may only sign one employment contract that will last several years. That is why contractors need just enough contract law knowledge to ensure that they're aware of the point when they need to seek professional help. That's the point of this chapter.

In fact, it is hugely important for contractors to understand that, at times, there is absolutely no substitute for professional legal advice. Legal experts are expensive, but such is the law of market forces that if their services were not of such high value (although generally modest compared to the much more costly alternative of you getting it wrong) they wouldn't be able to charge so much.

To put a contractor's legal expenses into context, at the time of writing a simple contract review by a specialist solicitor might cost up to £200; if the legal representative is then asked to negotiate changes with the agency, the cost could rise to about £1,000. That might sound expensive, but these sums pale into insignificance when seen in the context of that same contractor being found to be within IR35.

In one case that a contractor lost at the High Court, being found to be within IR35 ended up with him facing a bill for back taxes and penalties of almost £100,000. Suddenly that £200 contract review doesn't seem quite so expensive, does it?

If you use an agency, then generally they will give you a contract to sign. If you go direct then you will need to prepare contracts for the client to sign. The best way to use your own contracts with a client is to use templates supplied by an industry organisation and get them checked by a solicitor.

7.1.1 How much law do you need?

To launch and maintain a successful contracting career, you only need enough law to be able to do two things:

- Understand and know how to use the law to protect yourself and negotiate your way through business life
- Know when you have reached the limit of your legal knowledge and that you should consult a legal expert.

As mentioned in the introduction to this chapter, there are some key areas where a small investment in legal advice will be more than worth it in the long run. These include:

- Checking final contracts, particularly with new agents and clients
- Evaluating IR35 status from contracts.

The old adage 'a little knowledge is a dangerous thing' is very true of the law, but there are some lessons that can be learned as they crop up again and again; so contractors with some basic legal knowledge will be in a better position to enjoy a successful contracting career.

However, the law changes on an ongoing basis and it is important to regularly check with a solicitor, whose duty it is to keep abreast of changes in the law. You should also keep yourself informed by following the contracting media, so that you have a good idea of when to ask your solicitor if a recent change in taxation, company or criminal law might affect you.

7.1.2 Understanding the law

To be convincing when you are negotiating legal matters, it is essential that you understand some of the concepts behind UK Common Law. Law in the UK, as in most Anglo-Saxon countries, is based on interpretation. Jokes abound about lawyers 'splitting hairs' but in fact the legal rights and wrongs of an argument are only rarely black and white, especially in business law.

It is easy, if you only have a little understanding and knowledge of the law to assume that 'the law says that x is allowed, and my contract says x, therefore I'm right.' The real situation is more complicated. Each statement and clause in a contract is interpreted in terms of the legal concepts behind it.

And this is also why it is important to get your solicitor to check your contract and not your accountant, as many contractors do. Your accountant is not an expert in contract law, in the same way that your solicitor would not be qualified to give you tax advice.

Another common misconception is that people imagine that the law is a long list of do's and don'ts. The law is more of a philosophy, a group of related ideas which judges interpret. Judges are guided and in some cases directed in their interpretation by case law. Case law is simply a written decision made by a judge on a similar issue in the past.

Judges judge arguments:

- You argue that 'x is allowed since there is a law that says it's allowed', and your contract says x, so you are allowed to do x.
- Your opponent will argue that either 'your contract doesn't really say x,' or 'the law that says x is allowed doesn't mean the kind of x in your contract,' or 'the law says that x is only allowed in different circumstances from the one in your contract.'

The judges will rule on which argument has the greatest merits according to the written legislation, or the rules, and the interpretation, or the case law.

Whilst the notion of a list of do's and don'ts and 'can dos' and 'can't dos' might seem attractive and certainly simplify matters, in practice the system of common law allows interpretation by judges which is a good thing. Life and society are complex and no one set of absolute rules can apply in every context. One day you might be thankful that, although the law says 'x', in your case, it might not.

It is worth noting that in some circumstances the Laws of Scotland are different from the Laws of England and Wales. However the broad principles remain the same. Some contractors working in the engineering and construction sector will already be aware of this.

7.1.3 Know your rights and protect yourself

As a contractor, a person who signs contracts with clients and agents, you need to understand how to read the contracts you are signing and to spot areas of concern that you may choose to fix yourself, or you may choose to seek the assistance of a legal expert.

It is important to remember that sometimes what contracts don't include can be just as important as what they do include. This is a good example where knowing enough about the law can enable you to push for any missing items to be included.

Contracts can also include dangerous or objectionable material that you need to have removed. This can happen sometimes through ignorance on the agent or client's part and sometimes through design, so having a basic understanding of how contracts are structured can be a valuable tool at this time.

Contracts are not the only area of the law where contractors may have to protect themselves, and this is where knowing enough about how the law works and how to use the law can be of immense value.

7.1.4 How the law works, or how to use the law

In the UK, the principal organisations for interpreting and enforcing the law are the courts and the judiciary. However, before you plan on taking someone to court, bear in mind that the civil courts in the UK can be very slow. Complex cases that involve attempting to recover large sums of money from debtors can take years and cost significant sums in costs.

For smaller sums under £5,000, there is a fast track service through the County Courts, often known as the 'small claims court' but still a part of the County Court system. There is even an online service available through HM Courts Service, MoneyClaim Online, which means you can file a claim against, for example a debtor who owes you money, and assuming it is uncontested and a low enough sum you never have to leave your office.

However, the courts like to see evidence of what is known as alternative dispute resolution (ADR), which basically means if someone owes you money, its best you talk to them first and ask for it nicely before you get tough and resort to the law.

It is therefore advisable to see if you can use your knowledge of the law to convince the other party to settle before resorting to the courts. It is surprising how effective this approach can be, because eventually, if the other party is really wrong, they could pay damages and costs. And if they know they are really wrong, and you call their bluff, they know they are going to lose and have to pay you anyway.

It is also possible to put indirect pressure on the source of your problems. For example, if an agency is requesting what in your view are unreasonable contractual changes and you are prepared to walk away rather than sign, it is worth talking to the client, who under some circumstances can be your best ally.

In this situation, if you informed the client that you are unlikely to be completing the contract because the agency has breached the terms of your contract or is planning to, the client is not going to be happy. They are expecting you to complete the work.

The client can read your contract and see what the agency is doing. The client also expects the agency to respect the law, and can pressure the agency with non-payment or worse if the agency doesn't get in line. You could not put that sort of pressure on the agency.

7.2 Contracts

Contract law is, alongside IR35, the greatest area of the law that a contractor needs to understand; because, by the very nature of contracting, contractors are frequently negotiating and signing contracts!

However, the lesson of knowing when to ask for expert help is also just as valid in contract law. There is no such thing as a standard contract for a contractor – any attempt by an agency or a client to insist on a standard contract should be fiercely resisted. Not only could the contractor find themselves with a contract full of unwelcome clauses but they could also seriously jeopardise their IR35 status, which is covered in more detail in chapter 8.

7.2.1 What is a contract?

A contract is a legally binding engagement between your limited company and the agency or the end-user client if contracting direct. If inside of IR35 and contracting through an umbrella company, the contract would be between the umbrella company and the agent or end user client but essentially the content is the same.

All contracts have two things in common:

1. You exchange your services for a consideration; technically the consideration need not be money, but in practical terms contractors want payment with money.
2. A contract is determined when an offer has been accepted.

These basic principles underpin every contract and they are hugely important because they will apply every time you negotiate a contract with an agency or client.

You will find yourself discussing 'which services were agreed to for a consideration?' with a client, the subtext being they want more than they are paying for. Your agent may come back to you with 'I agreed to your offer for a six-month contract, not a twelve-month one', the subtext being the agency wants you to renew at the same rate you started at, and you want a rate rise.

Naturally, being subject to the principles of common law, volumes of contract law and case law have been created. However, specific areas tend to come up again and again in contracting.

A contract is an agreement to do something in exchange for a consideration, usually in the context of contracting it is a payment. When you accept an offer, you agree to a contract.

If you receive an offer, and make a counteroffer, the other party may accept and a binding contract is the result. Usually the acceptance of an offer is indicated by the signature of a contract, which is described as a fully-executed contract when both parties sign. Both parties must enter into the contract freely, before it is binding.

This is important for contractors, because what you agree to do has to be carefully described in the contract. You should not agree to perform vague or general work, you must agree to perform a specific task or series of tasks for a specific fee, which is the consideration.

Having a contract relating to specific projects is also essential if a contract is to remain outside of IR35.

Once the contract has been executed, if you are asked to do more things than are listed in the contract, you have a perfect legal right to refuse. Of course you could re-negotiate the contract or even have an additional contract specifying a separate consideration for the additional work.

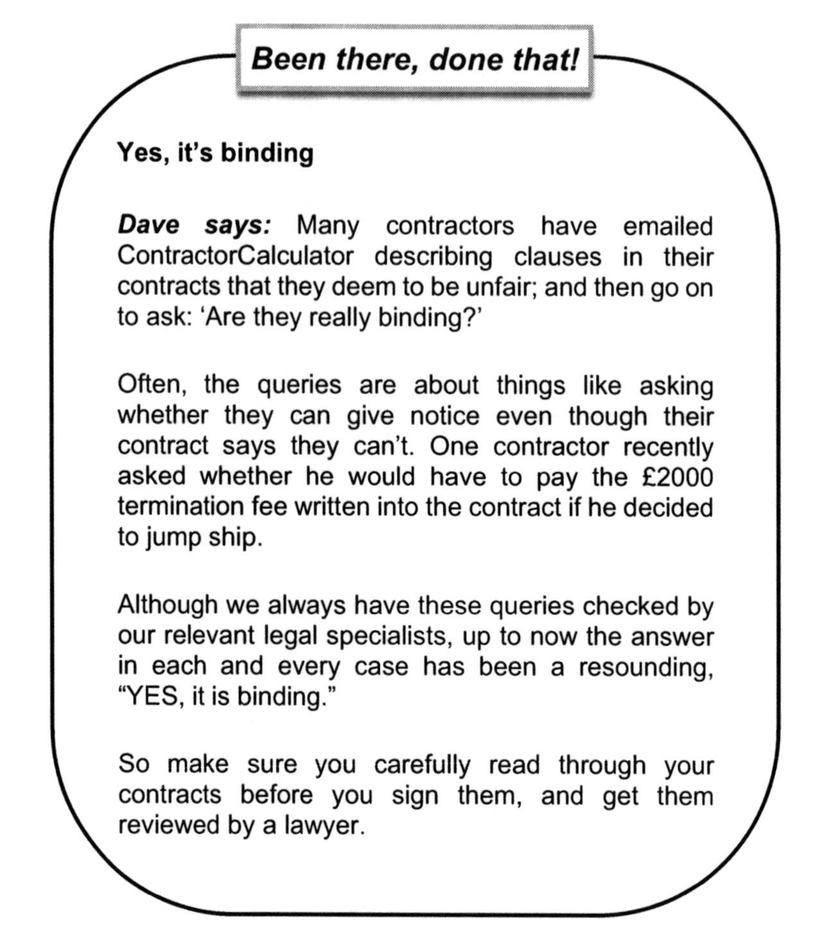

Yes, it's binding

Dave says: Many contractors have emailed ContractorCalculator describing clauses in their contracts that they deem to be unfair; and then go on to ask: 'Are they really binding?'

Often, the queries are about things like asking whether they can give notice even though their contract says they can't. One contractor recently asked whether he would have to pay the £2000 termination fee written into the contract if he decided to jump ship.

Although we always have these queries checked by our relevant legal specialists, up to now the answer in each and every case has been a resounding, "YES, it is binding."

So make sure you carefully read through your contracts before you sign them, and get them reviewed by a lawyer.

In general, avoid anything in contracts that you don't understand, or find odd. Never allow yourself to be told that it's 'normal,' or 'standard;' if you don't like it, have it taken out or renegotiate it.

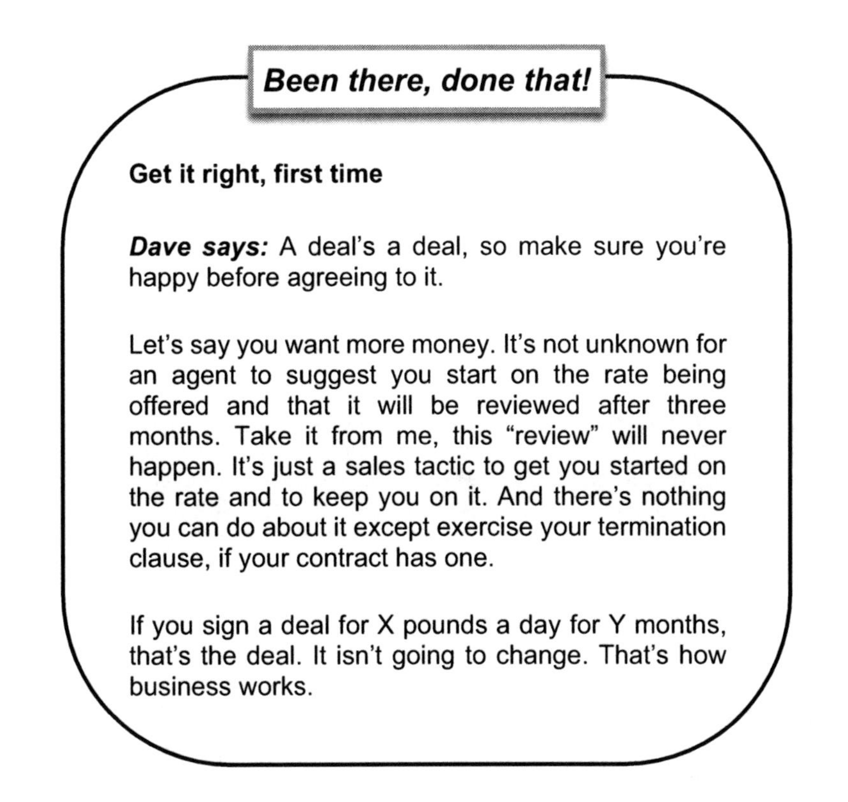

7.2.2 The difference between contract work and employment

Contractors are not employees. Previous chapters have laboured the point and highlight the differences. It becomes of huge importance in the contract between the contractor and the agent or end-user client that there is not even the slightest indication that you could be an employee.

However, HMRC can apply the tests of IR35 (see chapter 8) to a contractor to determine whether they are judged to be a disguised employee for tax purposes and if it is concluded that you are inside IR35, your net pay drops by a significant amount, up to 25%. Even if you think you are a contractor, if HMRC rules you are a disguised employee, then you have to pay tax like an employee. And you still won't get any employment rights.

You should understand the difference between a contractor and an employee, and you should scrutinise your contracts carefully for anything that makes you sound like an employee. And even then it is a worthwhile investment to have the contract checked by a specialist IR35 legal expert.

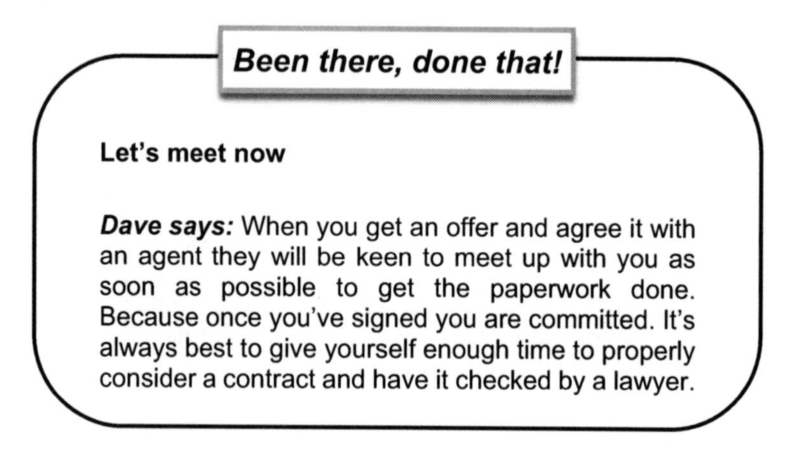

Being an employee is a special legal situation. Employees have a specific commitment to the companies they work for, and the companies have to ensure them a certain number of basic rights and privileges. These are detailed in the Employment Rights Act of 1998 and involve items such as holiday pay, sick leave and termination and redundancy rights. An employer cannot simply fire an employee for no good reason. Contractors, of course, have none of these rights nor do they expect them.

One of the most basic employer/employee rights is mutuality of obligation. Employers have an obligation to provide work for employees and employees have to do that work. Employees have an obligation to present themselves at their place of employment every day, they can't send someone else instead like a substitute, and they are expected to do whatever the employer requires of them, subject to their job description.

Contractors are engaged to complete a specific project for a client, usually a company that employs people. Contractors aren't employees, so they have no obligation to be at their client's site unless their contract requires them to be there, and they only perform tasks related to the specific project that is described in their contract.

If the project is cancelled or if the tasks on the project run out, the client has no obligation to the contractor to provide more work. Contractors in turn have the right of substitution; they have the right to send a suitably qualified replacement to continue and if necessary complete the project.

Contractors have control over the way they complete their tasks. The work an employee does is controlled by the employer.

The employer also assumes all the risk involved with the business, not the employee. Contractors are responsible for the business risk on their projects (but see section 7.2.5 regarding liability).

Employees do not have expenses directly related to their day-to-day work (in practice of course they do but claim them back, so don't really have expenses). Contractors supply their own equipment at the cost to their business and pay their own expenses.

To make the essential difference between a contractor and employee perfectly clear, consider what happens when you hire a plumber to fix your boiler. You don't employ the plumber, you engage the plumber's services for a specific task for which the plumber bills you.

You don't offer the plumber holiday pay, nor does the plumber expect you to supply equipment, nor for you to guarantee work for a given period – they usually do. The plumber does the job for you and goes on to another one for someone else. If, after you have the plumber fix the boiler, you want the pipes fixed, then you agree another contract.

The difference between an employee and a contractor is that an employee has a *contract of service* with their employer and a contractor working through their own limited company or umbrella company has a *contract for services* with an agency or an end user client. This is defined in more detail in section 7.2.4.

7.2.3 The different between contracting and temping

The term 'temp' means that a worker accepts assignments on the basis that they will not become a permanent employee. The temporary worker is paid by an agency, but their work is not under their own control.

The temp works for one agency, and then perhaps does other work for another. Temping is a very flexible form of work, but one that is changeable and, as its name suggests, is not one to take a worker through their entire career. Temps do have one advantage though: if they work for one agency on a regular basis they are able to claim benefits like holiday pay and sick pay under the Employments Rights Act 1998.

The term 'agency worker' is one used by a number of sources, in particular the trade unions and the Labour government. Trade unions like to feel they have a role to protect vulnerable agency workers, often on minimum wage doing low grade jobs.

However the issue is what kind of agency is described? A temporary work agency uses temps; an employment agency may handle a short-term assignment, such as maternity leave cover, interim executives and there are, of course, agencies that place contractors. 'Agency worker' is used to describe people who work through agencies, but temps employed by an agency are a world apart from interim executives and contractors working through an agency.

This difference is very important in legal terms for contractors. A contractor either works for their own limited company, or for an umbrella company which simply keeps the accounts for the contractor.

7.2.4 Contract for service v contract of services

The distinction between the employed and self-employed and businesses has long been characterised by the nature of the contract they have with the organisation requiring the work, or services.

Contract for service: A worker with a contract for services is employed. They satisfy all the tests of employment described in section 7.2.2. Their contract is with their employer.

Contract of services: A major corporation can have a contract of services with a customer who is also a major corporation. A contractor has a contract of services with their client, if contracting direct, or with their agency. This is an arms length business to business arrangement (including the self-employed) where services are provided by a supplier to a buyer. There is no question of any employment relationship.

Although only differing by a few letters, these two phrases describe fundamentally different contractual relationships and it is vital that any contract between a contractor and an agency or client makes it completely clear that it is a contract of services.

7.2.5 The elements of a contract

It has been stressed that contractors should never use standard contracts provided by an agency or client. Whilst this is a good rule, most contracts will have a broadly similar structure and content.

In fact, some parts of a contract with one client may be virtually indistinguishable from a contract supplied by another. After all, most UK companies work within the jurisdiction of the courts of England and Wales and want the contracts to be subject to the laws of England and Wales.

Most contractor contracts are divided into two sections: the standard or permanent section and the schedule. The permanent section includes all the standard clauses that relate to both parties, such as jurisdiction, liabilities, termination and so on.

The schedule defines the precise deliverables for the specific project the contractor will be working on. If the contractor is engaged by the same client through the same agency, the permanent section can generally remain the same and a new schedule is issued to reflect the new project and deliverables.

Either part of the contract can be changed when renegotiating or a completely new contract can be issued. However the division into contract and schedule helps significantly to demonstrate that the contractor is working on a specific project and not just working on whatever the client needs doing. This is essential if the contractor has any chances of remaining outside IR35 if they are investigated by HMRC.

Schedules and deliverables: This section is generally found at end of most contractor contracts and corresponds to the basic contract theory of an offer of a consideration (payment) and acceptance with supply of services. The front of the contract has details of the parties, such as the contractor and the agent, plus all the standard clauses.

Most contracts begin by defining the two contracting parties and the consideration/acceptance:

- The contractor - you
- The 'contractee' - the agency in most cases, sometimes the client
- What is the nature of the offer; a certain hourly or daily rate you get paid
- In exchange for what; specific services as part of a specific project, what you have to do.

The time period is generally next: for how long must you provide these services.

This should be fairly straightforward. If it gets any more complex then start asking questions.

This section of your contract just defines how you should perform our work, and what you can expect from the contractee (agent/client). It will normally require that the work be done with reasonable skill and care and to the timescale agreed on in the schedule.

The schedule would also include a number of warrants: you are warranting, or confirming, that you can perform the skills required to complete the contract. Be careful not to warrant anything you cannot provide. For example, do not warrant that you can speak Russian if you can't; you may be held responsible for damages if you warrant you can speak Russian, but actually you can't.

Schedules generally oblige you to provide your own insurance, administration, support, and equipment. If it doesn't, it should state specifically why this is being waived for the purposes of the project. If there is no reason given, start asking questions.

It should also state what the client will provide. The agency has the right to certify this in your contract, but you hold the agency responsible if the client doesn't provide it. Remember you have no contract with the client, and the client has no legal obligation in your regard.

Payment: This section of your contract simply lays out how and when you get paid. Billing is most often monthly (but need not be) and you are usually obliged to submit time sheets to the agency to justify it. The client must sign these time sheets. You have every right to assume, as a result of this clause, that when you submit a signed time sheet, you should be paid.

It is best that the contract states billing dates without equivocation. If billing is linked to your completion of certain milestones, which does happen on occasion, see that these phases are accurately described.

Right of substitution: As case law grows around the IR35 tax legislation, the importance not only of having a Right of Substitution clause but, and this might sound odd, the right to exercise it, are becoming increasingly important.

Having the right to substitute is a key test of employment status and partially determines whether a contract is of service or for services. However it is put, contractors must have a substitution clause in the contract with their agent or end user client.

The elements of correct Right of Substitution are:

- You must have an unfettered right to substitute yourself for someone else
- You should pay for the substitute (not the client), since you are effectively subcontracting the work
- You should pay for the handover period (for example a training period) for the substitute to replace you
- The client must not have the right to refuse a substitute without reason. Bear in mind that if the substitute does not have the necessary skills and cannot fulfill the contractual requirements then the client reserves the right to terminate the contract.

Some clients have not investigated the law in sufficient detail and form worrying, often emotional, conclusions from the right of substitution clause.
For example, they infer conclusions like:

- "I don't want that, they could bring someone in less skilled."

- "I don't want that, if they arrange a substitute it could cost us a lot of time and expense in handover costs."
- "I don't want that, if they arrange a substitute close to a deadline, the time taken to handover and train could jeopardise it."
- "I don't want that, if they cannot do the job anymore I'll simply find someone else who can."

Although these arguments are contrary to what could be exercised legally based on a proper substitution clause, they are nevertheless real and need to be dealt with if you are going to have a chance of getting the clause into your contract.

These objections can usually be countered if the client is made aware of the full range of issues. The suggested responses include:

Objection 1: "I don't want that, you could bring someone in less skilled."
Answer:
I legally cannot do that, because you have hired me to perform a specific function. If I bring in someone less skilled you can terminate the contract immediately and also sue me for damages for not fulfilling the contract.

Not only that, but as my skills inevitably increase on the project and my value on the market, you can be assured that if I do exercise the clause that you will only have to continue paying the original rate for my increased skills. This is better than me exercising a termination clause because it will cost you money to find and retrain someone, and you will have to pay more to hire them in the first place.

Objection 2: "I don't want that, if you arrange a substitute it could cost us a lot of time and expense in handover costs."
Answer:
The contract legally states that I must fund the entire handover and cover all training costs. This is better than me exercising a termination clause whereby you would have to incur this cost.

Whilst I personally intend to fulfill the services myself throughout the contract, unforeseen circumstances could arise where this is not possible.

Having the clause in the contract protects you throughout the contract should something like this happen. Think of it like car insurance. You don't intend to crash, but if someone crashes into you, you are covered.

Objection 3: "I don't want that, if you arrange a substitute close to a deadline, the time taken to handover and train them could jeopardise it."
Answer:
I am equally committed to meeting deadlines and do whatever is required to meet them. The handover and training of a substitute will never be allowed to jeopardise a project deadline.

In the event that I exercise the substitution clause we will both be able to plan accordingly to ensure that the project continues to run smoothly. There won't be any surprises.

Depending on the level required a handover period would normally last one month, and a vast majority of the handover training is done outside of normal working hours.

Not only that, whilst they are training, they will also be able to provide extra input into the project which you will be getting for free, which I shall be funding.

Objection 4: "I don't want that, if you cannot do the job anymore I'll simply find someone else who can."
Answer:
I have every intention of fulfilling the contract personally until the end. However, there could be unforeseen circumstances which mean that I will no longer be able to do so.

If you allow me to terminate the contract you would then have to fund the recruitment and training of someone to take over from me. Without the ability to terminate early together with a Right of Substitution clause the onus will be on me to find a replacement and train them, all at my expense.

This will reduce the exposure for you.

Mutuality of obligation: As explained in section 7.2.2 about the difference between employment and contracting, if mutuality of obligation can be established then the relationship is almost certainly one of employment, or a contract for service.

There may not be a clause specifically called mutuality of obligation but the following clause is typically used in contracts to ensure there is no contract of employment (contract of service):

"The client is not obliged to offer ongoing contracts or work to the company nor is the company obliged to accept such contracts or work if offered"

As long as you ensure you work on a project basis and do not take any work that needs doing, then this points strongly to a contract for services, putting you outside of IR35.

Control: To contribute towards establishing that a contract is outside IR35, the written contract must have no indications that the contractor is under the control of the end-user client. So it must not detail a line manager that the contractor reports to and should not indicate that the contractor's work is regularly checked.

The contract must also be specific about what the contractor can and cannot do. A manager at the end user client has no right under the agreement to insist that the contractor takes any work that is available, only that they work on the project covered by the contract.

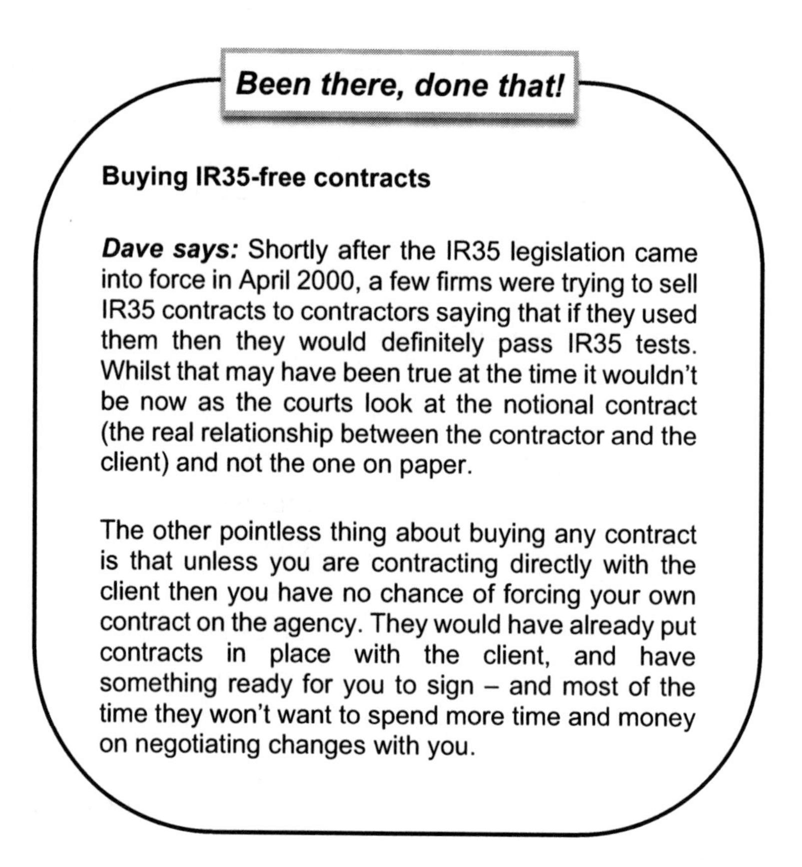

Except for reasons of health and safety and security, the contract must not specify hours to be worked, such as nine to five. The contractor should be free to take holidays and work at home according to their requirements without asking permission from the client, although it would be professional courtesy and good client management to negotiate time away from the contract and any days working off site.

If a contract is within IR35, then it may include clauses saying the contractor must work under direct supervision and control of the client.

Termination: Most contracts include a termination clause for both parties. Contractor contracts are often different. Quite often, the agency retains the right to terminate, but the contractor is not permitted to do so.

This is acceptable because one of the services demanded of a contractor is to be available for the full length of the project. It is simply part of what you do.

This is not usually an issue and all goes smoothly: you finish the project so the termination clause will never be brought to bear. Should, however, the agency wish to terminate early, they do have the right to do so.

The agency must pay you for all time through the termination period: this means that if the agency commits to a two week notice before termination, then they pay you for those two weeks whether you work or not, and assuming no other factors intervene like the quality of your work.

You are however bound by a "duty to mitigate", which means that you need to go looking for more work after you stop working under this contract regardless of the termination period. You can't just sit around and watch the television and expect the agency to pay you for it. Courts won't enforce your payment for the termination period if you cannot demonstrate that you have tried to 'mitigate.'

Always make sure that the termination clause clearly states what notice must be given. Under no circumstances should termination be permitted without notice. Technically, the only way your contract can be terminated without notice is if you are in serious breach of contract, and it must be a pretty major breach for the client not to allow the contractor to remedy the breach. In this instance you would probably be marched off site and not paid any more.

Restrictive covenants: Contracts with agencies often include what is legally defined as a 'covenant in restraint of trade'. They are more commonly known to contractors as 'restrictive covenants'.

Covenants are a form of protection for the agency. Typically, they restrict you from working for the client directly without going through the agency and they are sometimes extended to client subsidiaries. Covenants should have a period of usually no more than a year.

Restrictive covenants are enforceable in law, so it is advisable that you don't try to circumvent them. They are a reasonable form of protection for the agencies, which spend money and time getting you your first contract with the client. They have a right recognisable in law to continue to profit from the effort they have made.

If covenants had no teeth, every contractor could cut out the agency and work directly for the client after the first contract period and no agencies would be left in business.

An important point to remember is that the restrictive covenant can only be used for its original purpose and in the specific circumstances for which it was drawn up. Some agents might try and tell you that you have to reduce your fee if you want to continue working for a client, or they will exercise their rights under the covenant. That's completely unfair, and you can ignore the threat with complete safety.

The covenant is not a bargaining tool. If the agent wants to continue under the same contract terms, then the covenant has force. If the agency wants to change the terms, by making you take a rate cut for example, then the covenant has no value.

The application of covenants in restraint of trade, is, however, a very complex and difficult area of contract law. There is relatively little case law to depend on, and the number of challenging exceptions continues to arise: does it apply in public services where there is no competition? Does it apply if the agent does not make a good faith effort to renew the contract?

There are no exact answers to these questions but the rule of thumb should be to assume the covenant has force if the agency respects the terms of the contract and does not attempt to change them. In situations where you believe the covenant should not apply, enlist the help of a professional.

Potentially your best ally in conflicts involving the covenant is the client. Explain to the client what the agency is doing and see if you cannot get the client to negotiate on your side.

Intellectual property rights (IPR): Intellectual property can be an issue in contractor contracts. Problems arise as sometimes the contractor brings their own IPR to the table.

The most effective approach to this section in the contract is simply to set out what belongs to your company, and what belongs to the client. The agency has no rights in this area. If you are working with client-developed material, clearly you won't obtain any rights to it. But see that it is all clearly stated.

Liability and indemnity: You are a business in your own right and you are therefore liable if you cause loss or damage. If you call a plumber to install the dishwasher and they then flood your kitchen, they will have to pay for the damages and clean-up. You will have to indemnify the client or the agency or both if you do something you're not supposed to.

However you are not responsible for third-party liability. You are responsible to the agency through your contract; you are not responsible if the client takes action that brings in the lawyers.

It should clearly state in this section in the contract that you are liable for yourself, but not for anything else. If the client sells a product you worked on to another company and they then get sued it is not your fault. It is the client's responsibility to ensure that the product works before selling it.

Many contractor contracts call upon the contractor to 'indemnify' the client or agent if something goes wrong. The one thing that you have to make sure doesn't go wrong is your providing the deliverable on time: should you have doubts about your ability to do that, include them in the contract, or just don't take the job. If you foresee problems, you should get the client to agree in the contract that they may arise, and that you expect to be paid anyway.

Obviously, things do go wrong. However it is unreasonable to expect the contractor to pay for it if the contractor hasn't been dishonest about the services provided.

Some agents or clients try to include 'indemnification clauses' in contractor contracts. These clauses oblige the contractor to pay for losses incurred under specific situations. You should try to renegotiate these, as they are very easy to abuse and it is the responsibility of the client to pay for business losses. The client is in a better position to handle these situations than the contractor. What the contractor can and should do is to agree in the contract to cooperate with the client to help make good the loss.

Governing law: Most contracts will state the legal system to which appeal may be made if there is a problem. This is only to prevent parties from claiming that they want to go to court in Singapore if the work takes place in the UK. For the most part, you will want UK jurisdiction and indeed the legal system works better here for litigation than in most other countries.

Confidentiality: Confidentiality should not prove to be a difficult issue. You will probably be contractually bound to keep all your work confidential. If a non-disclosure agreement is added to the contract that should also pose no great problem. However always check the 'field' of the confidential material and the term.

Force majeure: This is a standard clause in nearly all contracts and essential allows for the unexpected and catastrophic events that can't have a separate clause to themselves. If your client's offices are destroyed by a hurricane, you will not be able to enforce your rights.

7.2.6 Things to avoid

To ensure that the contract is one for services, not one of employment, there are some clauses that should not be present, as they may point towards employment.

Holidays: Contractors are not employees and do not receive paid holidays. Any reference to holidays must be removed.

If you want to take a holiday during a contract, then the best option is to informally discuss this with the project manager and if it can be accommodated take the time off. Obviously you won't be able to bill for that time.

Ideally take time off between contracts. That is one of the benefits of the contracting lifestyle.

Ongoing contracts: If there is reference to ongoing contracts, the inference is that this is ongoing work and not project work and thus implies a mutuality of obligation and thus employment.

Make sure there is no mention of ongoing contracts anywhere in your contracts.

Automatic renewal clauses: If the contract is automatically renewed, it suggests that there is ongoing work and a mutuality of obligation exists – there will always be work for you if you are always there to complete it and you are not working on projects with a defined completion date.

Remove any mention of automatic renewal clauses, however tempting they may seem, from your contract.

8.

IR35

8.1 What is IR35?

IR35 is tax legislation aimed at identifying individuals supplying their services to clients via a limited company or partnership who, in the eyes of the Treasury, are actually 'disguised employees' and should therefore be taxed as employees.

However, although these individuals might be treated as employees for tax purposes, they do not qualify for any of the rights associated with employment from their client or agency 'employers'.

So why should you be worrying about a complex piece of tax legislation? Well, for the very good reason that getting caught by the legislation could result in you experiencing a serious decrease in your take home pay, to the tune of up to 25%.

And whether a contract is within IR35 or not is not a black and white decision for you and your accountant, or your agency or client for that matter. You need to take reasonable care to make a judgement on behalf of your company based on the advice from an IR35 and employment law specialist and ultimately it is your responsibility.

However, you may still be investigated by HMRC at a later date and the taxman could decide that you had made the wrong decision; that you had, in fact, been working within IR35 for some of your past contracts. This might lead to you owing a fortune in unpaid back taxes, interest and penalties.

That is why it is so important for you to understand IR35, how it works and its potential impact on you and your livelihood.

If you work through an umbrella company, you are already technically an employee subject to full PAYE and National Insurance Contributions (NICs), so you are not affected. IR35 only applies to contractors who operate via limited companies, the majority of whom run their contracts and their companies entirely legitimately.

Whilst all contractors using limited companies need to be concerned by IR35, not all contractors are automatically caught by it. With forethought and correct planning you can ensure you remain outside IR35 throughout your contracting career and never have to worry. That is one of the main objectives of this chapter.

The idea behind IR35 is sound: to stop people who are really employees pretending that they have rights to all the tax breaks that limited companies get, without having to take on the risks that companies run. In other words, it's the Treasury's and HMRC's way of making sure people pay the tax they're supposed to.

Sadly, the way the IR35 legislation is used is not only far from that simple, but is also often interpreted by HMRC and the law in ways that appear, at best, unfair, and, at worst, tantamount to state harassment and bullying.

But those caught would not even have been in the taxman's steely gaze if they'd followed the advice in this book. It's not difficult, you just have to be aware of the ways in which you work, how they might be viewed by the authorities, and how you should respond in each case.

The name, IR35, stems from the original Inland Revenue (now HMRC) press release announcing the new tax rules. Its more formal name is the 'Intermediaries Legislation', which was first announced in the Pre-Budget speech of 1999 by then Chancellor Gordon Brown, and adopted as part of the Finance Bill for April 2000.

The motivation of the Treasury at that time was to tackle what they perceived as tax and National Insurance (NI) avoidance schemes through the use of intermediaries, such as partnerships or limited companies.

And there was a serious problem, where lax tax legislation was leading to employees being able to change their status to limited companies or partnerships, thereby considerably increasing their take home pay, almost overnight. They did this by paying considerably less tax, which was not only a problem for HM Treasury, but also put additional burdens on PAYE taxpayers.

But despite their new limited company or partnership status, many of these contractors were really still employees – in the most blatant cases still working for the same boss, doing the same work, at the same desk, in the same way they had done before, and at the same company!

The limited companies used by individuals to offer their services to clients became referred to as personal service companies (PSCs). A typical PSC is a limited company with a sole director who owns all of the shares and who provides services via the company.

Contractors who work through limited companies and take some, most or all of their remuneration in the form of dividends pay far less tax. HMRC's aim is to keep those it sees as employees from 'pretending' to be contractors and thereby reducing considerably the tax they must pay to the taxman.

So the Treasury's view was that a large number of IT consultants, engineers, non-executive directors and "one man band companies" were often treated as employees and shareholders of their own companies, with the resulting low tax regime, when in fact they should have been treated as employees of the end client.

If the intermediary, such as the limited company were removed, the Treasury argued, a large number of these workers would be 'disguised employees' who should therefore be included on the client payroll and have income tax and NICs deducted at source each month.

From its inception, the Intermediaries Legislation sent shock waves through the contracting sector. IR35 originally had a noble purpose and was designed to address a very real problem – that a minority of workers were abusing the system to avoid paying tax and NICs, whilst at the same time employers were turning their employees into contractors to save on taxes and costs.

Unfortunately, most now agree that the legislation was poorly thought through and badly drafted in the rush to get it onto the statue books. In addition, the Treasury's use of the then Inland Revenue as a blunt instrument to enforce the legislation resulted in its virtually indiscriminate application.

As a result, IR35 is often characterised as a 'sledgehammer used to crack a nut', largely because it threatened not only the majority of contractors, but also the livelihoods of other occupations and professions that had used limited companies and partnerships for over a century to legally ply their trade.

There are many critics of the legislation, the majority of whom conclude that the whole idea of IR35 is unworkable. But, unworkable or not, it is law and HMRC has to apply it, and apply it rigorously, in order to meet its revenue-collection targets.

Most people are aware that the UK tax authorities have the powers to investigate an individual's or company's tax affairs going back six years. The same is true of IR35, so HMRC can look at past contracts and, if it successfully proves that you were inside IR35, you will have to pay back taxes, plus National Insurance Contributions, interest and penalties. This can amount to a great deal of money.

The danger is that nearly any contractor could be considered 'caught' by IR35, and become the subject of an HMRC investigation. That's because the Intermediaries Legislation is based on the model provided by employment law, and employment law has very extensive and often contradictory case law (see section 7.1 for an explanation of case law).

Whilst investigations are rare, and only a few contractors find themselves in the courts each year, you must ensure you take adequate precautions to stay outside IR35. In one past case, where HMRC has been successful, the contractor had to pay £99,000 in back taxes, interest and penalties for being caught, because he had not made sure of the fundamentals.

Defending your IR35 status is very much a pre-emptive strategy. HMRC's inspectors are looking for easy targets – don't be one.

8.2 The financial impact of IR35

If your contract is caught within the IR35 legislation, then all income for that contract is 'deemed salary'. In other words, income tax and National Insurance Contributions should be deducted as if you were an employee.

A contractor caught by IR35 will typically receive up to 25% less take home pay (the 'cash' left in your pocket after paying all your taxes and National Insurance Contributions) than they would if their contract was outside IR35.

For a contractor on £40 per hour, the difference would be approximately £800 per month or £9,600 per year after taxes – not an insignificant sum! And many contractors can earn considerably more than £40 per hour.

As you can see from table 8.1, the financial impact of a contractor being inside IR35 is considerable. But don't fear – not all is lost, because avoiding IR35 is certainly possible if you are clear about how to demonstrate your non-employee status.

To avoid IR35 requires you to understand not only the legal aspects of the legislation, but also how and when to negotiate with clients and agents to avoid it.

Rate per hour	Monthly take home pay	Impact on monthly take home pay after taxes
£20	£2070	Decreases 21% (£439)
£30	£3144	Decreases 22% (£714)
£40	£3959	Decreases 20% (£828)
£50	£4773	Decreases 20% (£960)
£75	£6810	Decreases 18% (£1,289)
£100	£8847	Decreases 18% (£1617)
£125	£10885	Decreases 17% (£1946)

Table 8.1 Typical reduction to net take home pay for a contractor inside IR35

8.3 Factors determining status

IR35 has evolved considerably since it first came into force in 2000, although it still suffers from being poorly drafted and decidedly opaque in areas!

As chapter 7 outlined, no law contains a definitive list of do's and don'ts, and IR35 is no different. So to prepare an effective IR35 defence, contractors must effectively maximise the chances that they are working outside IR35 by having as many 'contra-indicators' in place as possible.

That is to say, contractors should stack the odds in their favour to prove that they are outside IR35. This is not about trying to prove that white is black or vice versa – if your contract means that you are effectively an employee then you must pay taxes as an employee. But if your contract places you outside IR35, you must ensure that there is no possible room for misinterpretation by a tax inspector. That's what we'll go on to discuss.

8.3.1 Key factors overview

Determining whether one of your contracts is caught by IR35 (or is 'inside IR35') depends on a number of factors. It is not entirely objective whether a contractor's contract is caught and depends on the terms and conditions in the contract, together with the contractor's actual working arrangements.

It is also important to understand that it is not the 'contractor' being judged on IR35 status, but the specific contract. So, you could have three contracts in a year two of which are outside of IR35 and one of which is inside.

There is no single reason why a contract fails IR35 and it is normally a combination of reasons. One has to stand back and consider the whole picture to arrive at the decision.

The key factors in an IR35 decision, some of which will be familiar from chapter 7, are:

- Contract – has the client hired your company or you personally?
- Control – does the client control you?
- Mutuality of obligation – are you obliged to accept work offered, and is the client obliged to offer you work?
- Right of substitution – can you provide a substitute to do the work?

Other factors include:

- Financial risk – do you risk your own money and is there opportunity for you to gain financially through sound management?
- Part and parcel – are you a 'fixture' of the client's organisation?
- Being in business on your own account – are you really running a business?

- Provision of equipment – do you use your own equipment to do the job?

If you come under tax investigation and are suspected to be incorrectly paying tax as if outside IR35, all these factors will be examined to decide your true IR35 status – firstly by an HMRC inspector and then, if you choose to fight it, in court.

All these factors are based on case law – previous employment status cases that have been in the courts – which is why it's worth you knowing a little bit about how we've got to where we are now.

8.3.2 IR35 case law – a brief history

There is no definition in law for 'employment' and 'self-employment'. The definition of who is an employee and who is not depends heavily on case law, or jurisprudence, which is basically a set of principles of law established through precedent by judges over the years, decades and centuries.

HMRC itself makes this clear in leaflet IR56, which deals with employment status:

> *"The law for tax and social security legislation does not define 'employment' and 'self-employment'. But, over the years, the Courts have considered this issue and their guidance on whether an individual is an employee or self-employed is known as case law."*

So it is this case law that is used to determine whether a contractor is either employed, inside IR35, or self-employed, outside IR35.

But don't worry. You certainly don't need to learn all the case law surrounding employment status; the subject is vast and best left to experts. It is more productive for you to engage professional lawyers who specialise in employment law and IR35, although you should read on so that you understand the basics.

If you decide to fight status disputes with HMRC yourself, your chance of success is significantly reduced. Leave it to the professionals! The costs of professional help can be insured against, but the very best insurance is to not get yourself into bother in the first place!

It is certainly both possible and useful to gain a basic understanding of the factors determining IR35 decisions without learning about each and every court case. The following factors in sections 8.3.3 to 8.3.11 are the current guidelines based on an analysis of all the existing case law.

Once you have learnt the factors involved it is very useful for you to keep abreast of any IR35 cases that go through the courts to see if any precedents are set. There is only a handful of these each year and the results and analysis are widely reported.

8.3.3 Notional contract – it's not a paper exercise

Unfortunately IR35 can seem to come at contractors from all angles. If a contract is badly written, HMRC will flag this as a reason why the contractor must be inside IR35. If the contract is well written, then HMRC will fall back on what is called the 'notional contract', or the hypothetical contract that is formed by the taxman after examining the true nature of the relationship between the contractor and the client.

This means there is an increasing tendency on the part of HMRC inspectors and judges to look at what actually happens in the workplace and to base much of their decision on testimony that reflects the day-to-day operations on the job. When judging a contractor's IR35 status, an inspector or judge will form a notional contract that expresses the real relationship between the contractor and client.

This means that a contractor may have a written contract with all the right clauses regarding control, right of substitution and mutuality of obligation, but if the client thinks differently – and tells HMRC investigators so – implying that the notional contract is different from the written contract – then the contractor could be in trouble.

On the reverse side, the concept of the notional contract has saved many contractors from falling within IR35. An example would be a contractor whose contract did not explicitly include a substitution clause. However when investigated it was discovered that the contractor had actually used a substitute, and that fact put the contractor outside IR35.

The other defence against a badly worded contract is to seek a written "confirmation of arrangements" from the client, detailed in section 8.4.5.

An added complication is that most contractors have no idea of the exact contractual relationship between their agency and client. So contractors are advised to obtain a copy of the contract from their agency, highlight any areas of concern as soon as possible, and at least keep that copy in their contract file.

HMRC will certainly want to see the agency-client contract, known as the 'upper level contract', while the contract between the contractor and the agency is known as the 'lower level contract'.

This is another reason why the notional contract is so important. If the upper level contract between the agency and the client differs from the lower level contract between the contractor and the agency – for example by not including a right of substitution – the notional contract could work to the contractor's advantage.

8.3.4 "Contract for services" versus "contract of service"

This key issue has been introduced in chapter 7 and it's a fundamental underlying concept for determining whether a contractor is inside or outside IR35.

To recap, a "contract for services" is where the client engages your company to provide services to them. You then decide how and who is going to provide those services.

A "contract of service" is where the client engages you as a named individual to provide services to them. This is employment.

As highlighted in chapter 7, your contract must show that your company, not you as a named individual, is providing services, and you therefore need a "contract for services".

Your contract should state the terms for the services that your company provides, but should avoid any mention of personal service. It is not you the client wants. The client wants an action performed. Your company decides all the rest.

8.3.5 Control

The issue of control is a key factor that determines whether or not you are an employee.

Many contractors assume that they have control of the limited companies they have created to run their businesses. But how much decision-making do they actually exercise? Is the client, through the agency, telling you when to work, how to work, and where to work?

Should it become obvious that you are simply behaving like a regular employee for a given company, but are being paid like a contractor, HMRC will rule you are caught within IR35 and you will pay tax accordingly.

Clauses in the contract showing that you have to regularly report to the client are not going to help you. The more control is mentioned in the contract and the more control the client exercises in the actual relationship, the more HMRC will believe you are an employee.

If you look like an employee, are dealt with like an employee, and act like an employee, then in the eyes of the taxman you are an employee, whether or not you are working through your own limited company.

It should be clear from the contract that most decisions about how that service is to be provided are yours to make, assuming they do not affect the final deliverable. You should decide what hours you work, choose who else from your company can do the job, select a substitute if needed or appropriate for a specialist part of the job, and provide your own equipment.

Nothing in the contract should suggest that the client can approve or disapprove of your actions, or your means of performing the project the client requires, as the client might for an employee. Unless the means of performing the action is directly related to the outcome, the client should have nothing to do with it.

For example, if it is clear that you report your progress during early morning team meetings to the project leader and you are monitored regularly for the quality of your work, the implication is that you are controlled by your client.

The issue of control, because it has much wider implications in employment law, is a particularly large and complex area of employment law; as such, it is one area where the advice of a professional is highly desirable.

8.3.6 Mutuality of obligation

Mutuality of Obligation (MOO) is one of the key tests of employment status. As outlined in section 7.2.2, mutuality of obligation between an organisation and a worker implies a contract of service and that the worker is employed.

Under normal conditions of employment there is a mutuality of obligation between worker and employer. The employer is obliged to provide work for the employee, and the employee is obliged to accept it. There is an expectation of regular employment by the employee until they are made redundant or leave of their own accord.

For most contractors this status does not exist, and is one factor towards arguing that the contractor is outside IR35. After an initial contract, the contractor is not obliged to accept another one and is free to go. Neither is the company obliged to offer a new contract or continue paying the contractor.

However, when the contractor regularly works for the same client on new or rolling contracts, HMRC will say this suggests employment. If you are doing whatever work is available and not specific project work, this makes it worse.

In one IR35 judgement, the judges cited a statement by the client manager calling the contractor a 'tail-end Charlie', meaning that the contractor did whatever other members of the team didn't complete. That is powerful evidence of you being treated as an employee, and will therefore act against you in an IR35 case.

You should show that you have the right to refuse further work from the client. You are not obliged to turn up at the client's office every day and just work at what is assigned. You pick and choose your assignments: you accept one, perform it, and then choose whether or not to accept another.

Contractors who operate more as consultants with a multiple client base will be at less risk of IR35, since they regularly accept or refuse work from different companies.

8.3.7 Right of substitution

If you are genuinely providing a service then another contractor with your skill set able to provide the same service could take your place. In addition, you should have the choice of the substitute, not the client or agency, to ensure that the right of substitution is 'unfettered'.

Chapter 7 shows that your contract should have a right of substitution clause and your company should be able to substitute another contractor at your own expense, who can provide the services instead. Case law suggests this is one of the more important tests demonstrating that you are outside IR35.

Remembering the concepts introduced in section 8.3.3, any clause in a contract must be based on the real situation. Can someone else really substitute for you? If you are a famous television personality, a world-renowned expert on a recondite subject, or the last-surviving programmer in a software language that no one uses anymore, the court is likely to rule that you have no possibility of substitution, although this does not necessarily mean you are within IR35.

On the other hand, if you have the right to replace yourself with another contractor who has much the same skills that you do, then you are obviously not providing the services 'yourself', as an employee would. This strongly points away from employment and that you are outside IR35.

In chapter 7 it was stressed how important it is that you retain full control over any substitution. Clauses that require client approval or satisfaction, usually worded: '...the right to substitute another representative of the Company to provide the Services provided that the Client is satisfied that the proposed substitute possesses the necessary skills, expertise and resources to perform the Services' are to be avoided.

If the client has too much control over the substitution process, the court may claim that the client is simply looking for another employee like you. So ensure you retain the right to find and furnish the substitute yourself in the contract – you must maintain an unfettered right of substitution.

Restrictive clauses are not necessary, because if the client is not satisfied with the substitute's services, then your company is responsible no matter what and could be in breach of contract. You should at no time suggest that the client has control over the provision of services that you make.

Therefore, a more relevant phrase in your contract might say something like: '...any costs incurred in providing a substitute will be at the expense of the Company.' That nullifies the risk of sending in a substitute who cannot do the job.

8.3.8 Financial risk

Your own financial position will be examined if you are required to contest your IR35 status. Employees are protected from any exposure to financial loss, whatever involvement they may have in a given project.

This is not the case for a contractor, who may find a project terminated before completion and who then may not collect the full fee. Exposure of this kind is a key factor in determining IR35 status and it should be clear in any contract that you sign. If you appear to have the same protection as that enjoyed by an employee, HMRC and the judge may consider you one.

A contract that does not show a price for the work and an approximate date for completion implies there is no financial risk. It would simply state that you will work a set number of hours per week for an hourly rate.

8.3.9 Part and parcel

Want to use the company canteen when you're working on assignment? Want to share car rides with other employees when you go home? Want to get a security pass to avoid the bother of signing in each time you have to get in to the office you're working at? Well, don't even think about it, because even these small things can help to put you inside IR35.

Unfortunately, when you are working on site under contract, you can easily get mistaken for an employee. It can be hard to distinguish what you are doing from what the permanent employees are doing.

You can also find yourself being sucked into the employee workforce: eating at the company cafeteria, being added to internal phone directories and organisation charts and even given business cards to use.

Yet another of HMRC's tests of IR35 is whether you are 'part and parcel' of the client's organisation or not.

HMRC will contend that the provision of work by a contractor is the same as that of an employee and that the contractor is part and parcel of the end user client's business. In other words, the taxman will see that contractor as an employee, with all the tax implications that brings with it.

In case law there are no clear determinations of what 'part and parcel' means. In fact, some judges don't consider this test a very useful one in determining employment status. But others do, and

HMRC certainly use part and parcel as a test of IR35, so you need to be careful in how you manage the relationship with your client.

To make certain that you avoid the attention of HMRC inspectors, simply avoid looking like an employee and don't accept any of the conveniences that employees take for granted:

- Don't accept a pass that lets you into the building through the employee gate; sign-in every day
- Don't allow yourself to become listed in the company telephone directory
- Don't get your business cards from the company
- Accept no sick pay or holiday pay from the client
- Don't eat at the company canteen
- In so far as possible, see that you're not listed on company materials as part of the organisation.

If you have a management role, make it clear in written form that this is strictly related to the project you have contracted for. In general, it is best to avoid written materials that put you in the light of being an employee in any way; this is just what HMRC will be looking for.

Make sure you document some facts to back up your arguments during the course of your current contract in case of an investigation – which could be six years from now and you may have forgotten the details if you haven't added them to your contract file.

Draw up a list of the differences between the contractor and the client's employees. As the contractor is not an employee, there should be some fairly obvious differences, such as not having set hours, benefits, pension arrangements, access to social clubs, parking, expenses arrangements, use of a subsidised staff canteen and so on.

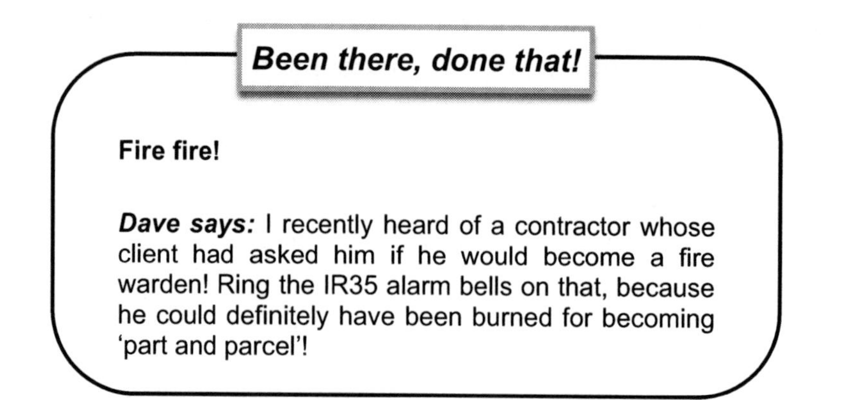

Try and keep any correspondence with the client that shows clearly you are not under complete control of the client's project manager. Keep this file safe with the relevant financial records from the same period. If HMRC come knocking, you can simply reach out and produce the file. Section 8.4.9 details setting up and maintaining the right records to support your case if you come under HMRC investigation.

8.3.10 Provision of equipment

This is a particularly difficult test of IR35. For the vast majority of contracts, contractors will need to use the client's equipment. For IT contractors in particular, using the client's computers and networks is just a basic requirement of IT security; an IT director would be irresponsible to let hundreds of contractors into the organisation using their own equipment and posing a huge range of risks to mission critical operations.

Unfortunately, several conclusions can be drawn if you use a client's equipment:

- You are part and parcel of the client's business
- You are taking no financial risk by investing in your own equipment
- You are being controlled by the client.

However, if HMRC can draw conclusions about your use of the client's equipment there are actions you can take to counter the conclusions.

Section 8.3.9 details how to avoid being labelled part and parcel. Section 8.3.11 details how, by demonstrating you are in business in your own right, which might involve you buying equipment that you simply do not use on the client's networks, you are taking financial risks.

To demonstrate that you are not under the control of the client, section 8.4.5 details how to ask a client to confirm this statement in a confirmation of arrangements letter.

8.3.11 Being in business on your own account

If you are in business in your own right, then you are clearly not an employee – you are a legitimate businessperson supplying services via a limited company.

There is a range of activities that can demonstrate that you are in business in your own right, rather than a de facto employee. Initially, these activities are likely to take the form of marketing – after all, if you were not in business, why would you market your company? Simple steps include:

- A website, business cards and company stationery
- Listings in business directories like Yellow Pages and yell.com
- Advertising in trade publications.

There is of course a cost associated with each of these activities, but compared with what you would lose if found within IR35, the cost is trivial. Not only that, as you've seen in chapter 4 and will learn in Chapter 10, marketing your company and services effectively is a crucial part of being a successful contractor.

When naming your limited company, avoid using your own name, as this implies you are only providing your own services. If you have Jane Smith Ltd on your business card, the implication is that Jane Smith will be completing the work. If the right of substitution is exercised and John Smith turns up, this might, understandably, cause some confusion.

It is also recommended that you do not use a company name that clearly says you are a contractor, such as IT Contractor Solutions Ltd, as this could also imply that you are the IT contractor, leading to similar confusion.

If however, you call the company ABC Computing, you are simply providing computing services that could be supplied by anyone from your firm, John or Jane Smith or, indeed, another contractor that you might sub-contract some or all of the work to.

Contractors who can show they have invested in business equipment also demonstrate that they are running a business. Business equipment could include:

- Computers, software, peripherals and consumables
- Business telephone and broadband
- Office equipment, such as a desk, office chair and a filing cabinet
- Stationery, such as foolscap files – that is not the sort of stationery you would normally use in the home
- Business insurances, including professional indemnity, public liability, employee liability and business contents.

A library of training material, investment in membership of a professional body, training courses and subscriptions to trade magazines all paid for by your limited company can all be indication that you are in business for yourself. Never charge materials like these back to a client, even if they offer, as it could be used as evidence of you being an employee.

Some contractors, particularly in the engineering field, are required to invest in personal continued professional development (CPD) in order to retain their chartered status, and payment for CPD by the contractor can be used as another indication of being in business.

Having concurrent clients can be a strong indication of being in business for yourself, but as evidence it tends to be treated on a case by case basis. For example if you are earning £75,000 a year doing high end development work for a corporate client, and maybe £5,000 per year producing websites for family and friends, then HMRC would not take this as evidence by itself that you are in business for yourself.

However, if you work two days on one contract for £35,000 per year and three days for £40,000 on another contract for a separate client, then this is strong evidence of genuine concurrent clients.

8.4 Ensuring IR35 doesn't affect you

The best IR35 defence begins before an investigation even starts and, ideally, before you even accept a contract. If you invest time in engineering out the risk of IR35, as you would engineer out risk in your work as a contractor, it is likely to save you money, time and considerable stress.

This section is not about pretending to be in business for yourself if you are not. If your contract and working conditions put you inside IR35, then you must pay tax as an employee; it's as clear-cut as that. But what this section is about is making sure that in your legitimate work as a contractor running a limited company there can be no room for doubt by HMRC or a judge that you are clearly not an employee.

There is a range of strategies you can adopt. Have them prepared in case you come under HMRC investigation, and the chances are that investigation will never happen. Or if you do come under HMRC scrutiny and you've prepared well, the tax inspector is likely to look into your case, quickly conclude that you're acting in full accordance with the law, and move on.

The other key fact to consider is that an investigation can go back six years. Can you remember exactly what you were doing on every contract six years ago? Will your client be able to remember? Keep some simple records and you won't have to.

8.4.1 Steps to avoiding IR35

Firstly, under no circumstances sign a contract without being fully aware of the IR35 implications. It does not matter if you are within IR35 or outside, as long as you know and you can plan for it.

Never, ever accept assurances from agencies or clients that you are outside IR35. Agencies are not particularly interested in your IR35 status – they get paid the same regardless. Some might even try and tell you the contract is outside IR35, but review it yourself and get the contract checked out by an expert if there is even the smallest sliver of doubt.

Remember that the agent is not your friend, but a salesperson whose interests are likely in places to conflict with your own. They are certainly not experts in employment law, and even if you are convinced they know what they're talking about and are sincerely giving you correct advice, don't trust it! Otherwise, you could find yourself in court saying something the equivalent of, "The big girl told me it was alright." The judge might find it amusing, but it certainly won't help your case.

Once you have secured an interview, or even beforehand if you have sufficient information, start evaluating your IR35 position based on a very realistic evaluation of what you will actually be doing on the contract. Make sure the client describes this clearly and unequivocally in your meeting. Use the questions in your interview to clarify what you will be doing and how you will be working.

Once you are offered the contract and get the contract paperwork you now have everything you need to review your decision. Your written contract will need to cover all the key IR35 concepts already discussed, such as project-based work, control, mutuality of obligation, right of substitution, use of own equipment, financial risk and so on.

If possible, you should also try and get a copy of the agency-client contract (the 'upper contract') to check that it mirrors your own.

You can try and evaluate the position yourself, but if you are in any doubt, get professional advice. In fact, even if you are not in any doubt, it is generally advisable to ask a lawyer who specialises in IR35 to review your status, and give you an accurate assessment based on your situation.

To avoid any further penalties on top of the extra tax if you are caught by IR35, you will need to show 'reasonable care' has been taken when evaluating your IR35 status. If you have done it yourself this isn't as strong evidence as getting a professional to do it. If you get a specialist to do a review you can mitigate any need to pay penalties if you are caught, because you can show you have taken 'reasonable care'. It will cost you a fee, but this is nothing compared to the extra tax you would pay if you are caught by IR35. This assessment, along with other testimony and materials, can also be useful to you if HMRC comes knocking at your door. At the very least, you can consider it investment in your own peace of mind.

If the agency won't budge on changes to the contract then insist on getting the client to sign a confirmation of arrangements, covered in more detail in section 8.4.5, which clearly states the real relationship you have with them.

Your accountant will ask you to declare your IR35 status for each contract so they can process your tax correctly. You may also be asked to sign a statement saying that the accountant is not liable for a false declaration.

You should not be afraid to sign this, as the accountant is in no position to assess whether or not you are 'inside' or not. IR35 is primarily a legal issue, not an accounting issue.

Always, on every contract, create a compliance file, containing every piece of useful proof you can get. This can be enormously important in a court case. Keep all the paperwork from every contract for six years.

While at work, obtain and save as much paperwork as you can that shows that you are doing a project and not working as an employee. Also, don't get involved in any activities that might make you appear as part of and parcel of the client's company – see section 8.3.9.

8.4.2 Getting the contract right

Many contractors, particularly if it is their first or second contract, wait until they have signed a contract before they start addressing IR35, significantly increasing their chances of being caught by IR35.

If you sign the contract without getting it reviewed you will eliminate any opportunity to negotiate the contract for IR35 compliance. Whilst you can provisionally check the contract yourself to determine if you are outside IR35, make sure you get any new contract and your working arrangements professionally reviewed before you sign it or agree to it verbally.

If the contract is not genuine (ie you are working as an employee, whatever the contract might say); has been copied and presented as a 'standard contract'; or is a 'do it yourself IR35 contract', HMRC will identify it, and disregard it as not being 'a live contract'. For example, in one case a judge ruled that the substitution clause was 'window dressing'. So beware and take care!

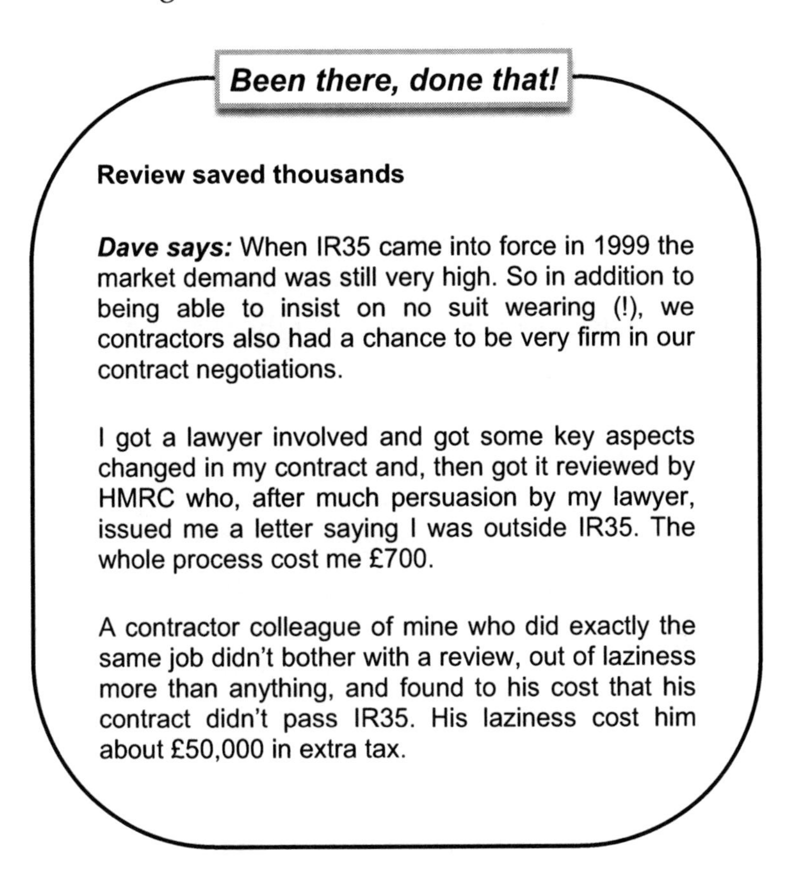

Although HMRC will consider the notional contract, that is the real relationship between the contractor and the client, it is vital that contractors get their written contracts reviewed by a specialist before they sign it. A poorly worded contract will immediately attract HMRC's attention.

Avoid buying 'IR35 proof' contracts. Passing IR35 is not a paper exercise and the agency is unlikely to accept a new contract replacing theirs. There is no such thing as a standard IR35-free contract. In fact, the most important thing you should know about IR35 compliant contracts is that there really aren't any.

The contract you use should be custom-made for your work with this particular client or agent. And when working through agencies you should also ensure the agency's contract with the end user client does not impact on you.

In the event of an investigation, HMRC – and later on a judge if it goes to court – will expect to see that both you and the client have made a special effort to come to a specific agreement for this particular project. You may create a different one for a different project, or you may use a similar one, but the contract should reflect the specific intentions of you both.

In the light of the High Court's ruling in 2008 on Dragonfly Consulting Ltd, if you have a series of contracts with a client renewed over time, but that were not correct from the start, HMRC (and subsequently a High Court judge) can take this to mean later contracts were purely cosmetic or "window dressing", as the judge in that case called it. So it is vitally important to get the contract correct, right from the start.

Beware of contracts that are home made and based on a normal employment contract. These contracts are dangerous and will not only put you inside IR35, but could also contain clauses you don't want, and be missing clauses that you really need. A lawyer who reviews your contract will easily be able to spot this. Large agencies are unlikely to send out contracts like this, but some of the smaller ones might.

The contract should be between the client/agency and your limited company; under no circumstances should the contract mention a named individual. The schedule should describe the work to be done, preferably referencing a project by name, and the skills/services supplied.

In addition to the general points above designed to minimise IR35 risk, you should consider the following specific points that should appear as clauses or within the schedule of the contract:

Intention of the parties: Your agreement should specify the intentions of the parties, that you are offering services through a limited company and the client is engaging your company to perform those services.

Contractor engagements should be fixed term: As a key test of employment it is very important that your contract is for a fixed term and not renewable. If you have a two-year contract with one client and it is renewable for two years, HMRC is going to ask some questions, particularly if you have few or no other clients.

Mutuality of Obligation: You should display clearly in the contract that there is no 'mutuality of obligation' between you and the client – sample text has been provided in chapter 7.

Setting own hours of work: Demonstrate in your contract that you are able to set your own hours of work. If you work on the client's premises, make it clear in the contract that at least part of the work may be performed in your own offices.

Contractors pay their own expenses: Some clients are prepared to pay certain contractor expenses. This can attract attention as it can be seen as a sign of employment. You should include expenses as part of your rate.

Contractors don't get to take holidays: You should not expect clients to pay for holidays, nor should you expect to take a break during a contract. To allow for holidays, fix your contract periods with gaps in them so that there are breaks in between. Paid holidays are a certain indication of employment status and should not be accepted under any circumstances.

Contractors do not receive sick pay: The same rules apply to sick pay as those previously explained for holiday payments. This does not mean that you cannot get sick. It means that you should not expect to be paid for the time you cannot work. Ideally, you should arrange for a substitute, if you get sick.

Contractors supply their own equipment: This may be difficult for contractors to arrange in practice, but the contract should at least state that contractors are responsible for the supply of their own equipment. You may well find yourself working with the client's equipment, but at least you have undertaken to supply your own.

Contractors find their own substitutes: One of the key tests of employment status is whether you must provide the services yourself, as an employee would, or whether a substitute can provide them. You should plan to find suitably qualified and experienced substitutes and be prepared to provide them if necessary.

Upper level contracts: If you are not contracting direct and are working through an agency, which is very likely, you may encounter problems with the agency-client, or upper level contract. There may well be important differences between your contract and the one the agency has with the client.

For example, you may have done your best to show in your contract that you are outside IR35, but there could be elements in the agency-client contract that contradict those in yours. HMRC will try to show that the real contract is reflected by the agency-client contract and not by your contract with the agency.

HMRC will claim that your contract does not mirror the real situation in your day-to-day work, and that the agency-client contract does. There is unfortunately very little contractors can do to protect themselves in this situation.

In almost all of the IR35 cases reviewed by Special Commissioners, the judges take the agency-client contract into consideration and quote it extensively in their final judgement. This may seem unfair, since the agency-client contract often covers a large number of contractors, and not just the one hit by an IR35 case. Unfair or not, though, that's the situation.

The main issue is that the language of the agency-client contract can be directly contradictory to that of your contract with the agency. And if you are facing an IR35 investigation by HMRC, discrepancies between the agency-client and agency-contractor contracts add weight to their conclusions.

8.4.3 Contract reviews for IR35 status

The first key fact to remember about contract reviews is to get the contract reviewed before you sign it. If you have it looked at after you have signed it, and there are IR35 issues, it is too late to renegotiate. The agency will simply say it's too late and there will be nothing you can do about it.

When reviewing a contract for a new assignment you have four options:

- Don't review your contract (a horrifyingly common approach)
- Review the contract yourself
- Get the contract reviewed by an IR35 legal specialist
- Ask HMRC to review your contract for you.

Choosing not to review your contract at all is almost certainly going to cost you money in the long run. The contract may be within IR35, you may get investigated and you have no idea about the facts. Remember that HMRC has six years to review your contract themselves.

Been there, done that!

Ask the taxman?

Dave says: I actually used the Revenue's IR35 review service in 2000, shortly after the rules came into force. I wanted peace of mind and thought that was the best way to get it. It turned out to be both a good idea and a bad one. Bad in that their default reaction was 'you're caught' but good in that after much persuasion by my lawyer I got a letter stating I was outside.

Still, I wouldn't recommend any contractor do the same, particularly now after several years of IR35 legislation. It's the notional contract that is important, so until the contract has been completed a proper judgment can't be made anyway; therefore, why stick your neck out?

If you choose to conduct your own preliminary review that is quite sensible, as it will prepare you for any future legal expert view. However, to rely completely on your own knowledge, no matter how experienced a contractor you are, could backfire, as it has already backfired on others. To their considerable cost.

When you get your contract reviewed by a specialist make sure:

- You are using a legal specialist and not an accountant, because IR35 is a legal and not an accounting issue
- The legal specialist you use is highly experienced in the IR35 arena; your local family solicitor is unlikely to have that experience
- Ex-revenue inspectors are an excellent source of expert IR35 assistance.

It is very strongly recommended that you do not use HMRC's contract review service. Think about it.

Even if you have not reviewed contracts in the past, it is a valuable exercise to review them now so you can accurately plan for any tax implications and structure your payments and tax savings accordingly.

There is also the issue of reasonable care. If you self-evaluate your status and you lose an investigation ruling, then HMRC may well add insult to injury with increased penalties for you failing to take reasonable care.

8.4.4 Negotiating IR35 compliance with agents and clients

The important thing to remember when trying to negotiate IR35 compliance into a contract with an agent or directly with a client is that IR35 does not matter to them.

The agent gets paid the same whether or not you are inside IR35. And not only do they not care, but it is generally in their interests to get you to sign the contract as quickly as possible, so that they can start taking their cut and then move on to another 'sale'.

Similarly, the client probably won't have any real reason to negotiate with you on your contract – after all, they're not going to pay any less for your services; they're likely to have a million and one other priorities; and some of the things you might be talking about, like substitution, could get them worried about the project being satisfactorily completed.

If there is nothing in it for them why should the agent or client change the standard contract they are comfortable with just to please you?

Agencies have a number of tactics they use in an attempt to grind you down into submission so they don't have to change their standard contract. Often, according to the agent, it is the client who won't change. Sometimes, even if the contractor and client are in agreement, the agency won't change the contract.

There are also underlying issues for the agency, such as trying to reduce their liability because if something goes wrong, the client has the relationship with the agency and can sue, leaving the agency to chase the contractor.

A typical example of an agency mitigating this liability is when it attempts to write into its contract with the client a clause saying the contractor is under the client's control. Obviously, as the contractor, you simply must not accept this clause as you are in business in your own right and not controlled by the client.

Negotiating with the agency is often the only way to remove such risky IR35 clauses from the contract, and the discussion must happen before the contract is signed. Afterwards, the agency won't be interested, unless you threaten to leave, but of course you may not have a termination clause so could be in breach of contract.

There are key occasions when you may wish to negotiate with the agent about contract clauses: when you are discussing a new contract or when a contract is being renewed.

How receptive an agent is likely to be to such IR35 contract negotiations depends largely on the market conditions. In a depressed market where there are lots of contractors chasing few contracts, agents will not be interested in holding conversations about contract amendments. If you try, they will move on until they find a contractor who will accept the contract as it stands.

If the market is buoyant, and agents are desperate to fill positions, they will be much more likely to compromise about specific contractual clauses. The same is true at renewal time if the client is keen to renew the contractor. In fact, if the client fears losing your company's services, they may well put pressure on the agent to make the changes you are requesting.

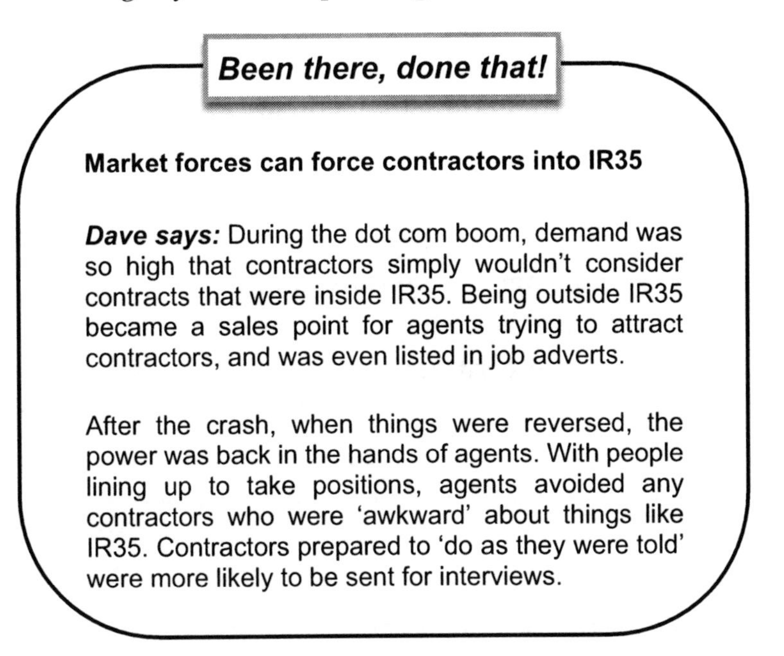

Ensure you have had expert help in preparing the negotiation; prepare a list with your legal adviser of what you want removed and what you want included, down to the specific wording. Also make it easy for the agent by preparing clauses in bite-sized chunks that integrate seamlessly with the original contract.

Trying to negotiate your way out of an 'inside IR35' contract at renewal time also depends on the state of the market, and the same principles apply. However there is a different process for making what are likely to be substantial changes, and having a legal expert involved in the process is well worth the investment:

- Get legal help to compile a list of the changes that need to be made
- Speak to the agent first and request the changes for the renewal. After they refuse them (most likely) ask to speak to the person who deals with the legal aspects of the contracts. Trying to negotiate contractual issues with an agent can prove

unproductive, as they just want you to sign again and have other more pressing things to attend to

- Get your lawyer to speak to the agency's legal person on your behalf. This is much more effective than trying to do it yourself
- Speak to your client directly if you are not getting results. Tell them you desperately want to renew the contract, but give the impression that you might be forced to consider your renewal position if they cannot get it sorted out. They might then put pressure on the agency to compromise
- You can also use the same 'I'm not sure I want to renew unless you sort out the contract' tactic with the agent. They don't want to appear bad in front of their client by not treating their contractors well. But be careful with this tactic: you don't want to give them a month to find someone else to replace you!

You could spend a tidy sum in legal fees being given the run-around. So try and establish early if the agency is paying lip service and trying to stall you, in the hope that when renewal time comes you'll just sign the contract again.

At some point it could become clear that you are going to be unsuccessful with the changes. There are a few options:

- Grin and bear it. You tried
- Threaten to not take (or renew) the contract. This might make things happen. Beware of burning bridges though
- Ask for a rate rise. It's unlikely to cover the whole gap, but you might get something.

If a month before renewal you feel you are getting nowhere and could get a better contract elsewhere, then it might be worth looking for one. Having a back-up plan is always useful.

Bear in mind that getting individual contracts changed for contractors at a site where the agency has many other contractors is hard. They will have their upper level contract with the client and the lower level contract with you. Changing your contract means either opening up a risk to them if they don't change their contract with the client, or spending money changing it.

Also, as most agencies don't have separate legal departments and lawyers are expensive, agents will try and prevent any changes getting made. Understanding this when you approach them, and making it as simple and inexpensive as possible to make the changes you want, will give you a much higher chance of success.

8.4.5 Confirming arrangements with your client

Even if you have a first class contract with all the correct clauses and wording, HMRC and, at a later stage, a judge, will examine the real nature of the relationship between you and your client, and then come to conclusions about the nature of your 'notional contract'.

You might find it shocking that a judge could conclude you are employed, when neither you nor your client had any intention of creating an employment relationship. In other words, your supposedly legally binding contract could be judged to be not worth the paper it is written on. But whatever your views on the fairness or otherwise of this, accept that that is the law and you must look after your own interests in light of it.

It is therefore very important that as much evidence as possible is available for each contract demonstrating the true nature of your working relationship. Items such as emails between you and the client over key issues can help.

What has happened in several high profile IR35 cases is that the contractor has believed, and has on paper, that the contract is outside IR35; that they are not controlled by their client; and that they have an unfettered right of substitution. But when the client has been asked about these matters during subsequent investigations, they have directly contradicted this.

In addition, upper level contracts between the agent and the client can contradict lower level contracts between the contractor and the agent. HMRC use these contradictions against contractors, even though they have no knowledge of these documents.

One tool that contractors can employ in a number of circumstances is the confirmation of arrangements letter with the client. This is basically a document that outlines the working practices of the contractor, confirms there is no control and that the client is aware that the contractor has an unfettered right of substitution in their contract with the agency, and so on.

The objective is for the client to sign and date the letter, so if you are asked by HMRC in the future the exact nature of the relationship you had with your client on a given contract, you have written evidence to back up your claims.

Although the letter confirming arrangements should remain valid as long as the original contract is in force, if the project manager at the client changes it is important to ensure they understand the situation, as they may well be giving evidence at your hearing if you get investigated.

Where HMRC try and use a contradictory upper level contract against you, you can use the notional contract in your favour in this context by producing the confirmation of arrangements that shows the true nature of the relationship.

You also have a handy summary that you can keep in your compliance file (section 8.4.9) that will still be valid in six years if HMRC decide to go back that far.

Ideally you should draft the confirmation of arrangements, perhaps exchanging a few drafts with your immediate project manager who actually knows what you do, and then ask them to sign it. Don't ask someone from the human resources or legal department to sign it – they don't know how you work.

A typical confirmation of arrangements would contain the following:

- The precise nature of the services you provide
- The exact dates of your contract
- Confirmation that a substitute can be supplied, at your expense and your choice
- The financial arrangements, such as daily/hourly rates or a fixed fee
- The location of the contract, including other client sites
- Confirmation you can work from your own office
- If you need to be on site what is the reason
- Confirmation you can't be asked to do something not in your contract
- You work according to your own hours
- Your client does not instruct you on how to perform your tasks
- Confirmation that you are not governed by the same rules as permanent employees, except for obvious exceptions, like health and safety
- Confirmation that you supply your own equipment, and if you have to use the client's equipment why, for example reasons of security or health and safety
- Confirmation you are liable for damage or loss through negligence
- Confirmation you have to rectify defective work at your own expense
- Confirmation you can work for other clients during the course of the contract
- Confirmation you do not receive any form of benefits enjoyed by full time employees, not even use of the company canteen

- Confirmation that you do not take work not specified in the contract
- Confirmation that if you do not work, you do not get paid.

This is becoming an increasingly important document in proving that a contractor is outside IR35, so it is important to have a copy on record for each and every contract you undertake.

8.4.6 Setting and managing client expectations

Many clients simply do not know what IR35 means, or choose to ignore it. The sooner you are able to set and manage your client's expectations, the better. Speak to your main contact with the client, probably your project manager, and explain to them very briefly about the key issues covered so far in this chapter.

Ideally, you should broach the topic of the confirmation of arrangements as soon as you feel comfortable, which can be daunting, especially the first time you do it.

Whatever you do, don't allow yourself to become a 'tail-end Charlie' and take on tasks outside of your contract to please the client, or to ramp up billable hours. If HMRC or a judge creates a notional contract on that basis you will be inside IR35.

Remember some client managers might simply be inexperienced at hiring and managing contractors, or divorced from what they mean by the human resources department. To them you might be just like an employee who will do any work they choose to send your way. Contractors need to set expectations right from the start, and throughout the project, and also keep evidence (emails etc) that conversations like this have gone on.

This tactic is all about one thing: mitigating the chance that the manager/client says something untrue – sometimes in the mistaken belief they are being helpful to you – if HMRC comes knocking on the door. HMRC has been known to ask questions like, "So, tell me Mr Z, how do you control your contractors?" Your client needs to know right from the start that they don't control you.

Follow these steps to ensure the client knows exactly how the relationship works:

- Get the confirmation of arrangements signed
- Make sure you read through this with the manager so they digest everything in it
- Make minutes about what happened in the meeting when the letter was signed
- Send a copy to your project manager – and keep a copy of the email in your contract file
- If you are asked to do something that is not part of the services you are contracted to do, make it clear verbally that you won't/cannot do that. Then send a further email to your boss – and keep a record of that email and any responses.

8.4.8 More on being in business on your own account

As well as ensuring you have in place all the requirements of section 8.3.11, such as your own business cards, laptop, home office and so on it is important to act like you are in business in your own right. Because, actually you are and every day you are on the client's site you are 'client facing'.

This means ensuring that your working practices change so that you run your company and your work like a proper business, and that your professional working practices and standards adhere to the content of the contract document.

Avoid becoming 'part and parcel' of the organisation by distinguishing yourself as an independent contractor. And if that means you have to wear a smart suit to the office every day when all around you are in casual clothes, then do so – stand out as a professional contractor.

Your working practices will contribute to any construction of a notional contract by HMRC, or a judge. If your working practices fail to adhere to the contract and to your position as an independent, professional contractor, it could be deemed not to be genuine and ignored.

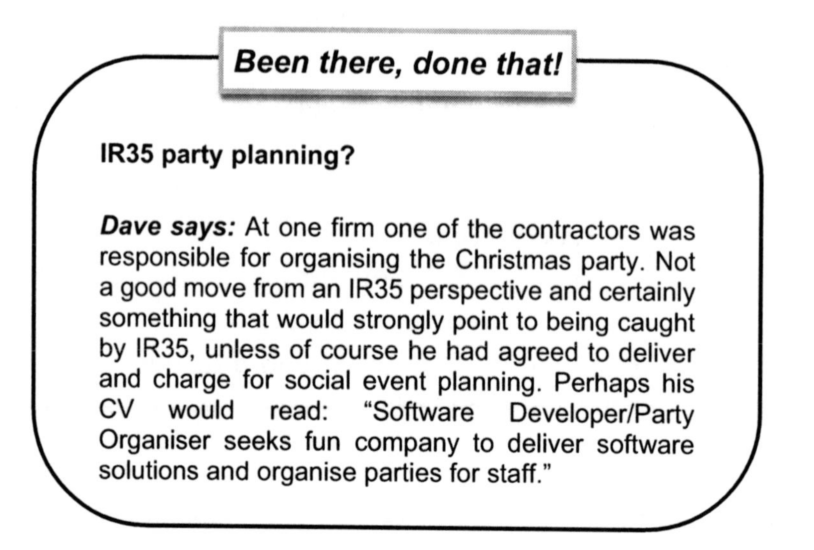

8.4.9 Building an IR35 compliance file for each contract

Should HMRC start an investigation, then your comprehensive, well-organised and accurate business records could make the difference between you winning or losing your case. It could also make the difference between a quick and straightforward investigation that HMRC will take no further, and a full investigation that could lead to a judgement against you and a court case.

So it is essential that you keep a record of each separate contract and schedules for each different project going back six years. It's not a difficult task, and well worth it.

HMRC will look for every opportunity to justify its inspection by claiming back-taxes, NICs and penalties, so investigators will want to go through your trading history in detail.

Should HMRC conduct a tax inspection and dispute your status, you will be faced with your local tax inspector, who will look at your evidence, and then eventually with the Special Commissioners if you appeal. If you go to appeal, you are likely to face a judge. They will all need convincing, with as much proof as possible, of what actually took place between you and the agency, and between you and the client.

You may have some proof in your letter of engagement. Again this may not be specific enough, but it may help.

If you can't get terms into the contract that clearly put you outside IR35, you have to find other means of proof. And even if you have a sound contract, you might need to back it up. So aim to achieve the following:

- Get a signed confirmation of arrangements letter
- Bring some of your own equipment and get some proof that it is used in the project by, for example, sending emails showing that you are using it
- Get your project manager to let you do some of the work at home, and see that the email record shows this is taking place. Or simply get a note saying you can work at home
- The right of substitution is a very important proof of being outside IR35. Send the client or the agent emails about this. If you get a reply, that may prove extremely useful. Any other proof of that kind, like letters or notes from the agent or client could help too
- Keep any proof you can get that you've paid your own expenses. Not just receipts, but also any requests for materials needed from the client, any email asking you to pay expenses and so on.

Make an effort to get as much proof as you can. Remember, HMRC may go back six years if it decides to review your status, so you will need to save everything relevant. Make sure that you get proof while the project is taking place, as you'll certainly struggle to obtain it six years later.

8.4.10 Insuring yourself against IR35

An investigation can take years and, if it goes as far as Special Commissioners and appeals, can cost tens of thousands of pounds in defence costs. And this doesn't include back taxes, NICs and penalties you might have to pay if you lose. The financial cost will be considerable; the emotional cost to you and your family could be even greater.

In the UK, tax law says that you are guilty until you can prove your innocence. If you do not mount a defence, you are assumed to be guilty and automatically have to pay any outstanding taxes, NICs and penalties that HMRC demands.

Contractors subject to tax investigations have no protection under the law, as someone accused of a criminal offence would have. HMRC's investigators can delve into every aspect of your life and use any evidence against you. And because the investigations can take so much time and have such potentially dramatic consequences, the stress for the contractor can be incredible.

Fighting inspections and rulings by HMRC is not for the uninitiated. Many cash businesses, even small firms like corner shops, have tax enquiry and investigation insurance that can remove some of the stress associated with the process. If you choose to take out a similar insurance, do it sooner rather than later so you have maximum cover by investing in a good policy before an inspection starts.

In addition to investigation insurance, you may be able to take out a tax liability cover policy too, which, in addition to paying the costs associated with running a defence, would also pay out if you lost the case and owed money to HMRC.

8.4.11 IR35 Issues for contractors working overseas

IR35 can follow you across borders when you go contracting overseas. If you remain liable for tax in the UK, then you are liable for an IR35 re-assessment of whether you were actually an employee of a foreign company or whether you were a genuine contractor. You will only cease to be tax-liable on earned income in the UK after a full year abroad.

When you cease to be liable for taxes in the UK, you can forget about IR35, but you will have to think very carefully about the rules in the country you are now working in, because these can be quite restrictive. The same rules for best contracting practice apply, and an IR35 contract-assessment can be made based on contracts drawn up anywhere in the world.

HMRC will follow the same procedure that it always does if it wishes to prove that you are caught by IR35. The first step is to obtain a copy of the contract between your end client and the agency you worked for to compare it with the one you have with the agency. If the agency-client contract sounds a lot like an employment contract, you will almost certainly experience the start of an IR35 investigation.

In practice, HMRC may not find it easy to obtain contracts drawn up between two foreign companies, that is, the agency abroad and the end client abroad. HMRC has no jurisdiction outside the UK, and foreign tax authorities are rarely cooperative with each other.

But don't count on avoiding the IR35 issue in this way. Should HMRC manage to obtain what it needs, you could be in trouble. It is best to ensure that your contract clearly addresses the IR35 issues, just as if you remained in the UK.

8.5 IR35 Investigations

For most contractors, an HMRC inspection is possibly one of the worst things that *could* happen to them in their professional lives. And for many contractors an HMRC inspection *has* been the worst thing that has happened to them.

When you first find out about it, is likely to come as a tremendous shock. However, if you have taken all the steps recommended in chapters 7 and 8, it can prove a relatively quick and easy process.

If your evidence and defence are already in place – because you've taken care over things like your contract and your working arrangements, plus kept a detailed contract file – there is every chance that the investigators will be satisfied that you have been correctly working outside IR35, and therefore move on to another case.

Nevertheless, even if you have done absolutely everything as you should, you should still tread very carefully throughout every step of an investigation. Remember, unlike other parts of the UK law, when you are dealing with HMRC you are guilty until you can prove yourself innocent.

The rules of evidence are not as strict as they are in criminal law, so even a light-hearted, off-the-cuff remark while you're offering the tax inspector a cup of tea can take on huge significance if your case goes to court. So take great care.

It helps to have an understanding of what is going to happen so you can prepare yourself.

8.5.1 How HMRC might challenge you

An experienced HMRC inspector can glance at the profit and loss account of a large business, like an engineering firm, oil company or bank, and immediately spot unusually high bills in the professional services costs line. That means the firm probably uses a lot of contractors, which will be of immediate interest to the inspector.

HMRC then only has to identify the contractors from their invoices in the firm's accounting records, and for the inspectors it has suddenly become a target rich environment – with contractors firmly in their sights.

The investigation starts when the inspector reviews the contractor's accounts. HMRC has an extremely sophisticated IT set-up (ironically, largely built by contractors!) that allows it to drill down into your accounts and compare you with thousands, possibly even tens/hundreds of thousands, of very similar businesses.

Any discrepancies in your accounts will be quickly and easily spotted – almost like a big red flashing light next to your company name saying, 'look at me, look at me!'.

There are a number of instant giveaways that a contractor might fall within IR35 and merit an inspection:

- No employees, other than directors
- The directors pay themselves the minimum wage as salary
- The directors, possibly husband and wife, take most of the cash out of the business as dividends
- There are no or few materials charged through the business.

HMRC will view each of these factors as pointing to a personal service company, which will almost certainly result in an inspection.

Warning bells should ring the day a contractor receives a letter from the HMRC informing them of an Employer Compliance Review.

This means the early stages of a status inspection has begun and the inspector will be out to prove the contractor falls within IR35 – classic HMRC tactics.

HMRC will look into all the points highlighted in the bullet points above, along with your contract with the agency and/or client, and the contract between the agency and the client.

The agency-client contract can cause you a great deal of trouble, and there is nothing you can do about it. While the agency may have agreed to good contractor contract terms with you, the agent may have promised the client all sorts of things in terms that make you sound like a 'disguised' employee.

You can always ask for a copy of this contract when you are negotiating with an agency, but most will refuse as it is probably confidential and protected by a Non-Disclosure Agreement.

You can also ask the agency to include a clause in your contract saying that it is faithful to the agency-client contract, but this is of little use in court as HMRC will argue that it may say so, but it really isn't. There is, in practice, little that you can do involving the agency-client contract to protect yourself.

Most of all, HMRC will try and get your on-site manager to describe what you do. This is the most important aspect of the case, because the courts will base their judgement on what actually happens in the workplace – to the best of their ability.

They will ask about how the work is controlled – do you decide or does the client? Is it project-based, or are you just doing whatever the manager asks? Are you supplying your own equipment, or if you must use the on-site equipment, is there a good reason why?

This is where a confirmation of arrangements letter can be so useful if the client inadvertently says something to HMRC that sounds suspicious, although it could be perfectly innocent.

The worst of all this is that HMRC has the right to go back six years into your records and try to prove you were 'inside' IR35 on any given contract. So you may wind up trying to find people at the client who can remember back that far just to state what you really did.

The review is contract-based, so you may have had 20 contracts that were clearly not caught by the legislation, but HMRC can still come after you for the one that sounds like it was.

You can fight an HMRC judgement in court, but it's going to take a long time and cost you a lot of money. If you win, you may or may not be able to collect costs from HMRC – the law on this is not black-and-white.

So, it's best to find ways to avoid an HMRC inspection in the first place, or to make sure you can effectively defend your position as being outside IR35 on all the relevant contracts.

8.5.2 Steps to mitigate a challenge

The ideal strategy to avoid an investigation and challenge by HMRC is to avoid being noticed in the first place. This is subtly different from ensuring your IR35 defence is in place before you get inspected, although of course you must keep on top of IR35 issues. The object is to do nothing out of the ordinary to attract the attention of HMRC, by truly working as a contractor and not a 'disguised' employee. Basic practices include:

- Take professional advice before you sign any contract from either an agency or a client

- The contract should make it clear from the clauses and conditions that you are an independent contractor and not an employee
- Ensure all tax documents are completed accurately and do not have mistakes on them with crossings out and a lot of correction fluid
- Ensure that all tax demands are paid on time with all payments being sent to the correct office or processing centre
- Make sure all expenses are categorised correctly on any Self Assessment (SA) return – ask your accountant if in doubt
- If there are any significant changes to any expenses on the SA return, include a note in "additional notes" as this can make it clear to HMRC that there is a perfectly good explanation for these changes
- If you have ever been instructed by HMRC to make changes to your records, make sure these are done. If they're not, then you will be listed for another review.

If you are contacted by HMRC about an inspection, do not to speak to HMRC or contact them in any way. You could inadvertently say something, however innocent it might appear to you, which is later used as a central feature of the evidence against you. If you have tax enquiry insurance, now is the time to get in touch with your insurer.

Ideally, all contact with HMRC should be through your specialist IR35 lawyer, accountant or approved advisor, again to ensure you don't say something that might harm your case. Personal contact could jeopardise the chances of successfully defending the inspection.

Even a chance remark to what sounds like a friendly enquiry from a tax inspector can become the basis of a strong case against you. This is so important because HMRC will start the investigation before they even arrive at your premises.

HMRC will have already considered the main issues and great care needs to be taken at the initial meeting – that's when you really need your expert adviser present.

Just to give a real-life example: a contractor who uses a lot of sub-contractors on various projects had their tax adviser present. The sub-contractors were not employees. However the first question the inspector asked when the meeting began was, 'So, Mr Smith, how exactly do you control your employees?'

Two key IR35 tests were satisfied in that statement; employment status and control. Had the tax lawyer not intervened at that point and halted the meeting, the client would have responded to the inspector's question as he was invited to do. The inspector would have written in the notes of the investigation: 'When we arrived, Mr Smith explained to us how he controlled his employees'.

And this simple statement would have become a conclusive piece of evidence throughout the case, alongside the HMRC inspectors' account of the meeting, during which they would have used similar questioning.

The key lesson is, in order to mitigate the impact of a challenge you need professional advice.

8.6 If HMRC rules against you – the appeal process

If everything you have tried in creating an IR35 defence, avoiding notice by HMRC and defending yourself during the investigation fails, there is still the appeals process, where you can appeal to the Special Commissioners. So how does it fit into the overall picture?

Well, HMRC conducts its investigation and gives a Notice of Decision, which says whether you are inside or outside IR35. You have 30 days to appeal the Notice of Decision from the date it was issued. Should you appeal, HMRC is then required to look at the situation again. Once you hear back from HMRC, if you still disagree you can appeal to the Tax Appeal Commissioners. There are two types of commissioner and both are independent of HMRC:

- *General Commissioners* – three laypersons assisted by a clerk, who is usually a solicitor. This is typically an informal tribunal held in private
- *Special Commissioners* – three full-time commissioners appointed by the Lord Chancellor. This is a more formal tribunal and can be held in public, unless a request is upheld not to.

You can choose either. You will need to be represented unless you feel extremely confident about conducting your own case. You can also make an application of postponement to pay, so that you don't have to pay your outstanding tax until after you've had a ruling from the Tax Appeal Commission. Be aware, though, that your application could be refused.

If you are not happy with the decision of the Commissioners you can then appeal to a court of law. At this point, however, you will have to pay the amount asked for; it will be returned if you win. The appeals are held in the High Court. As such, they can only be heard on a point of law.

The tribunal of the Special Commissioners is the fact-finding body and the appeal court cannot interfere with a decision made based on the facts, unless the decision was so unreasonable that it points to an error of law. The contractor has 30 days to appeal to the High Court. The clerk of the court then has 56 days to draft the case. There are then a further 56 days to make representations based on the draft. And then an additional 28 days for further representations to be made.

When the Commissioner has signed the case in its final form the contractor then has 30 days to appeal to the High Court. So, roughly speaking, this process will take about six months. The decisions in the court are based on 'the balance of probabilities'.

To go through this entire process you will need good case law, very good representation, personal strength and conviction, and cash (unless you've taken out insurance).

Some of the contractors who have taken their cases to the High Court have been backed by industry bodies, which have seen those contractors' particular cases as tests on a point of law. Most contractors are not that lucky and have to pay for the costs themselves.

Either way, should the case go against the contractor, any back-taxes, interest or penalties will need to come out of their own pocket. The only exception is if the contractor has taken out insurance against this; but the reality is that the requirements of the insurers are likely to be so strict, in terms of dealing with the issues covered in chapters 7 and 8, that the contractor probably wouldn't have suffered an IR35 investigation in the first place.

8.7 Contractors Caught by IR35

8.7.1. Treatment of expenses and the 5% rule

If you are caught by IR35 and use your limited company and your trading option and payment structure, you need to take into account the HMRC 5% expense allowance rule.

Basically if you receive income caught by the rules of IR35, you must carry out a deemed salary/Schedule E calculation each tax year, based on income received from relevant engagements. It's worth checking with your accountant about this calculation, but the basics follow.

HMRC allows an expense allowance equal to 5% of the income received from relevant engagements in calculating the deemed salary. This is intended to cover the following 'administration' costs:

1. Premises costs, including home as office
2. Administration and secretarial support
3. Accountancy and tax advice
4. Costs of seeking contracts
5. Printing, postage and stationery
6. Employer's and Public Liability Insurance
7. Training costs
8. Computer equipment (if not eligible for capital allowances)
9. Bank and overdraft interest
10. Hire purchase payments.

The 5% deduction is given at a flat rate on gross fees receivable and is not available to employees as an expense which they can draw from the company. It is simply allowed in the deemed calculation of IR35 salary as a fixed and limited claim against the above expenses. In granting the 5% allowance, HMRC does not require proof of expenditure and the full 5% is granted, even if there is no actual expenditure whatsoever.

The 5% allowance is only for 'administration' and is to cover the ten points above. In addition to the 5% for administration costs, a contractor can also claim direct costs such as travel, computer costs, subsistence, direct training, sub-contractors and so on. So basically, legitimate business expenses not covered by the ten points can be claimed on top.

If you are caught by IR35 and using a PAYE umbrella, then the 5% rule is irrelevant as it only applies to limited companies. Umbrella companies have different rules for processing expenses. The actual costs of travel, subsistence, computers and so on can be claimed in full and tax/national insurance relief obtained on them.

8.7.2 How your taxes are calculated – the deemed payment

There are some odd terms used, like 'Net Result' and 'Deemed Payment', but actually the concept is very simple. Basically, the way it works is you run your company as normal, paying yourself a salary, and claiming the expenses that you are allowed to, then see what is left in the pot at the end of the year.

This then has to be considered as paid as salary from an employer. So a calculation is done to work out what the salary would be ("deemed payment"), a figure which employer's National Insurance Contributions (NICs) would then be applied to.

Eg Net Result = Deemed Payment + Employer's NICs

Then the employee's NI and PAYE is applied to the deemed payment, just as taxes are applied to salaries.

In practice, most contractors caught by IR35 take everything they earn as a salary along the way, so there is only a small deemed payment, if any, at the end of the year. Your accountant will be able to help out with all this, and you really don't have to worry about it yourself. But here's a typical example:

Contractor details:

£80K annual revenue, £5K salary, and £5K legitimate expenses.

Revenue	£80,000
Allowable Expenses (5% of revenue)	£4,000
Salary	£5,000
Legitimate Expenses	£5,000
Net Result	£66,000
Additional Employer's NI due	£7,849
Deemed Payment	£58,511
Additional Employee's NI	£4,037
Additional PAYE	£16,030

8.7.3 When you have a mix of contracts – some caught, some not

During your accounting year you may earn revenue from several contracts, some of which will fall inside the scope of IR35 and others outside. When this occurs it is important to arrange your records to clearly record both types of income and the expenses which relate to 'inside' and 'outside' IR35 contract work.

Receipts and payments for IR35 contract work will need to be identifiable for use in a year end calculation – your accountant will have to do a different set of calculations for each contract. At the end of each tax year an IR35 calculation for 'deemed salary' will be done, which takes into account the IR35 contract income and expenditure relating to those specific contracts.

Any salary you pay yourself during the year can be allocated to your IR35 income, so that any profits, excluding salary payments generated by the non IR35 work, can be either paid out as dividends to shareholders or carried forward for distribution in a future year.

The IR35 status of one contract does not affect the IR35 status of another. Each needs to be judged on its own merits.

9.

What to do when things go wrong

9.1 Contract search

The key to maintaining, enjoying and profiting from your successful contracting career – even when things might appear to be going wrong – is not to take anything personally.

Whether you are working for yourself through your own limited company or an umbrella company, there can be times when it seems like the agent and client are conspiring against you.

Remember, for them it is just business. And it is important that you stay focused on the fact that, for you, it is just business, too.

9.1.1 When an agent sends out your CV without your permission

Your relationship with an agency usually begins with you sending them your CV in response to an advertisement, or with the agency finding you from a job board listing.

An agent may send your CV to a client and then find that another agency has already sent it, even though you never gave them, permission to do so. No one has the right to distribute your CV without your permission. If you do find out who was responsible – which may happen if, for example, the client tells your agent that they have already received your CV from XYZ agency – then you must call them and tell them you have not given your permission for them to use your CV. They will need to prove that you did, which of course they won't be able to.

Agencies cannot send your CV to a specific firm without your permission. So they cannot ask, 'Can I put your CV forward for a few roles next week for the banks in the City?'.

You are caught between a rock and a hard place because you need your CV to get maximum exposure, but you want protection from unscrupulous agents. It could lose you the contract, so you need to take action. Politely put in writing a request to that agency that you would not like it to happen again, then move on.

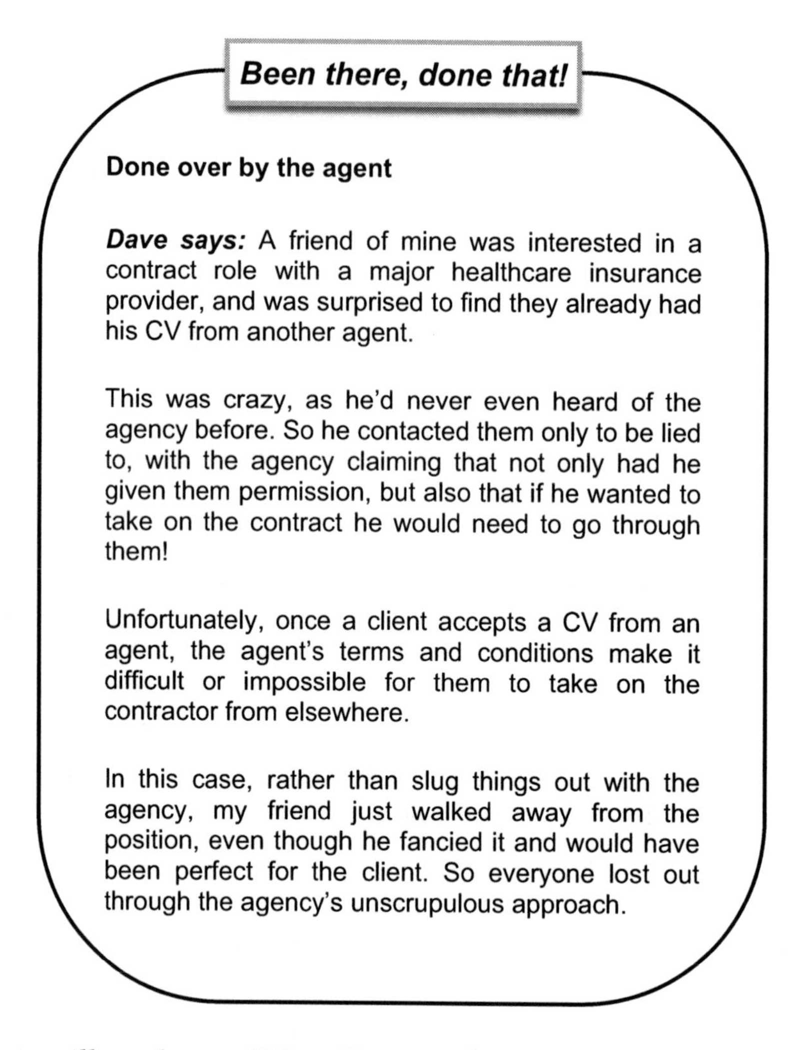

Agents will send your CV to clients without your permission for two reasons:

- To demonstrate they can find really good candidates. Then, when the client wants to interview you, if you won't play ball the agent will simply say you have accepted something elsewhere; but it's given the agency time to be noticed by the client

- To be the first in the door. This is totally illegal, very rare, but a pain to fight.

However, fight you should and if the agency refuses to take you seriously, your ultimate recourse is the recruitment agency industry body, the Recruitment and Employment Confederation (REC).

9.1.2 When an agent or client cancels your contract at the last minute

You have just signed a contract with an agency and cleared your calendar for the period when the agent calls and tells you that the contract is cancelled. The client had their budget cut or changed their mind.

You point out to the agent that you have a contract offer and acceptance, which you can prove because it is signed, and you've given up other work to take it. You expect some payment. You should certainly get the full value of the termination period, provided you can show that you actively sought work during the period as part of your 'duty to mitigate'. The client has to pay for the termination costs and any costs you incur to put you back where you started.

The approach to the agent should be a formal letter, preferably written by a lawyer, explaining the legal position, and that they have to pay you for the termination period. You should also explain you understand your duty to mitigate and that you are seeking further work, and would welcome their assistance.

You should tell them that once you have found further work you will bill them for the gap they need to pay you for. They may try to ignore this approach, or try to suggest they owe you nothing, but this doesn't comply with the law.

You can then take the agent to the small claims court and, if you do things right, you will almost certainly win; but it is essential that you seek professional legal advice if you are forced down this route.

Unfortunately, most contractors don't take any action and the client and agent walk away without paying the contractor a penny. The sad truth is, that's because many contractors don't know their rights, won't stand their ground, or, to be frank, are simply too lazy to claim what's legally theirs.

If the client had no termination clause, which is unlikely, then in theory the contractor should be able to claim the full value of the contract. In practice, though, they would be wise to focus on getting a new contract.

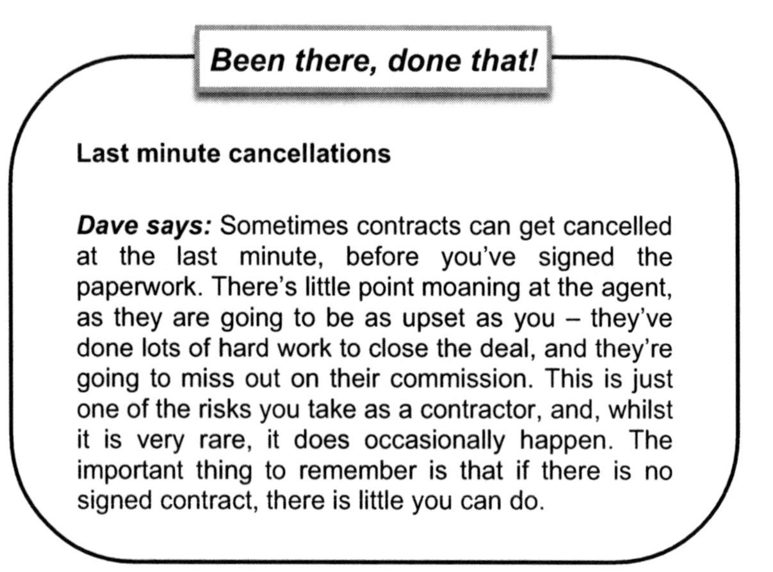

Been there, done that!

Last minute cancellations

Dave says: Sometimes contracts can get cancelled at the last minute, before you've signed the paperwork. There's little point moaning at the agent, as they are going to be as upset as you – they've done lots of hard work to close the deal, and they're going to miss out on their commission. This is just one of the risks you take as a contractor, and, whilst it is very rare, it does occasionally happen. The important thing to remember is that if there is no signed contract, there is little you can do.

9.1.3 When an agent insists on you giving references before any interviews

Agents have a right to ask for references. Just like any other recruiter, an agency dealing in contractors has the right to be sure about whom they are sending to their clients. But they might just be 'phishing' for valuable information, including the names of people who will give you references and might therefore be in a position to make hiring decisions – such information is like gold dust to an agent.

It's not a good idea to keep giving out reference information all the time for the simple reason that your ex bosses won't take too kindly to being rung up all the time.

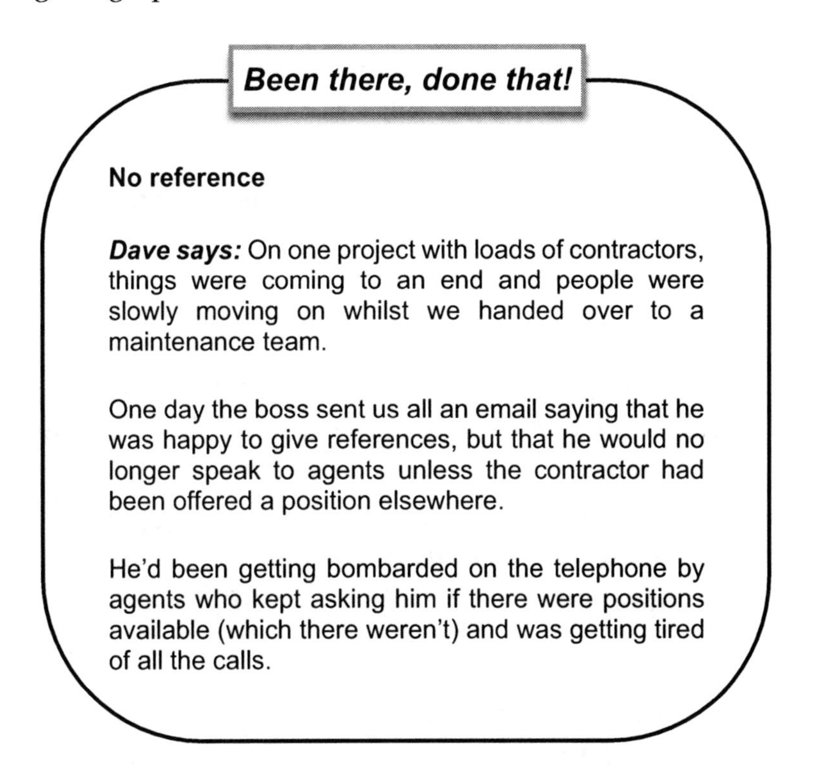
Been there, done that!

No reference

Dave says: On one project with loads of contractors, things were coming to an end and people were slowly moving on whilst we handed over to a maintenance team.

One day the boss sent us all an email saying that he was happy to give references, but that he would no longer speak to agents unless the contractor had been offered a position elsewhere.

He'd been getting bombarded on the telephone by agents who kept asking him if there were positions available (which there weren't) and was getting tired of all the calls.

You do not have to give references before an interview if you don't wish to. There is no legal requirement for the agency to provide references to the client, and clients won't expect it. Agents are almost certain to put you forward even if you hold back on references. They make their money by placing you. Therefore, a good agent will get you the interview first and then, only if it is necessary, check your references when it looks like you'll get the contract.

Remember, you are a contractor and if you don't perform your contract is terminated.

As you don't want to offend legitimate agents while looking for contracts, here is an easy way to be diplomatic about not giving references. Say that your former clients and/or bosses have requested that you do not give reference information out until you have been offered a position, and you have to respect these wishes.

Tell the agent that if there is an interview and offer, you will provide not only references, but also the names of some firms that might be looking for contractors. They will be able to read between the lines. If they then put your CV forward without references, it is a real job. If you were suitable for the position, and they don't, then you can assume they were just on a phishing expedition.

9.2 Contract terms

As indicated in chapters 7 and 8, it is very important that you get your contract right before you agree to it, either verbally or in writing. This sometimes requires negotiation with the agent. Once you have been offered a contract you are in a strong position and so should stick to your guns over the finer points of the contract – after all, it is very important to your earnings and IR35 status.

9.2.1 When the agent promises to make changes to your contract and doesn't

The interview went well, the client liked you and you've had an offer from the agent which you accept. Then you receive the contract to review and it is full of holes so large you could drive a tank through them. You request changes, and the agent promises they will be made, so you start work. And then the agent does a U-turn, and claims that because you have started work, the implication is that you have accepted the terms of the original contract, as it was before you requested the changes.

Agents will not make changes to contracts for a variety of reasons, quite often because they don't wish to have to change their standard contract. They also may not wish to run the risk of a conflict between their contract with the client, known as the upper level contract, and their contract with you, the lower level contract. And there are a host of other issues that a contract review by a specialist legal adviser might identify.

Remember that the contract is not valid unless you have agreed, either verbally or in writing, to the terms. You can hold out for the agent to make the changes, and they may give in and agree to your terms to avoid upsetting their client and missing out on their margin.

Should they refuse, point blank, then you should be prepared either to walk away or to compromise on the contract. Should the agent agree to the change, though, you must ensure you get the agreement in writing, and that it is on the final contract.

Whatever you do, don't start working without the contract finalised and signed. If you have started work, you may find that you are stuck with the contract, unless you can categorically prove that the agent has been wilfully dishonest.

9.2.2 When the agent or client tries to changes terms or rates during a contract

Some agents will always try it on with you and the most common way they do this is to try and change the deal mid-contract. Usually, any proposed deal would end up with the agent enjoying a higher margin. You have no obligation to accept any changes to a signed contract during a contract. Diplomatically, tell the agent not to try it on.

If you are contracting direct and the client comes up with a really good reason for a contract change that you are prepared to accept – perhaps relating to the evolution of the project – you might want to offer to renegotiate a new contract.

This is a perfectly reasonable scenario but you must be sure the new contract will work for you and does not place you at a disadvantage compared to the original one. If the proposed contract changes don't benefit you, you are perfectly within your rights simply to continue working to the terms of the original contract.

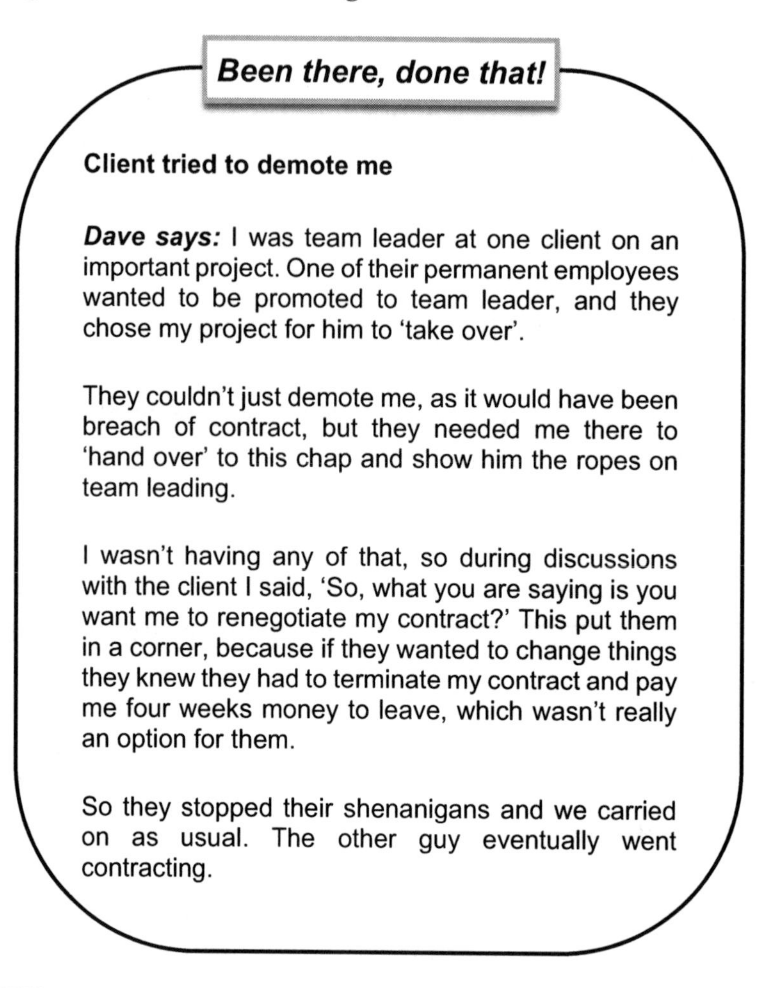

Been there, done that!

Client tried to demote me

Dave says: I was team leader at one client on an important project. One of their permanent employees wanted to be promoted to team leader, and they chose my project for him to 'take over'.

They couldn't just demote me, as it would have been breach of contract, but they needed me there to 'hand over' to this chap and show him the ropes on team leading.

I wasn't having any of that, so during discussions with the client I said, 'So, what you are saying is you want me to renegotiate my contract?' This put them in a corner, because if they wanted to change things they knew they had to terminate my contract and pay me four weeks money to leave, which wasn't really an option for them.

So they stopped their shenanigans and we carried on as usual. The other guy eventually went contracting.

9.2.3 When you sign a terrible deal and want to get out

You've signed the contract, you're on the job, and it's awful. You hate the client, you hate the work, and worst of all, you've discovered that you could have negotiated a much better rate with a contract on another client's project.

Can you get out of the contract? If your contract includes a termination clause that permits you to end it early, then you can give notice and leave. But if it doesn't, which isn't that unusual, then you are stuck unless you can replace yourself.

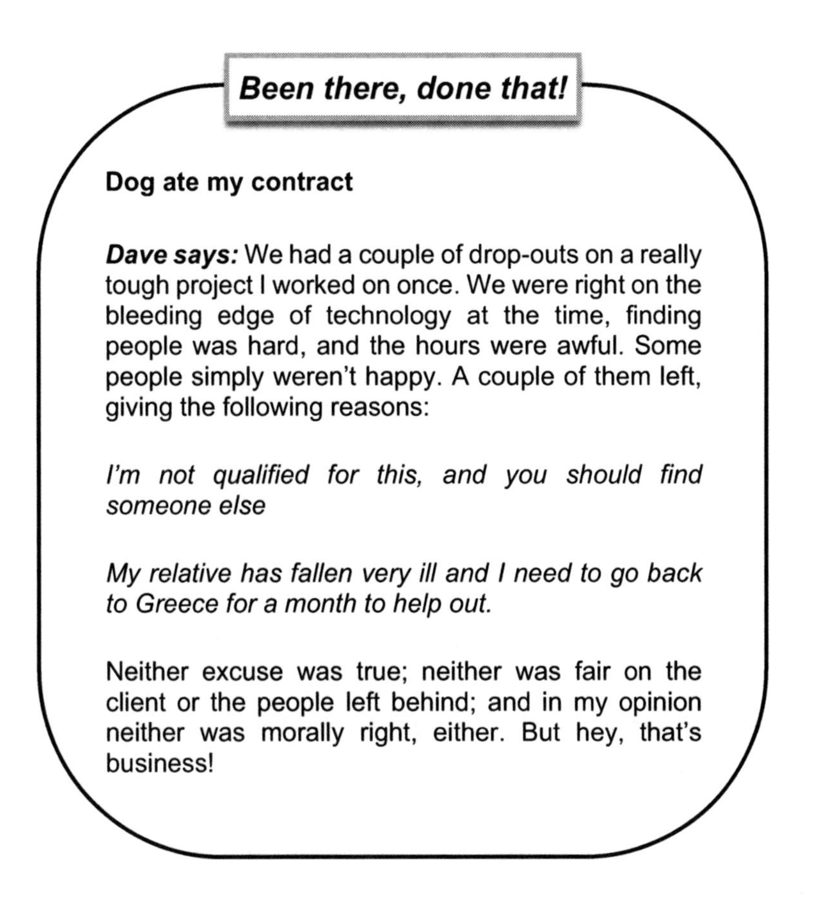

Been there, done that!

Dog ate my contract

Dave says: We had a couple of drop-outs on a really tough project I worked on once. We were right on the bleeding edge of technology at the time, finding people was hard, and the hours were awful. Some people simply weren't happy. A couple of them left, giving the following reasons:

I'm not qualified for this, and you should find someone else

My relative has fallen very ill and I need to go back to Greece for a month to help out.

Neither excuse was true; neither was fair on the client or the people left behind; and in my opinion neither was morally right, either. But hey, that's business!

Assuming you used a lawyer to help with your contract it should include a substitution clause and you could try and bring in another contractor to replace you. You would be responsible for training and paying that person and that would cost you time and money. If they didn't perform, you would be responsible for putting right their failings.

So you might be best to see the contract through and put it down to experience.

9.3 Contract renewals

When you come to renew your contract, this can be both an opportunity and a threat: an opportunity because you can use the renewal as a chance to increase your rates; a threat because the agent may try and increase their margins by reducing your rates.

9.3.1 When the agent or client tries to renew your contract automatically

When you have questions about contractual obligations, the first place to look is your contract. And when it comes to renewals, the advice in chapters 7 and 8 is that you should not have renewal clauses in your contract, as it may affect your IR35 status by making you look like a 'disguised employee'.

If your contract does have a renewal clause, check it carefully. It should state that any renewals will be agreed in writing between you and the agency.

But, instead of taking the trouble to negotiate a renewal with you, some agencies try to economise on time by sending you a letter and by ignoring your requests to renegotiate. A letter with terms proposed unilaterally by one party to the contract has no legal standing, so don't be concerned by it.

Ideally you should handle renewals before they come due. Don't wait until after the contract period is over; get all the paperwork straight the way you want it well before the current contract is due to expire.

So, you do not have to accept an automatic renewal and you should dig your heels in if the agent stonewalls. If you don't have the paperwork in place before the contract ends, stop working. When your client asks why, you just you tell them and, if they really want you to continue to complete a vital project, guess who they will call?

9.3.2 When the agent fails to get your paperwork in place by the renewal date

Following on from the previous section, if the agency does not send you the correct paperwork for signature before the contract ends, and you get to the end date you must stop working.

If you continue to work, you have effectively agreed to the agent's proposal, or according to the terms of the original contract and extended your contract on the same terms.

9.3.3 When the agent tries to force a margin increase at renewal time

Contract renewals are a subject area that generates lots of difficult scenarios. The most typical of these is when the agent wants you to renew on the same terms, whereas you want different ones, including a rate increase. The agent will want a cut of the rate increase.

Sometimes the agent will try and force a rate decrease, explaining that they are not making enough of a margin on the contract. The agency will try to tell you that you have to accept their terms, or you won't be allowed to work at the client anymore under the terms of the restrictive covenant in the contract – this is a standard element in all agency contracts and entirely fair, until the agent tries to use it unfairly as leverage.

If you want a rate rise you simply say, 'Pay it, or I will move on.' You cannot threaten to go direct because of the restrictive covenant in the contract. If you do they will sue you, and the judge will agree.

At renewal time, some agents may try and cut your pay claiming that they need to increase their margin of profit. Take the same approach and just say no. The restrictive covenant does not apply here, because it cannot be used as a bargaining tool.

Once the agency understands that you know your rights, they will become more reasonable.

9.3.4 When the client wants to bypass the agency and take you on direct

Another classic renewal scenario is when the client wants to renew, but does not want to use the same agency that originally found you, preferring to use a different agency or to renew your contract direct. In some cases, they may wish to change because they have been, or are, in dispute with the original agency.

Don't accept a renewal direct from the client or their new agency, as you will get in trouble. Both the restrictive covenant you have with the agency and the agency's terms and conditions with the client will place the agency in a position to sue both you and the client. Just don't do it.

9.3.5 When the agent insists you verbally agreed to a contract and threatens to sue

This situation can arise when you have talked to an agent about a contract, but you have accepted another one. The agent claims that you verbally agreed to the contract and insists you have to complete the contract they have negotiated.

Verbal contracts are, in theory, just as valid as written ones. The difficulty is in proving that there has been both an offer and an acceptance. If you have sent the agent an email saying you will do the job, that means you have accepted the offer and represents viable proof of the existence of a contract.

If you talk on the phone with the agent and say you'll think about it, that's not acceptance. Phone conversations would be very hard to prove without other evidence, and taped phone conversations are not admissible in court in the UK.

Provided you've not signed anything you can easily get out of the contract, because you can argue that they have not sent the paperwork over. A deal isn't really done until the paperwork is signed, and neither contractors nor agents take each other to court based on claims of verbal agreements.

9.4 Restrictions

9.4.1 When the agent insists you cannot work directly for the client

Clients may ask you to work directly for them in a permanent role. They may do this for a number of reasons, which often include the desire to save money and to have a leaner (i.e. cheaper for them) relationship with you.

If the client recruits you into a permanent role, they will be obliged to pay the agency a finder's fee. Depending on the volume of business the client has with the agency, the agency might let you become employed without the client suffering a penalty. But, it is down to the client to pressure the agency on this. You have no bargaining power as a contractor.

If the agency does agree, then you should get confirmation in writing from the agency that you have permission to work directly for the client in a permanent role and that the decision overrules the restrictive covenant in your contract.

Of course if you have not yet signed a contract with the agency, you do not have a restrictive covenant but the client will have terms and conditions with the agency that forbid them from recruiting you, if the agency introduced you, without the agency receiving a fee.

The restrictive covenant is designed for exactly these types of scenario, where you might be given the opportunity to work for the client direct. Quite rightly, agencies who have invested a significant amount in marketing the role and identifying you as a candidate want to be sure they profit from the arrangement.

9.4.2 When you are told you cannot use client facilities

Believe it or not, even small things like using the canteen, or having a badge that allows you access to the building without signing in, can become hugely important in determining your IR35 status. HMRC and a judge might consider that you eating in the company's subsidised canteen, or having a company swipe card to enter the building, point to proof that you might be a 'disguised employee'.

As discussed in chapter 8, the case law governing IR35 includes a test of whether a contractor is 'part and parcel' of an organisation. Unfortunately, there are no clear criteria about what being 'part and parcel' actually means, and the case law on the subject varies greatly.

So every little detail involved can be taken into account. In one case, a contractor was accused of being within IR35 because they had the same security pass that employees had and so could walk in and out of the building at will.

Other cases have included factors like eating at the company canteen, or sharing employee transport. Almost anything you do that makes you seem like an employee can be held against you, largely because the case law varies so much. This means that HMRC tax inspectors and High Court judges will look at everything.

So if you're told that you cannot use the company canteen or aren't entitled to a security pass, or can't use the staff car park and don't receive a gym pass, be grateful. And if you're invited to use the canteen, or given that security pass that will make getting into the building so much easier, politely refuse and explain why.

As a contractor outside IR35, you must always distinguish yourself as much as possible from the permanent employees, and make sure that both your contract and your actual day-to-day activities show that you are an independent contractor and not a disguised employee. Even if it means missing out on delicious, subsidised lunches!

9.5 Termination and breaches

When a project doesn't go well, contractors are often blamed for the problems, even when they are not their fault. This can lead to unfair termination, when the client or the agency simply blames you and puts an early end to your contract.

9.5.1 When your contract is terminated unfairly

There are several reasons that typically lead to unfair termination. A client can find that the original budget for a project has been drastically reduced, or that the original objectives have been changed. Your manager is now stuck with finding a way to make everything right, and blaming the contractor can provide an easy way out.

So the client's project manager calls you into the office, and says: 'You've made a right mess of this project, and you're fired.' What can you do?

If you've done the work, and you are being falsely accused, you have a right to compensation for unfair dismissal. This should include payment for at least part of the contract time.

The key issue is proving what you've done. The best strategy is to pull together the best dossier of proof that you can, so that when your manager accuses you of making a 'right mess,' you can say: 'Not only is that statement entirely false, but I can prove it. And if you don't change your tune, my lawyer will call the tune in court with a demand for compensation.'

Very often a simple demonstration of strength on your part will make the manager think twice, or at least get the manager to see that a compromise with you on this is desirable. Because if you are obliged to seek legal redress, the issue will be the subject of a complex debate, and when lawyers say 'complex' what they really mean is 'costly'.

If you are going to be able to enforce your legal rights, you will need documentary proof, compiled as completely as possible. You should also ask fellow contractors to write statements on your behalf, and you should create a chart of progress, a kind of 'before and after' scenario.'

This is not as daunting as it sounds.

First of all, you should have been careful throughout the project to document what you've done. Keep all emails, indications of milestones reached or phases completed, and as many records of your work as you can.

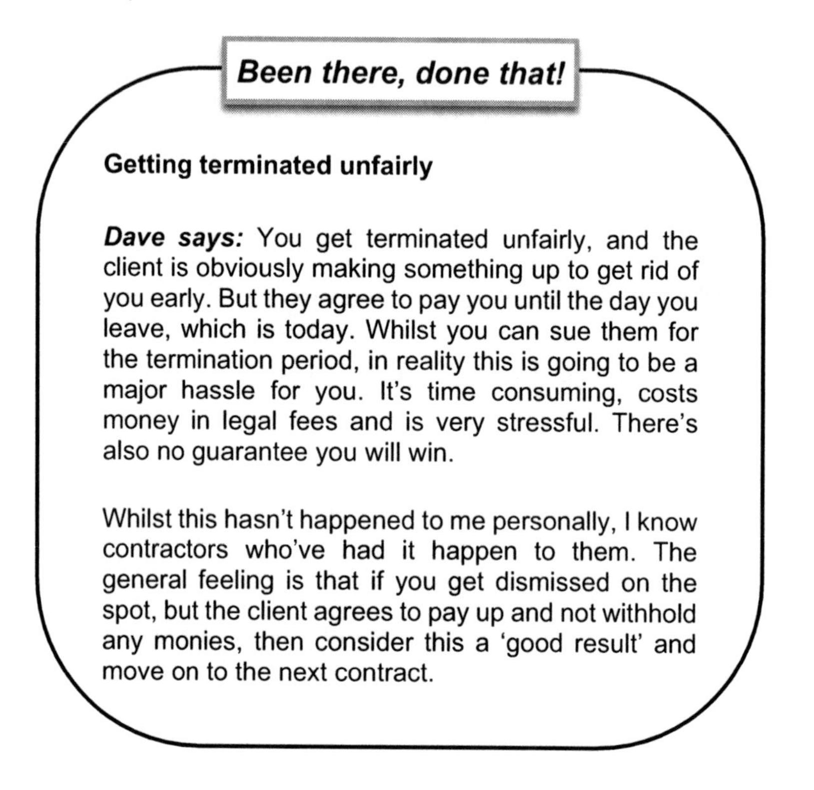

Been there, done that!

Getting terminated unfairly

Dave says: You get terminated unfairly, and the client is obviously making something up to get rid of you early. But they agree to pay you until the day you leave, which is today. Whilst you can sue them for the termination period, in reality this is going to be a major hassle for you. It's time consuming, costs money in legal fees and is very stressful. There's also no guarantee you will win.

Whilst this hasn't happened to me personally, I know contractors who've had it happen to them. The general feeling is that if you get dismissed on the spot, but the client agrees to pay up and not withhold any monies, then consider this a 'good result' and move on to the next contract.

Get as many of your colleagues on the project as you can to support you. If you are all being victimised in a group, that's likely to work to your benefit, because your combined testimony will be all that more damaging.

Use your own technical knowledge to explain what happened. You know what you were hired to do, and what the project was for. In the evidence, try to explain how things were at the start, what you did, and what was left to be accomplished. Use plain language. If the project's failure was due to negligence on the part of the client, explain what the client should have done and didn't do. Did the client fail to provide necessary materials? Were you given access to everything you needed?

Make the most convincing case you can. Then take it first to the highest-level manager you can reach, and lay out the case. Give them a good 'scare'. If necessary, you could consider paying the lawyers to contact them and help in the 'scare'.

It is of course frustrating to know that you are in the right but to accept less than all that you are owed. And, if the client refuses to negotiate, you should go ahead with the lawsuit if you've put sufficient proof together. But the best strategy is to get a reasonable settlement and to move on. Years of legal expense, frustration and health-damaging stress should be avoided if possible, even if you know you'll win in the end.

9.5.2 When your client breaches the contract

When agents or clients breach your contract, you should react with notification, and if appropriate and necessary, termination of the contract. You may also have the right to damages if your contract is breached, but these damages could be limited by your 'duty to mitigate' – you can't just sit around and collect damages, rather you have to make an effort to find a new contract and move on.

Remember that a contract is an agreement to provide goods or services in exchange for a 'consideration', which means money. This exchange is governed by terms: when will it take place, how will it take place, and so on.

Breach of contract occurs when one of these terms is not honoured by one or more of the parties to the contract. There are two ways in which this can happen: one party cannot do something they have promised to do; or one party can interfere in a way that jeopardises the completion of the contract.

There are two types of breach of contract: major and minor. A major breach allows you to terminate immediately, although this may not be your best option from a business point of view. If it's a minor breach, then you should certainly make a real effort to negotiate before pursuing damages.

For contractors, typical examples of major breaches of contract include:

- Non-payment or late payment
- Termination without sufficient notice
- Accusation of a breach on your part to justify early termination
- Cancellation of contract before work begins
- Client refuses to sign a time sheet when work has been completed
- Failure to provide materials or other conditions promised by the contract
- Demand for services not included in the contract.

The first thing to do if you are subject to a breach of this kind is to talk to the person responsible. Always try to avoid legal action in any case; going to court is a time-consuming, stressful and expensive process, and the results are never predictable no matter how certain you are of being right. Bring the matter to the person's attention, and see if you can work something out.

If that doesn't work, and you have to get formal, then notify the client or agent with a registered letter that you feel their action constitutes a major breach of contract, and that you will terminate and seek damages if they do not correct their actions.

The next step is either to take the matter to small claims court, if it involves less than £5000, or to seek legal advice. If the party in question settles with you, or if you win in court, you can expect to receive damages, and any costs in addition to of the small claims court charges and fees, but these will be subject to what is called your duty to mitigate.

For example, if you have been terminated after three months for no justifiable reason on a six-month contract, you should be entitled to payment for any termination period. You have to show the court that you've made a real attempt to find more work after the early termination, which demonstrates your 'duty to mitigate'.

So the rule is discretion: you don't have to accept breach of contract, but don't just race off to sue without very serious thought, or without trying to negotiate. It's easy to threaten to sue when you are angry, but doing it is a lot more trying.

Understanding your rights and stating them clearly is the surest way to resolving most contracts disputes.

9.5.3 When you want to leave early and don't have a termination clause

Having a friendly word with the client's project manager is the sensible option in such cases. They are unlikely to want to force contractors to stay who are unhappy and unmotivated. They could then terminate you early, assuming they have the option.

You could also offer to help find and fund someone to take over from you – a substitute. Incidentally, this would also help any future IR35 case, as it could be construed as your company providing a substitute. Your agent, if you have one, will not like you terminating as you are cutting off a source of income for them. The agent can also take legal action for breach of contract, so make sure you keep them informed about what you are doing.

However, if you provide a substitute, the agency will maintain their revenue stream and won't care who is providing it for them.

9.5.4 When you are terminated and think you should get employment rights/compensation

It's simple: contractors do not have employment rights from their end-user client, even if they are within IR35. Any contractor who wants to make a representation to a client about employment rights is asking to be caught by IR35 and, as such, will potentially end up being targeted by HMRC for back taxes and penalties. So the strong recommendation to all contractors is not to even consider it.

You should also be aware that the courts have ruled that contractors do not qualify for employment rights even if they have been working for a client for several years.

9.6 Difficult clients

Clients come in all shapes and sizes. Many are a pleasure to work with and provide years of stress free contracting, calling you up when they have moved on to see if you can come and work for them again. Equally, many can be a complete nightmare and are downright nasty. Some have simply never hired contractors before, so think you are an employee and treat you accordingly.

9.6.1 When you are asked to provide more services than you agreed

Often contractors are asked to provide more services than agreed, and this situation requires a business decision on your part. The law does not expect your work to conform strictly and absolutely to the letter of the contract description.

Reasonable allowances are made for the needs of the workplace, changes in demand and so on. You are expected to be flexible and reasonable, and, if there is a dispute that ends up in the courts, you will be sanctioned if you have been inflexible.

With that said, an agreement to perform service 'X' does not include your performing services 'Y' and 'Z' too. You should feel free to point this out to the client's project manager if too many demands are made. This can be quite important for your IR35 status: to retain your contractor status you must focus on your project and not just do whatever comes down the pipe, or you could easily be judged a 'disguised employee'.

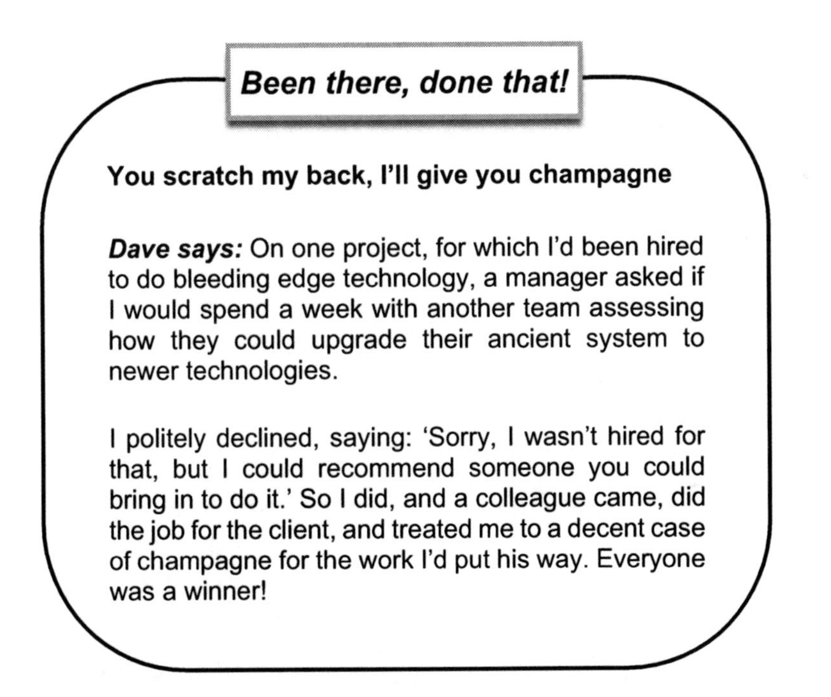

If the client threatens to terminate if you don't go the extra mile, you should point out that they are threatening a breach of contract, and that you will quit and demand compensation if they do not drop the unreasonable demands. If the contract is breached in this way, and you can prove it, you should notify the agency and client by letter that there has been a breach, or the threat of one.

Most of the time this threat will suffice to get the client to drop the unreasonable demands.

9.6.2 When the client won't let you take time off

Normally contractor contracts do not include time taken off from work except for standard holidays, and even these are not always included if the project is urgent. So, if your contract doesn't specify you can take time off, you can't.

If your contract does specify holidays then this would put you inside IR35.

The only way around this is to declare up front that your firm will not be able to provide services between certain dates and have those dates written in the contract. On the whole clients are pretty reasonable, and will let you take some time away, but they don't have to.

If you want to take off for extended leave, and not just a couple of weeks here and there then you need to substitute yourself. Holidays are covered in detail in chapter 11.

9.6.3 When the client forces you to take time off

Unless your contract specifies that you should expect periods of suspension, or that your period of assignment could be abbreviated, you are not obliged to take time off if you don't want to. This does not include time off for national holidays, like Christmas and New Year.

But for the rest of the year, if it's not in your contract that you can be suspended for periods of time, just say no. Your contract probably does include terms for termination, but if you are terminated, the client will probably want you back again when the project starts up again. You will be well-placed to demand a higher fee.

Should the client insist, point out that it breaches your contract and that you will take action. Warn the agency, and they will intervene. They should be made to understand that you will seek damages for the time lost on the contract.

If your contract does provide for such suspensions, obviously you are obliged to accept them. What would be perhaps the best solution is to talk the whole thing over with your client, and see if you can't find a compromise that works for you both. After all, you may want to work for the client again. But don't allow your rights to be impugned without a reasonable solution; ask up-front before signing the contract if time off is anticipated and get it confirmed in writing, at the very least in an email.

9.6.4 When the client threatens to terminate if you don't adhere to their unfair requests

If a client requires you to perform tasks that are well outside your remit, you always have the option of declining. If the client makes an issue of it, then you can remind them that you have a contract and what they are asking you to do is outside of the remit of the contract.

Should the client threaten you with termination the first step is to try and talk to them and negotiate a settlement. It might be that you can negotiate an additional contract to, for example, train the client's employees in a new skill. If the client terminates your contract unfairly, see section 9.5.1.

9.6.5 When your client decides to relocate and insists you must also move

You've been working on a contract for some months, based at a client's site within a reasonable journey from your permanent place of residence. Then you learn that the client is closing down the site you work at, and relocating the project to another part of the UK, or even, in extreme cases, another country.

If your contract requires you to complete the entire project, and the client is inflexible, then you might have to consider relocating. If you do, remember that as a contractor you will get no financial assistance from the client towards relocation.

In the unlikely event the client offers assistance, you have to decline it because to accept relocation expenses, or compensation for them, would immediately put you inside IR35 – don't go there.

The up-side is that, whether you are contracting through a limited company or an umbrella company, a significant amount of your relocation expenses, or extended travel and accommodation expenses if you choose a weekly commute, are tax deductible.

Some contracts specify the location where you will be working. This will give you the option of not completing the project and being able to claim a reasonable notice payment.

If you think this might be an issue from the start, say you heard that the parent company had been going through a major restructuring, then make sure there is a termination clause and that the location is written into the contract, with an exit option if this location changes.

9.7 Payment problems

Contracting is inherently different from permanent work in that there is more risk of not getting paid for the work that you do. Whilst this is rare, it does happen. Agencies and clients sometimes go bust and occasionally refuse or delay payment. However, in most scenarios, short of the agency or client going bust (which is covered in 9.7.4 below), there is something you can do to claim all or part of your fees.

9.7.1 When you don't get paid

In the event of payment being delayed by the client or the agency, then it is a breach of contract and you do not have to continue working. They will still owe you the money if you refuse to continue working. This is your legal right.

If this happens to you then the suggested course of action is to demand in writing that they pay you within three working days or you will terminate the contract. Your agency may counter this by saying they have not been paid by the client. However, this is not your problem, as your contract should not have a 'pay when paid' clause. Also, in practice, most agencies factor their invoices so get the cash immediately anyway.

If you are still not paid then simply withdraw your services. The more time you spend working for nothing, the more time you are losing looking for a new contract.

Having withdrawn your services, send them a letter explaining why and inform them that you have commenced legal action. Wait a week and if you still have not been paid then start legal proceedings. It rarely gets to this stage.

9.7.2 When you are consistently paid late

This is probably one of the most common 'when things go wrong' scenarios. Agents often don't pay on time, even when the contract specifies that they should.

Send a letter before action stating that you consider late payment a breach and that you will seek damages if it continues. That will usually resolve the issue.

Most small businesses have to deal, at one time or another, with the problem of late payment. It's an awkward situation: on the one hand, you need to get the money that you live on; on the other hand, you don't want to go overboard chasing agencies and clients so that you become known as strident and unreasonable.

Nonetheless, it is wise to know your rights, and then to decide whether you want to play it soft or hard with a given agency or client.

Repeated late payment might well merit your attention for another reason, though. When it comes time to get the last payment under the terms of the contract, it may not just be late, it may never come. To remind the agency that you are very determined to receive what is due to you, a firm line on late payments can be useful.

Or you may feel that repeated late payment is reason for terminating the contract. This is harder to do, but you may be justified in doing so under certain conditions.

First, what does the law say? Under the terms of the 'Late Payment of Commercial Debts (Interest) Act of 1998', you have an implied right to interest on debts that are older than 30 days, unless your contract specifically sets a different term.

You have to show that you are a small business and that the debt is due for more than 30 days. If your contract states that payment of your invoice is due after seven days, then you must wait 37 days before claiming that it is overdue.

Satisfy these conditions, and you're entitled to interest at 8% over the 'official dealing rate' If that rate is currently 5%, the interest rate you are entitled to is 13%.

If this begins to add up to serious money, send an invoice for the interest with a polite reminder letter. The law has been in force for some time, and many companies are aware that they have to pay this. Usually it will act as a wake-up call and they'll start paying you on time, and probably start showing you a bit more respect, too.

Remember that if the company refuses to pay, and the amount is less than £5,000 (at the time of writing), you can use HM Courts Service's

Money Claim Online, which is there to help you collect your debts without resorting to using a collection agency or solicitor.

But what if you want to terminate the contract?

It is possible to treat late payment as a breach of contract, but it must be of the essence of the contract. That means, for you, getting paid on time is absolutely essential, critical to the work you agreed to undertake when you signed the contract.

Some contracts have terms that make this clear in themselves. But if you need to prove that it is essential that you be paid on time, write a letter to the company and remind them that this is essential to the contract, and that you will consider it a breach of contract if they continue to pay late.

If the company still pays you late, you have the right to terminate without further delay, and you can seek to recover damages. If the amount is large, you should probably take professional advice at this point.

So know your rights, evaluate what you think is the most important aspect of the problem, and proceed accordingly.

9.7.3 When the agency or client withholds money from you, citing reasons

This is something that sometimes happens when, for example, a client claims that you have not returned a piece of equipment you have borrowed. Ideally, you should not use clients' equipment as this could be a contributing factor to putting you inside IR35. But if you do have to use your client's equipment, then you should always obtain a receipt on its return.

When a dispute arises and the client claims you have not returned equipment, the issue becomes a question of evidence. You must prove that you returned the equipment, which might require a statement from the person you returned it to.

Where it is not possible for you to prove you returned the client's equipment, then the client company has the right to 'set-off' the costs of the equipment. In other words, they can claim compensation from you for the cost of the equipment 'lost'.

However, this does not mean the client can withhold payment from you, which may amount to thousands of pounds in lieu of equipment worth a few tens of pounds. If the client withholds payment on the basis of equipment not returned and which is worth far less than the amount you are owed, then you are perfectly within your rights to take legal action to recover unpaid fees.

In this case, you should get in touch with a credit collection agency, or with you solicitor, or, if the amount of fees owed is less than £5,000, you could make a claim through HM Courts Service's Money Claim Online. Naturally, before taking such action, you should try alternative dispute resolution by, for example, negotiating with the agency and/or client.

In a perfect world, contractors should not put themselves in the position of using client's equipment, because it could be used as evidence by HMRC that they are a 'disguised employee', which could put them inside IR35. But when a contractor really does have to use the client's equipment, they should ensure that there is a paper trail of receipts to account for that equipment's whereabouts.

9.7.4 When the agent or client goes bust

If your client or recruitment agency goes bust, this is not great news for you, as contractors tend to be fairly low down the creditor pecking order.

However, there are steps you can take to ensure you do receive any funds distributed by a defunct company, and how you go about it is different if you are working through your own limited company or an umbrella company.

An agency or a client is insolvent if they do not have enough cash to pay their creditors or their net assets are less than their net liabilities. This usually means one of three things happening:

- Appointment of an administrator
- Appointment of a receiver
- Appointment of a liquidator.

If an administrator is appointed, it is usually good news for you as you may see a small amount of your fee. The receiver is responsible for either managing the company out of its financial difficulties or realising as much value from the assets as possible to pay creditors.

Most agencies have factoring arrangements with a finance provider, which means they receive payment immediately from the factoring agent, less a commission. It is this relationship that can often determine whether an agency survives or not.

The receiver, or liquidator, would usually have the task of attempting to realise as much cash as possible from the failed agency or client to disperse amongst the creditors.

You should find out who the administrator, receiver or liquidator is, and ensure you register your debt with the right forms and proof of debt. You should keep in touch with the administrator, receiver or liquidator, but not hassle them as they have a statutory obligation not to favour one creditor above another except as laid down in statute.

If you are working through an umbrella company, you should not contact the administrator, receiver or liquidator at all, as technically is it not your problem but your umbrella company's.

You should make sure your umbrella company is aware that your agency or client has gone bust and ensure they are taking action. Some umbrella companies do not pay their contractors unless they get paid, but others do; therefore, you would be wise to ask the question when choosing which umbrella company to use.

From a practical perspective, there may also be many contractors who work for the same client and agency under one umbrella company. The umbrella company can manage the process better as a single point of contact and potentially a larger creditor.

The order in which creditors are paid in the UK is clearly laid down by statute and guidance from the Insolvency Service shows the payments made by an insolvent agency or client in liquidation are:

- The administrator's/receiver's/liquidator's fees and charges
- Preferential creditors, such as government departments like HMRC, employees wages owed in the four months before the insolvency and contributions to occupational pension schemes
- Secured creditors with a fixed charge over tangible assets, such as a bank lending money by a mortgage on land owned by the company
- Secured creditors with a floating charge, such as a bank that has lent money against assets such as stock and assets not included in the list of assets with a fixed charge
- General creditors, such as suppliers, which includes contractors, and lenders who have greater rights for recovering their losses than shareholders, such as preference capital holders
- Interest payable on any debts

- Shareholders in the agency or client, who in practice almost always receive nothing.

Remember, you are not an employee and are therefore counted as just a general creditor, or supplier, and as a result are almost at the bottom of the chain when it comes to payment.

If the worst has happened and your agent or client cannot pay, you should register your debt, then move on and focus on finding a new contract.

9.8 Finances, accountants and umbrellas

9.8.1 When your accountant (or umbrella) messes up and costs you money in fines

Your accountant can be your best ally in your contracting career. Much useful advice about how to structure and grow your business is to be gleaned from the accountant, particularly if they've dealt with lots of contractors in the past.

But accountants do make errors. For example, you might find that yours has failed to file forms in time and you've been fined for it by HMRC or Companies House.

If this is entirely the responsibility of the accountant, and in no way the result of your failing to supply information, then you have a right to compensation. The accountant knows this, so a little insistence will suffice in most cases.

If you work with a chartered accountant, and you're not happy with the result, you have an inalienable right to change accountants. Notify the old one with a letter, pay the last of their fees, and switch to the new one. The old accountant is obliged to provide the new one with all necessary information.

You are paying your umbrella company to process your pay efficiently and accurately – that is one of their major reasons for existence. Should you spot an error or if you attract the attention of HMRC, then ensure they correct it.

Reputable umbrella companies have a finance and HR department, like a regular employer, who exist to act on your behalf as a representative to HMRC. If you feel like they are not doing this, either tell them firmly you are paying for the service or vote with your feet and change umbrella.

9.8.2 When your accountant makes it difficult for you to stop using their services

This is a rare occurrence, but it does happen. Moving accountants should not be a difficult process, in fact accountants have a duty to ensure the process is as painless as possible, but sometimes your old accountant can make things difficult if they hold a grudge against you, or more usually if they feel you terminated their services unfairly and/or that you still owe them money.

As with every dispute, the first step should be to ask nicely and try to settle the issue amicably. However, all chartered accountants are governed by the code of conduct of their professional institute.

If the dispute cannot be resolved amicably, then you should find out which accountancy body your ex-accountant belongs to and contact them regarding their mediation services. The institute will investigate the circumstances and arbitrate, so you should be very sure of your position and that you are in the right.

9.9 When you are being harassed and threatened by one of your client's employees

Contractors are not employees and have no employment rights. This means that if you are being harassed, physically threatened by, or suffering abuse from one of your client's employees, you cannot use your client's employee grievance process; in fact any attempt to do so could put your IR35 status in jeopardy (assuming you are working outside IR35).

However, although you may have no employment rights and want to avoid any indications that you are an employee, you do have rights under health and safety legislation, which applies to all workers and does not distinguish between employees and contractors. Your client has a duty to provide a safe working environment for you.

You should detail the situation in writing to your project manager to inform the client about your concerns about health and safety. In the event anything should happen to you, the client will be liable and in default for not taking reasonable action despite being warned by you.

Many contractor and consultant contracts include clauses that place an obligation on the client to provide a safe working environment. Contractors can, and should, have an added layer of protection by including a clause detailing that the client, their servants and agents are responsible for maintaining a safe working environment.

If you are assaulted by a client's employee you must report the incident to the police immediately. Then you are in a position to make claims against both the client's employee who committed the assault on you, as well as against the client.

The assault is not just a criminal matter, it is also civil matter. You can, in effect, make a personal injury claim and, because you had warned the client in writing and they have not taken reasonable action to protect you following your warning.

Of course the hope is that you need not take any action apart from warning the client in writing. In most cases the client will deal effectively with your concerns.

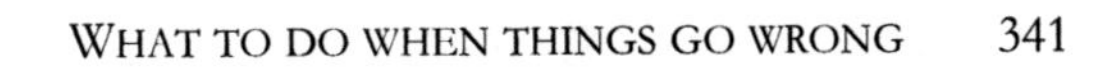

10.

Advanced marketing and sales

10.1 Marketing yourself

A new contractor often has red hot skills, and is in high demand, so even if they have objectionable personal habits someone is likely to hire them! The problem comes later when they have not kept their skills up to date and/or the market demand has dropped. An alternative scenario might be where there are plenty of contracts for everyone, but only a few plum contracts that everybody really wants.

In the run-up to the dot com crash, anyone with experience was being hired. After the crash, there was a mass migration of contractors back to permanent roles; but many of the most successful survivors were those best at sales and marketing and not necessarily the most highly skilled.

The key to success in contracting is to remain as a highly paid contractor for the long term, preferably for your entire working life. How do you keep your skills updated? How do you manage your money? How do you secure contracts when demand falls?

The main message is to learn some business skills that might be outside your core expertise – typically, this means getting to grips with marketing and sales. They are invaluable skills that are likely to keep you in profitable, enjoyable and rewarding contracts for as long as you want them. It's all about marketing and selling yourself better than anyone else.

So you've started contracting, had your first or second contract, and you're beginning to appreciate your new lifestyle and earnings. But key worries never go away: will you always get enough work? Will you always make enough money?

Being in business for yourself means that these worries are always there, especially in the early days. But your worst fears need never be realised if you market yourself well.

Contracting is a business like any other, in which you have to market your business, negotiate contracts, make sales and generally keep on top of many competing calls on your time. The contractors who learn these skills are the ones who stay in business, get the most contracts and get the best contracts. Those who don't often end up back in a permanent job, with the lack of flexibility and lower earnings that brings with it.

10.1.1 Your personal marketing plan

There is a discipline to marketing yourself. You need to constantly push yourself out into the marketplace, even when working on a contract, because that contract will eventually come to an end and you will need to have the next contract lined up. So here is a framework for your personal marketing plan:

Network: Keep in touch with your client contacts and other contractors you meet on the job. You need to be the first person the client thinks of when they are looking to fill a role. Maintaining contact with other contractors can mean you have a sales force in the field doing your marketing and selling for you. This also works both ways and if you can put in a good word for a fellow contractor that gets them a contract, they will remember you and are likely to return the favour. After about five years, you will find you win lots of your contracts this way.

Update your CV regularly: Make sure you update your CV with your latest contract details and skills. Ensure that your updated CV is also visible on the key job boards on the internet. Even if you are in a contract, your profile should be still highly visible. This keeps the calls coming from agents.

Meet with agents: Most contracts are secured through agents, so it pays to maintain a relationship with key agencies. Be helpful to agents when you can; for example, if they call and you are not available, then refer them to a friend who may be. The agent might return the favour when you are looking for a new contract. It is also well worth creating and maintaining a list of agents you get on well with and emailing them close to the time when you will be looking for a new contract.

Market yourself via a website and white papers: The cost of building and maintaining a website is small compared to the potential rewards of a new contract. In addition, having your own online presence reinforces your position of being in business in your own right, a strong factor in keeping you outside IR35. Take the opportunity to write and publish white papers on topics associated with your skill set. Many websites are desperate for good content and you can raise your profile by authoring thought leadership pieces. This will attract the attention of other people in your field who may contact you with work.

Work on your publicity: In addition to white papers, publicise yourself by writing articles for websites and trade magazines. Aim to become an industry commentator in your area of contracting and actively encourage journalists to contact you for expert opinion. The publicity will raise your profile and ensure your CV is top of the pile for agents and clients. You're also likely to be able to negotiate higher rates more successfully; after all, you're THE expert in the field!

Market yourself on the job: Make sure the client knows how much value you are adding to their operation and invest a little extra time in doing things that are not strictly in your contract – although not too much, for tax reasons that are explained in chapter 8. Let the client know what you are doing and blow your own trumpet, as no one else will; then ask for testimonials. Don't forget that other contractors can be a valuable source of leads, so cultivate your colleagues. If you can do them a favour, do it, as it will be remembered and could work to your advantage.

Look the part: Appearance is a large part of the battle. Get the look, and you'll get the work. It involves some effort, but once you've done it, you'll be amazed how a smart suit and the other trappings of being a professional businessperson will help you win contracts.

The objective of your marketing should be to ensure you have a stream of contract leads ready for when you finish the job you are currently on.

10.1.2 What are your features and benefits?

You will often hear sales or marketing people talking about 'features and benefits'.

As a contractor selling a 'product', your knowledge, you'll need to be aware of your own features and benefits and ensure you explain these to both the agent and client. You should also be able to recognise when sales or marketing people, like agents, are introducing features and benefits in an attempt to sell you something, such as a contract you wouldn't normally choose to take on.

Marketing and sales training allows people to use a process and a formula that provides the most effective way of communicating a message with a positive outcome. Part of this process will always include mentioning the features of a product or service and describing the benefits of each feature.

This may sound straightforward, but a common mistake made by many salespeople is to mention the feature and to forget to mention the benefit, or vice versa.

Remember that features and benefits enable a clear description of a product, like you, in such a way that it allows potential clients to easily and quickly agree to offer a contract. If parts of the process are missed out, the client may be confused and will probably not buy.

Firstly, what is a feature and what is a benefit? A good example to use is a car. The features of this product would include:

- Power steering
- Electric windows
- MP3 player
- Liquid petroleum gas engine.

It is important to mention these features to a potential customer, as they may not be aware that the product they are thinking of buying has them. When they discover these new features, the customer might be tempted enough to buy. However, mentioning just the features is not enough and will almost certainly not make the sale.

This is where benefits come in.

For every feature, there is at least one benefit and generally many. Benefits may not always be obvious, and what is obvious to you (the salesperson) is not necessarily so to others (your customers). The basic benefits associated with the features listed above are:

- Power steering – the key benefit to the customer being 'it's so much easier to drive'
- Electric windows – the key benefit to the customer being 'you never have to wind down the windows manually'
- MP3 player – the key benefit to the customer being 'you can listen to all your own music'
- Liquid petroleum gas engine – the key benefit to the customer being 'it's much cheaper than petrol or diesel, so travel costs come down'.

Much of the above will seem quite straightforward and largely common sense. All the same, many salespeople neglect this area of their pitches and lose sales as a consequence. When you are being sold to and features are mentioned without the benefits – ask the salesperson what the benefit is. If you don't have the facts, you cannot make an informed decision and the salesperson is not doing their job!

Often when people are trained on this area of a pitch, they make a massive list of features and benefits and then do little more than list them to their potential clients. This is not the way to sell. One of the most fundamental parts of the sales process is the fact finding – doing some research and listening to what features and benefits the customer actually wants.

Before presenting any features or benefits, a good salesperson will have already asked many questions of the prospective customer. The answers to these questions will suggest to the salesperson which particular features and benefits are likely to influence their decision, or not.

So, when selling a car, the salesperson will try and find out what is most important to their customer. If the customer indicates that they are conscious of high travel costs, then a car that runs economically on LPG is worth pointing out. If the customer mentions they're looking for something that's easy to drive, then power steering and electric windows are good features to introduce.

In the contracting world recruitment agents will try to sell the contract to you by first establishing which of your buttons to press, and then by explaining the features and benefits of the contract that align with your magic buttons. Conversely, you should do exactly the same with both the agent and client. This is why you need to ask lots of questions and listen carefully to the answers, to find out what those buttons are.

Your sales pitch should always be tailored to each customer as far as possible, be they a client or agent. Find out what they need or desire, and why, then clearly match the answers they give you with the relevant features and benefits you offer.

10.2 Effective sales

Part of the effort to secure lucrative contracts – a crucial part, in fact – is learning how to sell. To a highly educated and skilled contractor like you, selling may seem 'demeaning'. Get over it! Because, on the contrary, selling is the best affirmation that you are good at what you do. All it involves is you learning how to convince people of what you already know: that you can do a good job.

So, as a contractor marketing your expertise, you are going to have to sell yourself. Unfortunately, sales as a profession gets a bad press, particularly in the contracting industry. But there is a great difference between a salesperson and a conman. A salesperson knows how to best present what there is to sell; a conman lies about it.

You should not make the mistake of feeling bad about selling yourself, as all business depends on sales. Sales is the method of presenting a product or service in the most positive light, helping the potential customer see that the product or service meets or exceeds their needs, maintaining control over the 'sales process' and ultimately achieving the highest level of profit together with delivering the highest level of customer satisfaction.

Once you're in the game, the better you can sell yourself, the more work you'll get, the greater the number of contracts you can choose from, and the more money you will earn on each contract.

It's true that your skills are the principal selling point for your contracting. But there's no point having great cutting-edge skills if you're sitting at home waiting for an agent to call.

It sounds obvious, but is worth stating: the contractors who win the contracts are the ones who know how to find them in the first place and how to go about having them offered at a great rate. Something else to bear in mind is that these contractors are not necessarily the best candidates for those plum contracts; they're sometimes just the best when it comes to winning contracts. It's all down to their sales and marketing skills.

There are plenty of exceptional contractors who find it difficult to secure a regular flow of contracts, or are working for less than they are worth simply because they are unable to successfully sell their product – themselves.

Contractors with little or no sales experience often wrongly believe that competitive pricing is the sole key to securing business. This is untrue. Most clients will expect to pay the market price for the services they need, and they have budgeted for it, although bizarrely there are always a few clients who expect something for nothing. But that does not mean you have to behave like a monkey and get paid peanuts!

If you learn and apply sales techniques, you will maximise your chances of securing contracts and of making the most money. And in addition to the advantages of using a professional sales approach to your contract searches, you will also find the sales experience useful for other areas of your contracting career.

Being able to formulate and sell a winning argument will prove very useful for getting your ideas adopted. In addition, your sales knowledge will help you to build a good reputation and a network of contacts, which are invaluable in the long term for obtaining work directly or via recommendation.

10.2.1 Using a sales process

The sales process is a clear and structured way to introduce and to sell a product. It is a step-by-step approach that takes the seller from the introduction to follow-up on the sale. A typical sales process employed by recruitment consultants when selling a position to a contractor is as follows:

- The recruitment consultant will match a CV to a current position
- The recruitment consultant contacts the candidate and introduces themselves
- The introduction explains the nature of the call, the business of the agency and what the consultant is looking to do, to arrange an interview with the contractor for the position
- The contractor needs to be 'qualified' for the contract, which in the consultant's terms means: is the contractor looking for a new position?: are they qualified to carry out the work?: do they charge an acceptable rate?; and are they interested in the contract?
- The recruitment consultant then interviews the contractor, normally via telephone and in the same call
- The recruitment consultant assesses the contractor's ability to carry out the work and how successful they feel the contractor will be at an interview
- The recruitment consultant must 'sell' the position to the contractor
- The recruitment consultant must then 'sell' the contractor to their client. They will send over the CV for the contractor, which may well have been modified to represent the contractor in a better light for this position, and must convince their client that the contractor is worthy of an interview
- The recruitment consultant then prepares the contractor for the interview process. This will include providing background material for the contractor about the client and the role
- After being offered the position, the recruitment consultant will then attempt to negotiate the rate of pay for the contractor with the highest margin they can get for their agency
- The final job is for the recruitment consultant to further convince their client that the contractor is the best person for the job and that the rate is acceptable. At the same time, the

recruitment consultant must also convince the contractor that this is the best role for then and at the highest rate of pay
- On agreement from both sides, the deal is closed and contracts are signed.

Of course, this simplifies a much more complex process. But the advantage of this model is that you can track each stage of the sale and ensure that the necessary action has been taken for each step.

You need to maximise your impact in each step of this process. All experienced and successful contractors have developed their own sales process when searching for contracts. They might not have formalised it and written it down, but over the years they will have fine-tuned a process that works for them.

The agent will try to sell you the contract and you are trying to sell yourself to the agent. So there are sales techniques employed on both sides.

10.2.2 Fact Finding

When you are being sold to, be aware that you are probably not being presented with all of the facts. It is not the job of the salesperson to tell you everything about what you are about to buy, it is their job to sell it. Don't be too alarmed by this, it is just business and quite normal.

So when you are being sold to, it is your job to discover the information the salesperson has not told you. Ask lots of questions and always question detail. The agent might not have too much detail about the contract and could over-promise. You should ensure you verify these facts at any subsequent interview with the client.

In contracting this works both ways. For example, the agent might not want to tell you that the last five contractors hired by the client left in disgust after the first day. Similarly, a contractor might not want to tell the agent how they totally messed up their last project and were escorted off the premises!

10.2.3 Buying signals

When you are being sold to, the salesperson is looking for buying signals. These are signals that you make, often involuntarily, that indicate that you wish to buy the product. The buying signal relates to the reason you may have for buying.

For example, when buying a new car, it may be the running costs that are most important to you or it could be the speed at which the car drives. The salesperson does not know why each customer is looking to buy and so needs to find out by talking to you.

Once they have found your touch point, you are likely to give off buying signals. To make life hard for the salesperson, practice dealing with salespeople and giving away none of your feelings. This can be quite difficult, but you will see the salesperson get frustrated.

This is actually a very useful skill to develop. When you're speaking to an agent after an interview, for example, it may not be wise to tell them how ecstatic you are about the contract and that you would love to start straight away. This is sending the agent clear buying signals, that may result in you being offered a lower rate, with the agent enjoying higher margins.

Like all salespeople, agents have targets to meet and so want you to sign the deal now. Never allow yourself to be rushed into signing up for a position you have been offered.

Sophisticated closing techniques can often manipulate you into signing when you may not have been ready to commit. Take your time, digest the information you are receiving and try and take a balanced view. It is easy to be caught up in the moment and salespeople not only know it, but have also been trained to exploit it.

If you have been offered a position, agents will certainly try every trick in the book to get you to sign, as they are eager to earn their commission. You, of course, can use your own closing techniques to exploit their eagerness, and so obtain a higher rate or improved terms.

10.2.4 Body language

The majority of your discussions with agents will be over the phone, but body language will be important for you during the interview stage, when you become the salesperson.

Body language can reveal much that is hidden, a fact that is widely understood in the sales industry and manipulated by salespeople to good effect. A salesperson is often taught to mirror the same body language that their customer is displaying, as this makes people feel more connected and eases the atmosphere.

Your body language also gives away a lot about how you are feeling. When you are being sold to, be aware of your body language and make sure that it is neutral. Neutral means not sitting forward, rubbing your hands and looking like you are just about to reach for your wallet on the one hand, and on the other not slumping back in your seat and looking like you are about to fall asleep. You want something in between that does not give anything away.

Despite how professional you may look when turning up for interview, if you yawn and appear like you are not really listening, you will not be taken seriously!

10.2.5 Open questions

As a contractor trying to secure a contract, asking open ended questions of your agent or client during an interview is key to your fact finding, so that you can tailor your sales approach accordingly.

One of the most important aspects of sales is asking the right questions of your potential client. If you don't ask questions, you are merely guessing or assuming the needs and desires of the person you are selling to.

The answers you get will indicate which points to cover, and which to leave out. By asking the right questions, you can also control the dialogue and guide your customer into a closing situation, where you can ask for the business, having covered all the necessary points.

When you speak to agents over the phone you will quickly need to establish what the client is looking for and then convince the agent that you are perfect for the role. When you reach the interview you will need to do the same with the client.

So how do you do this? Well, in a selling situation, you need to allow your client to open up to you and give you the clues and insights into what will make them buy. This is achieved largely by using open ended, or open, questions. The opposite is a 'closed question'. Let's look at examples of both, from the situation when a recruitment consultant is pitching a new contract to you:

Open ended question: 'What type of role are you looking for?'
Closed question: 'Would you consider a role for £20 per hour?'

The major difference between these two is that one of the questions can be answered with a one word answer, or more dangerously in any sales situation, with the answer 'no'! That question was of course the closed question. The open ended question does not allow you to say 'yes' or 'no'; it prompts you to start opening up and providing the recruitment consultant with information that will enable him or her to sell to you.

With the closed question, the recruitment consultant may have lost the chance to place the contractor. It may have been the case that the contract being offered did not offer the best income, but perhaps the skills being used in this contract may have been of particular interest to the contractor, or the contract timings fitted in perfectly with a planned holiday. So, they may have considered the contract, but have already said 'no', and so the opportunity is lost to both parties.

You will almost certainly have experienced telesales representatives attempting to sell you all kinds of products over the phone. A well trained salesperson will always attempt to make you open up and start talking about yourself with open ended questions. A poor salesperson will simply ask something like 'are you interested in double glazing', to which you and 99.99% of the population will reply, quite simply – 'no'!

Understanding and recognising open ended questions can help you to make people open up, and as an added benefit can also help you to deal with irritating salespeople! The next time someone contacts you, introduces themselves as someone you don't know and then asks an open ended question, you have the ability to stop the salesperson from controlling the dialogue. Rather than answering the question (and of course there is no law that says you must answer questions at all), be direct and say: 'Please stop, and tell me what you are selling?'

This is likely to put the salesperson off their stride, as they won't want you to know the nature of the call at this stage. First they want to lure you in a little further before presenting their product or solution to a problem you were not even aware that you had! The salesperson's answer to the direct question of 'what are you selling' will often, again, not be a straight answer. So, ask again until the salesperson tells you what they are selling. Now, you have more control over the conversation.

As a contractor you will need to deal with open ended questions that the agent asks you, that perhaps you do not want to answer. For example, "what is the lowest rate you will accept?". You will also need to learn how to ask open ended questions to gain as much information as you can in order to tailor your responses to maximise your sales pitch, from securing an interview all the way through to negotiating the rate and the terms and conditions of your contract.

There is, though, an important place for the closed question. Once the salesperson has completed asking their open ended questions and extracted the information they need from you, they can then pitch their product and deal with any objections you might have, which is covered in the next section about objection handling.

It is then time for the 'close', which is covered in section 10.2.7. And here a close can certainly be a closed question like, 'would you like to order the product?', although more commonly the salesperson would ask, 'what quantity of the product would you like to order?'.

Open and closed questions are certainly not new and are found in many aspects of life. We have all attended dinner parties where you sit next to the boring guest who answers all of your questions with one word answers. The antidote to this guest is of course the open ended question. You can, with practice, learn to ask questions that do not allow a person to simply say 'yes' or 'no'. You can also spot an open ended question when you hear one and stop an unwanted sales pitch in its tracks.

10.2.6 Objection Handling

Inevitably you will come up against objections throughout the sales and marketing process. Good salespeople welcome these, because they are a very strong signal that the person is interested in buying from you, and giving you the opportunity to deal with their concerns. So you, as the salesperson selling your expertise as a contractor, need to recognise and handle typical objections that will be raised by both agents and clients during your contract search.

This is a well known and well studied area of sales. Anyone who has ever worked in sales will have had to pay attention to the typical objections found when selling their product or solution. For someone to be able to sell a product, they must engage the customer. For a customer to raise an objection, this demonstrates that they are considering the product for themselves.

Some common objections you will be faced with as a contractor trying to secure a contract are:

- “Send me your CV and I’ll consider it”
- "I don’t think you have the right skills for the role"
- "You’re asking for too much money and the client will not pay that"
- "The client needs someone to start sooner than you’re able to"
- "Your experience does not seem to be enough for this high-level role".

All objections can be distilled into two basic types: real objections and unreal objections. Let’s deal with the latter first:

Unreal objections

These are when the customer raises an objection that they may not necessarily feel, but they think the objection may get rid of the salesperson. This is the case when you have received three sales calls in a row and you just don’t want to listen to another sales pitch. You might say: ‘send me some literature in the post, I’ll read it and get back to you’. Salespeople know that in most cases the customer is not going to read the literature, they just don’t want to speak with you at that time.

As a contractor you will be faced with unreal objections when you are chasing positions with agents who might ask you to send your CV as a way of getting you off the phone.

Handling the unreal objection is reasonably straightforward. All salespeople are aware that they are often considered to be a pest. They know that you are not likely to read the literature they send you, but out of courtesy will send it through to you anyway.

Indeed, in many cases it is often not until the second, third or fourth telephone conversation that the salesperson actually gets to speak to their customer properly. That's why successful salespeople develop thick skins and remain patient when first speaking with prospective customers.

So the answer to an unreal objection is to be polite and friendly, to do as asked, and also to attempt to gain some kind of commitment to the next stage of the sales process.

For example, a salesperson might say: 'I'll make sure your literature goes in the post today – after you've received it, would Friday afternoon be a good time for me to call so we can have a chat?' Often the customer will recall they have agreed to a follow up call and will feel in some way obliged to at least listen to what the salesperson has to say.

As a contractor, you are the salesperson, so you will need to be patient, do as asked, and ensure you get a commitment to the next part of your sales process. Typically, this will involve sending a CV, then arranging to call back in a few days.

Real objections

The other type of objection – the real objection, is an objection that actually needs to be overcome and should be viewed as a buying signal.

Going back to our earlier example of a car, a potential customer might say: 'I've read that this model is extremely poor on fuel consumption, and my fuel costs are already too high.' This is a fact that the customer has stated. Be aware that for the car salesperson, this may be a good objection to be raised. The salesperson will now have a clearer picture of what their customer is looking for and can present a more suitable product. On the other hand, it is a problem for the salesperson if they only have one car to sell you. Here, they must find a way of demonstrating that the product is still the right one for the customer and make the sale.

You will be presented with many objections to overcome by both the agent and client. Typically these will involve your skills, experience, availability and rate.

The real objection must be handled differently to the unreal one, described above. On this occasion, this is a real objection that must be handled appropriately. Be aware however, that real objections are not always seen as the enemy to salespeople. Indeed, this may be the first time that the customer is revealing what they truly feel, and the salesperson cannot sell effectively if they have no idea about what the prospective customer really wants.

A good salesperson will have pre-rehearsed answers to all objections that arise and will not be caught by surprise – they might even appear to have 'the gift of the gab', although this is often the result of days, weeks, months and years spent carefully rehearsing answers.

Your preparation before applying for positions and attending interviews should involve considering all the objections that could be raised and preparing answers for them in advance. As you gain more experience it is advisable to keep a document containing all these objections and how they are handled, as part of your sales process.

A problem does develop, however, if the product being sold is flawed and the objection raised by the customer has identified the flaw. On this occasion the salesperson may have been found out and there is no 'magic sales wand' available that can help, other than providing the prospect with false information. So, as ever, be wary of disreputable salespeople, and beware of being one yourself!

Objections are actually a very useful tool for customers and salespeople alike.

As a customer, you should raise objections until you are satisfied that you understand the product or service you are considering sufficiently to make the purchase.

From the sales perspective, objections reveal who the customer really is and what they are really thinking. As long as the product or service is good, the salesperson should welcome objections.

10.2.7 Sales closes: theory and practice

When contracting, there are two primary situations where you will need to close a sale. The first is when securing an interview via an agent, and the second to secure the contract when you are at the interview with the potential client.

For salespeople all over the world, closing is often the most exciting and daunting aspect of doing business. It is, in essence, when and how you ask for the business. For most accomplished salespeople, closing is the part of sales they look forward to the most and once you begin to enjoy closing – you close a lot more!

A simple truth to bear in mind is that, very often, those who don't close a sale don't sell anything. The difference between a successful salesperson and a lousy one often comes down to the fact that the successful one closes, whilst the poor one doesn't. The lesson is not to expect agents to put you forward for interviews, or clients to offer you a contract, unless you actually ask them to; in other words, it's up to you to close the sale.

Much has been written on the art of closing and there are many well known and effective techniques employed. Closes often work differently in different market sectors. In the domestic and consumer markets, the most aggressive and manipulative closes exist. These closes however do not often work in the high level commercial world as more often than not, the buyer is trained to recognise them and so they are likely to have an adverse effect.

The most common closes include:

Assumptive close: This close involves the salesperson never actually asking their customer if they want to buy the product. Instead, they appear to assume that the customer is going to buy and closes with a statement something like: 'OK, I'll send the order to our delivery department and your product will be delivered in three working days." It is now down to the customer to protest that they have not indicated that they are interested in buying.

You would be surprised by how easy it is to be caught up in the moment and carried along with the sale. This type of close can even intimidate or embarrass customers, who therefore don't feel like they can disagree with the salesperson's assumption. This close is all about manipulating you into buying – be wary of it!

An example of an assumptive close an agent might use on a contractor is: 'I've spoken to the client, he is happy for you to work on the contract, and I've agreed with him that you will start on Monday.'

An example of an assumptive close a contractor might use on an agent is: 'I'm happy to be interviewed for this role tomorrow at 9am.'

Alternative close: A close relative of the 'assumptive close', this close is often used alongside it. Again, the alternative close dictates that the salesperson never actually asks their customer if they would like to buy. Instead, they will offer an alternative such as: 'Would you like to pay for this by cash or credit card?'

Again, the customer is being manipulated into feeling that they have already agreed to buying, it is just the payment terms that are left to be discussed. As with the assumptive close – be cautious of any salesperson trying to use it. And don't feel it's so obvious that you would never be caught, because many are!

An example of an alternative close the agent might use is: 'I've spoken to the client, he is happy for you to work on the contract; would you prefer to start on Monday or Tuesday?'

An example of an alternative close the contractor might use is: 'I'm looking forward to the interview tomorrow; would you prefer the morning or afternoon?'

Silent close: This is a fascinating aspect of closing and, as unlikely as it sounds, it really works. There is a saying in sales that says, 'He who speaks first, loses'. The silent close is based on this kind of psychology.

When the salesperson has made their final closing statement, they are taught to be silent immediately afterwards. If an uncomfortable silence follows, the salesperson must remain silent. The theory here is that whoever speaks first will 'lose', although the ideal for a sale is that everyone gets what they want.

There have been many documented cases of sales where agonising minutes have passed on the telephone before someone speaks, and it is at first not easy to hold your nerve in such situations. Should the meeting be face to face, the salesperson must continue to look straight at their customer, appearing neither too aggressive nor too passive.

Of course the silent close does not always work, but be aware that it exists and that it does have an effect. The next time you find yourself in negotiation and a silent close is used, you know the rules – do not be the one to speak first!

An agent might use a silent close on a contractor when asking what rate they would be prepared to accept. They will listen to your answer but remain silent afterwards, waiting to see if you crumble and offer a lower rate.

A contractor can use a silent close on an agent in a similar manner when asking what rate the client is prepared to pay. After the agent names a price, the contractor can remain silent, hoping that the agent will crumble and offer a higher rate.

Refractive close: This close is unethical, and you may have even come across it already. This is where the salesperson says, for example: 'Please buy the product, I have a family of eight and my boss will fire me if I don't make this sale.'

Of course, the salesperson's personal circumstances should have nothing to do with a sale and, if they are using this close, there is a good chance that there is no truth to the statement either. Be influenced by a balanced view of the product and your reasons for buying it; do not allow yourself to be manipulated in this fashion.

Within the contracting world it is uncommon to come across the refractive close. If you do, then be very cautious when dealing what that agency. Or avoid it altogether.

The closes described above are some of the most common and interesting ones used, but closing is an enormous aspect to sales and cannot be learnt over night. Often good salespeople close well purely because they have good presence and communicate confidently and in an effective way. Confidence is really what customers, and this includes agents and clients, want to see. When you buy from someone who looks nervous, you feel nervous about the sale.

But the opposite is also true. Try to be aware of what closing is and know when you are in a closing situation. This will prevent you as far as possible from being manipulated or tricked. For salespeople, closing is fun. After all, it really is all about asking for the business, which is, at heart, what business is all about!

10.3 Interviewing

The interview is the make or break part of the sales process. Sometimes it may just be a formality, but more often it is the part where you win the contract.

Chapter 5 provided an introduction to interview techniques together with some basic do's and don'ts. Now we'll move on to look at these in more detail.

10.3.1 Going to the interview

To reinforce the key points covered in chapter 5, there are some obvious things to remember about preparing for the interview:

- Dress properly
- Take an umbrella in case it rains
- Make sure you know where you are going and how to get there
- If you're driving, make sure you can park
- Make sure you have the names of the people you are to meet with. If possible, find out from the agency what their title is—Mr, Mrs, Ms, Dr
- Never be late for an interview. It is amazing how much executives hate lateness; it will probably cost you the contract. If you really must be late, call as soon as possible with a convincing excuse.

Your preparation will win or lose you the contract, so be thorough and professional about your research before the interview.

10.3.2 What the interviewer is looking for

When demand for contractors was outrageously high in the late 1990s contractors got snapped up quickly for simply having the buzzwords on their CV and being available, irrespective of their ability to perform at interview.

When the smoke cleared after the dot com crash the market was left with a large surplus of contractors. Good old fashioned commercial reality kicked in and the survival of the fittest contractors began. It still continues. So one crucial element to bear in mind when attempting to find a contract is this:

> *The contractor who wins the contract is the one who knows best how to win that contract, not necessarily the best contractor available for the role.*

To get the contract you first of all need to write a high impact CV that will get you put forward as a candidate – see chapter 4. You will then need to prepare for the interview and ensure you maximise your impact at the interview to ensure you get offered the role.

Good interview technique starts by asking the question 'What is the client looking for?' Look at the interview process from the point of view of the interviewer and use that to guide the approach to being interviewed:

The interviewer will be looking at the following aspects:

Likeability

- Do I like this person? Will they fit into the culture within our organisation?

- Will they avoid causing me trouble and making me look bad?

Specific skills

- Does this person have the relevant skills and experience for the role, or is their CV a work of fiction?
- Have they successfully completed a similar project for a company like ours?

Bonus skills and knowledge

- Do they have additional skills that would come in useful?
- Do they follow the industry and keep up with the latest advancements?

Initiative

- Is this person proactive, able to work alone and use their initiative?

Motivation

- Are they a happy and keen person or a lazy merchant of doom?

Communication skills

- Can they communicate with other human beings?
- Do they have the humility and confidence to ask questions if they don't understand something; or are they arrogant or shy enough to simply pretend that they understand perfectly?

Ability to listen and understand

- Can they listen respectfully and really understand issues, or do they jump in before people have finished to present solutions to what they assume is the issue?

Commercial awareness

- Are they commercially aware or have they no understanding of cost versus benefit and business goals?

Interest in company

- Do they know anything about our company or have they been interested enough to find out?

During the interview you need to address all the points listed above to give yourself the best chance of success. Basically, go through the list and tick all the boxes.

Based on the interviewer's motivation, your killer interview technique should:

- Demonstrate your appreciation of their problems and needs
- Demonstrate you have previous experience that is directly relevant to tackling those problems and needs
- Demonstrate you have extra skills that they might find useful
- Demonstrate that you are keen and motivated
- Leave out anything that is not directly relevant
- Demonstrate that you can fulfill all of their requirements.

This is not rocket science, but it is amazing how bad some people are at dealing effectively with all these points in interviews. Don't be one of them.

Chapter 5 discussed the need to prepare your list of questions tailored to the role based on the aspects the interviewer will be looking for and the entire preparation process up until the time you leave the interview room. Now we're going to cover how you should 'drive' the interview to ensure you are able to cover all the points the interviewer/s will be looking for.

If you get collected from reception by the interviewer then your interview has in fact already started before you've got into the interview room. By making casual conversation on the way you get the chance to tick the 'likeability' and 'Has interest in company' boxes.

There might be more than one person interviewing you and it may not be the decision maker who picks you up. Still, establish straight away if they are going to be in the interview room with you. If they are then start making conversation by asking them questions about themselves – 'how long have you been working here?' and 'what do you enjoy most about working here?'.

If you are led into the interview room by someone who is not going to interview you then still go through the motions of asking the questions. You never know. They might get asked their opinion of you.

Breaking down the interview: An ideal interview has four basic sections:

- Chat about company
- Discuss and understand needs
- Sell your solution
- Close.

You might think this looks like the sections of a sales meeting. That is because it is identical. The whole purpose of an interview is for you to sell yourself to the client. You are the product.

Chat about the company: They ask you about the company and you tell them what you know from the research you did in your preparation *[Tick – Has interest in company].*

They are impressed you know stuff, but tell you a bit more.

You listen, smile, nod your head, sound impressed and perhaps ask short questions. *[Tick – Likeability, ability to listen, has interest In company].*

Discuss and understand their needs: Driving point: You take control of the conversation and ask them what the business problem is they are attempting to solve, and how they envisage you helping them to solve it. *[Tick – commercial awareness].*

They will explain the business drivers, what the project is, and what they are hoping to achieve by bringing you in. Some might even ask you if that interests you. Whilst they do this you nod but don't interrupt, asking the odd short question to perhaps get clarification on some house jargon. *[Tick – Ability to listen and understand, good communication skills].*

You tell them it sounds exciting and interesting. You then summarise exactly what they have just said to show you can listen and understand a problem. You could then perhaps ask further questions about return on investment, expected timescales and so on. *[Tick – Good personal skills].*

Sell your solution: Driving point: Now for one of the most important parts of the interview: You then tell them what specific skills you have that will help them solve their problem, where you have used them before and the results that were achieved. You then summarise how you would tackle their problem. *[Tick – Specific skills, personal skills].*

If possible you then go on and explain how they could perhaps enhance their existing planned approach and use further skills and expertise that you have. Make sure you also mention that of course you would need to evaluate the timescales of doing so and justify the extra effort, since there is no point doing stuff just for the sake of it. *[Tick – Bonus skills, general skills, commercial awareness].*

After convincing them you are the person for the role you can go on to hammer it home by getting out your list of questions and asking them other questions that are more general to show that you have other areas of expertise. As an example, in IT you might ask about their project life cycle, testing approaches, methodologies, configuration management and so on. *[Tick – Bonus skills].*

Closing the interview: Driving point: The next thing is to say you have no further questions and state that you would be really interested in the role to show you
are keen.

Very important part – the close: Ask them 'Are you satisfied that I fulfill your requirements?' This gives them the chance to mention any areas they are unsure about, which you can then deal with to provide that reassurance. Leave nothing to chance here. You might not have covered all bases and there is no point missing the opportunity to deal with any nagging doubts they might have.

Finally, ask them when they are going to be making a decision. Unless you've had your eyes and ears shut the whole time you should be able to tell if they are considering hiring you.

In an ideal world you will work through each of the steps and secure the contract. However, sometimes everything does not go according to plan.

Poor driving: This means that the interview does not adhere to the format above because you failed to ask the correct questions at the right time and also steered away from some of their questions that were not on your ideal route.

Notice there are some key driving questions that lead you into each section of the interview. If you don't latch onto these then you risk veering all over the place.

Picking from the sweetie jar: This is where you fall into the trap of allowing the interviewer to say something like, 'Please talk us through the previous roles you have done', before you have even established their need.

You then end up describing what you have done with no understanding of what their requirements are or if anything you are covering is relevant. You are literally inviting them to have a look in the jar and take out anything they might find useful.

If they ask you that question then you can respond with: 'I'm happy to do that, but first I'd like to understand a little bit more about your requirements so that when I explain what I've done in the past I can discuss the stuff that is actually relevant and interesting for you.' You then get back to the second stage of establishing the need.

An equal trying to prove they are better than you: This is where there is someone else in the interview who is supposed to have the same skills as you and will try to test you. Sometimes they have no sense of commercial reality and might even consider you a threat to their superiority.

They can mislead you by taking you on wild journeys into detail for ages just to prove they are better than you. Don't fall for this. Have a little bit of a detailed discussion to prove your worth, but don't go on for ages. Flatter them and tell them how much you would enjoy working with someone like them then get back on track to selling yourself to the person who makes the main hiring decisions.

Timing: You might be doing great but if you don't get to do your whole pitch you won't get to sell yourself fully. Keep an eye on the clock and allow for a maximum of an hour. Ask how long they have for the interview when you arrive.

Failure to take into account the client's capability: You might be speaking to someone who is an expert in what you do, or they might not have a clue. However, there is bound to be a capability gap between yourself and the client, and you need to identify what that gap is.

If you are clearly more capable than the client you need to establish whether it would be risky to let your 'capability cat' out of the bag. They might feel threatened that you could make them look stupid.

More likely they will be impressed by your knowledge. In this instance the advice would be to perhaps pop out the cat's tail to test their feeling then bring out the rest of the cat and her kittens if it is appropriate. Basically you need to avoid not being hired because you are too good.

If they are more capable than you then just smile and say how impressed you are. But, don't say things like, 'Great, I'd like to learn xyz.' Mentioning how the contract will benefit you is of no interest to them and is a common BIG mistake during an interview.

You are the product. Sell yourself.

10.4 Negotiating

When negotiating, the key is to pitch to the decision maker, and that's the client. The golden rule in sales is: 'Always speak to the decision maker'. The agent has played an important part in bringing you and the client together, but they have little part to play in the decision making process once you and the client want to close the deal.

However, once the client has decided to hire you, the agent then becomes hugely important when it comes to negotiating rates. Remember, this is business: the agent will want to maximise their commission and minimise your payment. Accept this fact and deal with it to your best advantage.

10.4.1 Negotiating with the agent

Once you've 'secured' the contract at the interview, it's time to negotiate with the agent. Hopefully, you won't have committed yourself to any rate until that time. An agent will always ask you to name your rate in the hope that your demand will be lower than the market rate. That gives them the opportunity to charge the client the market rate (or above, if they can get away with it), pay you below the market rate (if they can get away with it) and 'pocket' the difference themselves.

Always try to avoid committing yourself to a given rate until you have to. If the agent asks you before you go for interview, just talk about accepting the market rate, and be as vague as you can. If the agent mentions a number, say something vague about that seeming to be the market rate and is therefore OK, but don't agree to anything.

Remember, at this stage you're in a weak position, and all you should be focusing on is getting the agent to put you forward to the client for possible interview.

But once the client has decided they want you for their contract, the game changes and you have the more powerful hand. It is now up to you to close the deal. This is business, so whatever you've said until now doesn't really matter, although if you've made the mistake of agreeing to a rate, you really should stick to it. But you're in a strong position: you've done the interview and you've either nailed the contract down, or you have a pretty good idea from the client's reaction that you will get it.

This means that the agent wants your signature on a contract. Now use your sales technique, and get really slow and deliberate about everything. Go over the contract, and make sure it has what you need in it. Check chapter 7 for the important clauses you want to include, and also those you want removed or altered.

Ask for a good high rate, and let the agent negotiate you down. The hard work will be on the agent's shoulders now. When you're close to closing, hold off. Pretend to reread something in the contract, and think the whole deal through once again. See if there is anything you think you could improve for yourself.

So, let's assume you've successfully achieved a decent rate and you're happy with the contract. At this point it is worth investing in getting an expert to review your contract, particularly from an IR35 perspective. No matter how experienced you consider yourself to be, and no matter how much IR35 knowledge you have, don't wing it – a small fee invested now could save you a fortune in the future.

Only after you've received the green light from the IR35 review should you verbally agree the contract, and then get your pen out and sign it.

If you are a first time contractor, then chances are that your sales and negotiation skills will be less developed. It takes time to learn how to do this. For that reason alone agents often enjoy securing contracts for first timers, since they can maximise their margins.

Don't worry if you fail the first time and the agent gets the upper hand. You certainly wouldn't be the first contractor this has happened to and it is all part of the learning process of going contracting.

10.4.2 Negotiating renewals

When you've completed your contract, you will often be asked by the client or the agent to sign on again for another period. This is called an extension or renewal.

From a legal point of view, you have no obligation to do this. And, importantly, you have no obligation to accept a given rate, or any specific conditions. You can seek to change everything in a renewal if you want to. Whilst the client or agent may refer to a contract extension, this is just the same as a renewal and so you have no reason to accept any conditions you do not wish to.

Been there, done that!

Renewal ransom or new contract?

Dave says: I started working for a client after the dot com crash, and the rate was at rock bottom – half what it used to be. After a year the market had picked up, rates were 35% higher, and the project was going great, so I figured that asking for an increase to market rate would be fine.

At renewal time the agent phoned me and said, 'Great news, they want to renew, but unfortunately there are no rate rises.' This was hardly surprising, considering the agent got paid pretty much the same regardless of my rate. So I started negotiating directly with the client, and basically said I wanted to stay, but expected to be paid market rate or I would leave. I had a few interviews lined up and was confident I'd get something. At the same time one of my fellow contractor colleagues was doing exactly the same thing – pay market rate or I walk.

Well, the client did some research and seemed to think we were asking for more than the market rate (which we weren't), and felt that both of us were holding them to ransom over the project, which was not yet completed. It was a messy business and we were both reluctantly given the rise to market rate, as they didn't want to delay the project. But the deal was that once what we were working on was released three months later, we had to leave. And that's exactly what happened.

Six months later we heard they had increased the rates of all their contractors to market rate, but the bridges were burnt. It seems that some clients are more than happy to cut your rate when the market drops. But they have issues raising your rate when the market picks up. Their view is that they're simply having to pay more for the same thing.

If you are going to insist on a rate rise and claim the market rate is higher than you're getting, you'll need to get some pretty strong evidence and start negotiating early to avoid the accusation of holding the project to ransom. But personal experience tells me that to get a higher rate when the market increases, the easiest way – and the one in which you won't harm your reputation or burn any bridges – is to simply move on to a new contract.

From a business point of view, you are in a much stronger position than you were when you first started out. The client knows you, and if you're wanted back you must have made a good impression.

A renewal can be a good thing for a number of reasons. It shows that you've done a good job and been seen as 'good to have around', so it looks good on your CV. It also means that you don't have to find another contract for a while and secures your income for another few months.

Furthermore, you can usually make your working conditions better when you renew, and you'll know the project and the client. All of these are advantages to renewals, but if you're not happy, don't feel obliged to renew. Just try to leave on good terms.

There are some key things to bear in mind when seeking or negotiating a contract renewal:

- **Blow your own trumpet – gently:** Discreetly remind the client of the value you've added to their business and what you can continue to offer
- **Judge the strength of your bargaining position if asking for a rise:** How keen is the client to keep you? Can they afford to lose you? Are you under-paid? Or over-paid if the market has dropped? Can the client afford to pay you more? Do you have other offers? What's the market demand for your skills?
- **Be realistic about agents:** Agents broker your services to clients and try to obtain the maximum margin they can. They earn significantly more focusing on new deals than renegotiating existing ones. They might not have your best interests at heart. The longer you've been with the client the more you can squeeze the agent's margin
- **Pitch to the decision maker:** The first thing professional salespeople learn is to pitch to the person who makes the decision and has the final say – the client

- **Appear indifferent to staying:** If you appear too keen to stay you will weaken your position
- **Timing:** Avoid getting into negotiations until four weeks before your current end date, otherwise you will not have a chance to line up alternatives
- **Avoid holding the client to ransom:** If your departure would damage the project then avoid holding the client to ransom by asking for a rise – "stick 'em up or the project gets it!". Burning bridges is not a good strategy – long term contractors get repeat business and referrals from previous clients
- **IR35:** If you are caught by IR35 then negotiating terms to place yourself outside IR35 will probably give you a better net return than negotiating a better rate. But remember, the project must be different; if it's more of the same, then IR35 will still apply
- **Don't continue without paperwork:** Don't continue working unless you have the contract terms agreed and the paperwork signed. There will be no legal recourse, and if you have a draft contract from the agent then they could argue that by executing the contract by starting it you have accepted the terms. This rarely happens, but is something you should be aware of
- **Renewal length:** When the market demand is high a renewal for six months ensures you'll get another bite at the cherry sooner rather than later. If demand is low then the longer the better (although bear in mind IR35 considerations, too, as you don't want to appear a 'disguised employee')
- **Do your sums:** Calculate the cost of downtime if you leave and have nothing else lined up – you might find the cost of sales and time without a contract is more than the rate rise you are pushing for
- **Don't burn bridges if you are leaving:** Ensuring a smooth departure will maintain a healthy client relationship. That's always advisable for providing good references and a source of future work. It will also help keep agents happy and, in most cases, they're the ones that help keep you in contracts.

Keep the client on side at all times, and the agent on side as much as possible, because the value of having positive referrals and testimonials could keep you in contracting for many years.

10.5 Evaluating your bargaining position

Maximising your return in negotiations is dependent on the strength of your bargaining position, and your sales skills.

The strongest bargaining position for you to have is, 'I have other options, so I will not renew unless you meet my demands.' This is a great position to be in, particularly if you already have another tempting offer elsewhere.

If you don't mind leaving the client and believe you can do better elsewhere, then try and line up an alternative contract. You can even hint to your existing client/agent that you are seeking alternatives. This tends to get things moving!

Seeking alternatives to strengthen your position is not unethical, and not disloyal to your existing client. It is simply business – playing the game and looking after your own interests.

If you are happy to stay at the existing client for the same money and terms, then avoid laying those cards on the table, otherwise you can consider yourself trumped. There is no point holding a begging bowl and entering into negotiations saying, 'I'll work for the same, but please give me more money!'

Understanding your bargaining position and negotiating a contract renewal is all about sales technique. You must know the strength of your position, play your strategy accordingly, and finally – above all else – ensure that you keep the client happy.

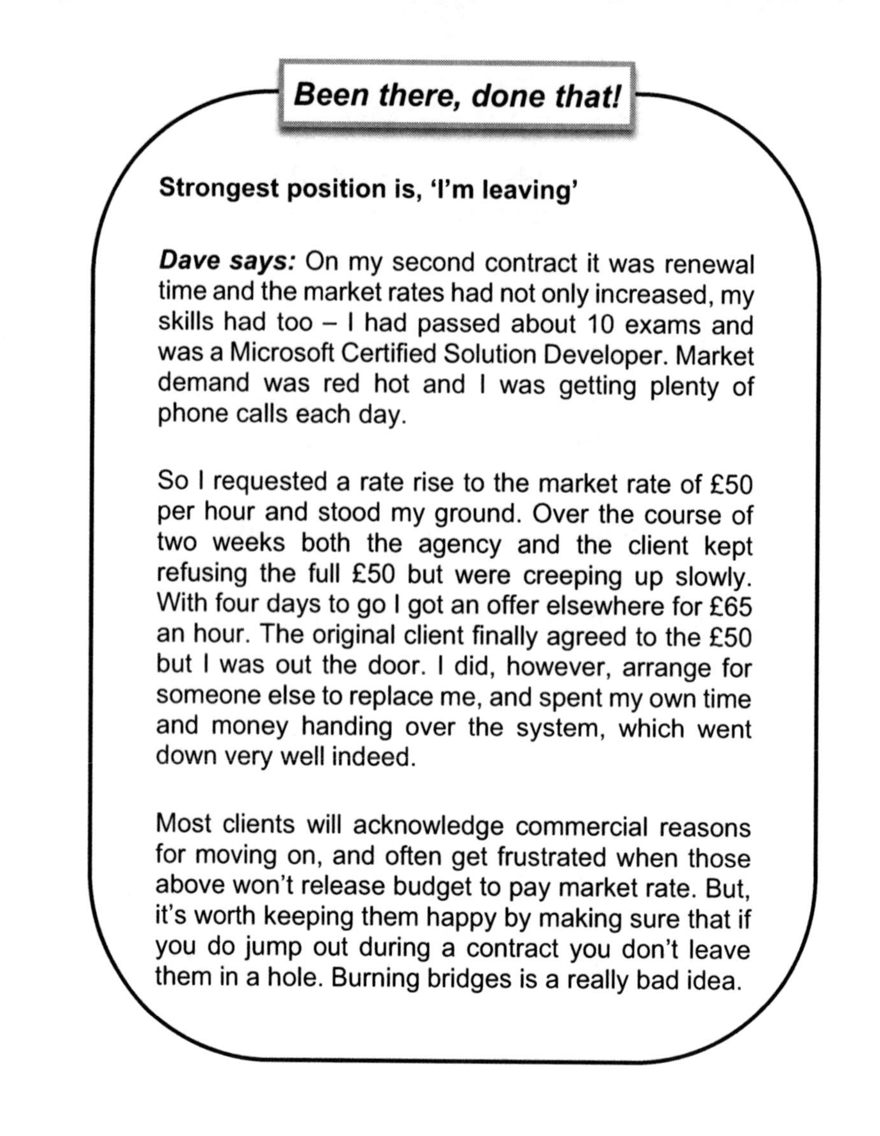

Two key strategies to improve your bargaining position are:

- **Line up alternative contracts:** Applying for other positions gives you a chance to research the market and line up an alternative contract, which enormously strengthens your position during negotiations – 'pay me the market rate or I'll go elsewhere to get it!'
- **Buffer of money:** It is always useful to have a buffer of six months money in the business bank account in case of surprises or future periods without a contract.

Then you need to consider the state of the market and your skills:

- **If the market has dropped** since your last renewal, or contract, then a rate rise is highly unlikely. After the dot com bubble burst and during the economic crisis that began in 2008, contractors found themselves negotiating rate decreases. If you are being paid over the current market rate, then your best strategy is to keep quiet and hope that you can renew at the same rate.
- **If the market has risen**, then the fact that you can earn more money elsewhere is a strong bargaining point and should be stressed. If the client is sensible they are unlikely to want to incur the cost of replacing you with someone who will, anyway, demand the same increased rate.
- **If the market is unchanged and you have not improved your skill set,** then the only justification for a rate rise would be the cost of replacing you. Taking this approach is not recommended at all – you should always seek to keep your clients happy and earn yourself good references.
- **If the market is unchanged but your skills have increased** and are worth more in the market, then you have good reason to request a higher rate. Tread carefully though, because from a perception standpoint clients are unlikely to agree with this. In this scenario, to get a higher rate might mean moving on.

The timing of your renewals also has a major influence over the strength of your bargaining position. Normally the contract renewal process is not started until one month before your current contract end date. If clients anticipate a risk that a contractor might not renew, resulting in a project schedule being affected, they might try to get a contractor to consider an early contract renewal.

If you have not heard from either the agent or the client at the start of that four week window then you should start the process yourself by asking both the client and agent if they are interested in offering you another contract.

If the client is slow to respond, start making hints that you are leaving. If the client is not planning to renew your contract, they do not usually tell you, so you will know the situation from the negative response after chasing them.

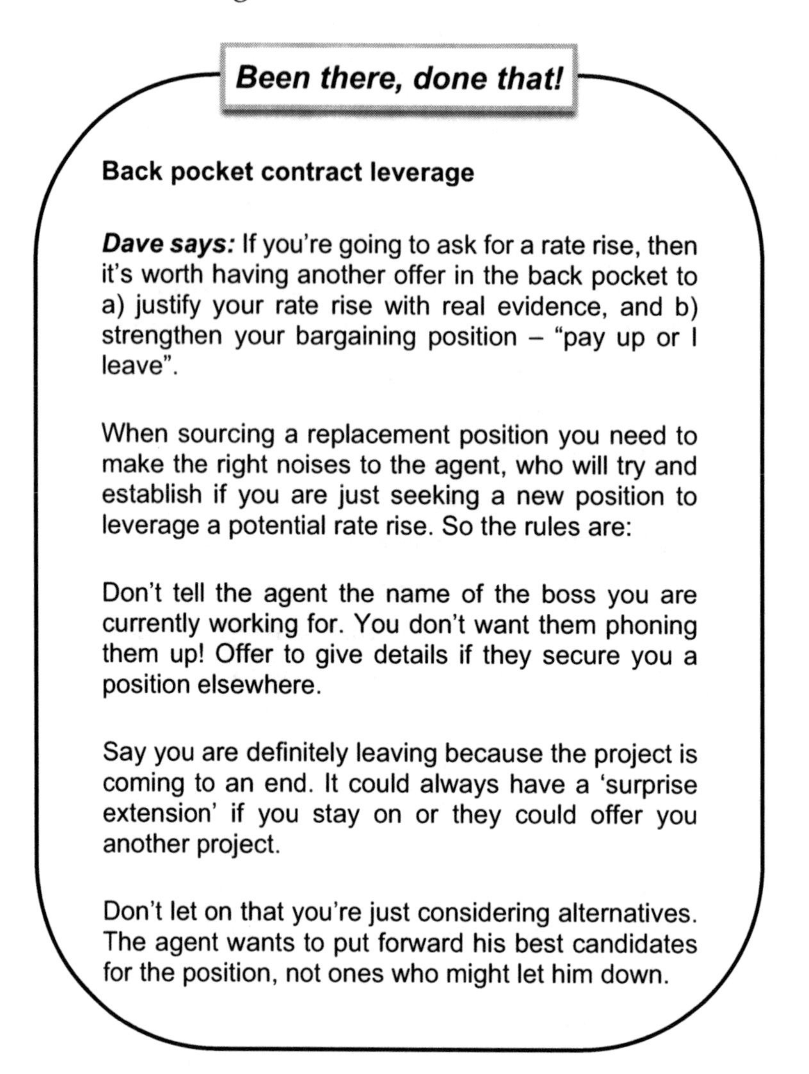

10.6 Seasonal factors

Like the best farmers, the best contractors know when to sow, when to reap, and when to stay indoors. The contract market has its own rhythms. A farmer knows when to plant and when to harvest. A contractor should know when to be looking for work and when to be safely in a long-term contract.

The contract market has *seasons*. Just as we know when winter is coming, contractors need to know when the market is slowing down. If you're reaching the end of a six-month contract, and your CV isn't generating the buzz it did before, you should focus on getting an extension rather than risk being left out in the cold.

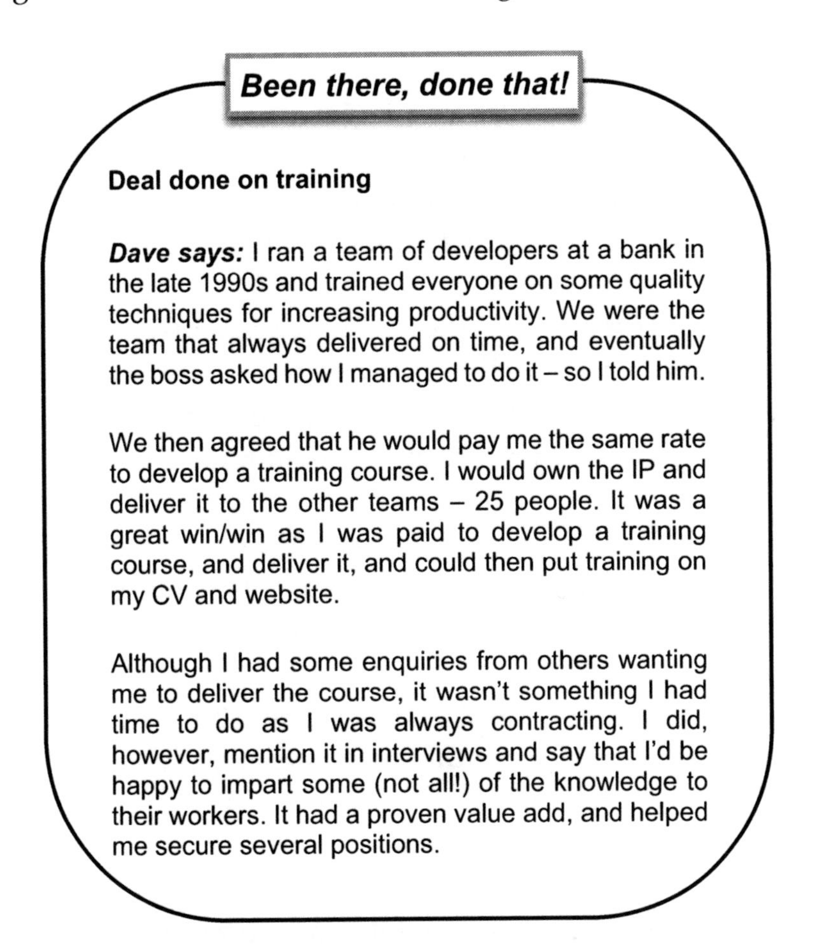

Been there, done that!

Deal done on training

Dave says: I ran a team of developers at a bank in the late 1990s and trained everyone on some quality techniques for increasing productivity. We were the team that always delivered on time, and eventually the boss asked how I managed to do it – so I told him.

We then agreed that he would pay me the same rate to develop a training course. I would own the IP and deliver it to the other teams – 25 people. It was a great win/win as I was paid to develop a training course, and deliver it, and could then put training on my CV and website.

Although I had some enquiries from others wanting me to deliver the course, it wasn't something I had time to do as I was always contracting. I did, however, mention it in interviews and say that I'd be happy to impart some (not all!) of the knowledge to their workers. It had a proven value add, and helped me secure several positions.

If you're reaching the end of your contract, and you're getting lots of attention from agents, then you can probably get more money somewhere else. It's worth putting out the feelers every now and again to see what the market temperature is. It's not because you want to finish your contract early. You just want to know what the weather's like outside.

The most successful contractors have a market barometer. They keep one eye on what's going on out there. By doing this, they build a picture of the seasons and rhythms of the contract market. With the wealth of online resources available to contractors, it is not difficult to keep abreast of developments and the personal networks of friends and colleagues can provide excellent 'human intelligence'.

Contracting seasons

Your own research will let you know what the 'weather' is like where you are. The range of sectors, clients and skills covered by contracting is so vast that it is impossible to give hard and fast rules; however, for many sectors, the seasonal pattern tends to be:

Spring – after winter, the market starts to warm up and flower buds begin to appear. Listen for the first cuckoos – your phone will ring just that little bit more often, and the rates on offer will be just that little bit higher. Keep your feelers out, as summer is on the way.

Summer – your skills are in demand and rates are looking better. This is the time to start a new contract, as for clients and agents it's all about finding the right people at this point.

Autumn – traditionally, this is harvest time. This is the best time to renegotiate. The highest contract rates are usually paid to people who've proven their worth. If your client sees you as too valuable to lose, you're in a strong negotiating position.

Winter – the best place to be in winter is indoors in the warm. Even if you're not 100% happy with your current contract, the weather outside can be far harsher. Hunker down and sit it out until spring comes round again.

Contracting Cycles

The contract market has short-term and long-term cycles. It also has two annual cycles, driven by the financial year and holiday seasons:

- **Jan/Feb** – after the Christmas holidays, clients start to galvanise into action. New budgets are approved and hiring starts. This is the equivalent of spring
- **Mar/Apr** – this is the equivalent of summer. Arguably the best time to look for a new contract
- **May/June** – time to bring in the autumn harvest. If you can secure a three-month contract in March, you'll be in a strong negotiating position in June
- **July/August** – Holidays break the rhythm of the market in what is effectively contracting winter, and hiring becomes a low priority. If you're not in a contract by the end of June, you could end up without a contract until September
- **September** –After the summer holidays, kids return to school and the HR department awakens from its slumber; it's contracting spring again
- **October/November** – another summer brings better paid contracts, making this a very good time to be on the market
- **December** – autumn and winter come around quickly. Many projects are scheduled to deliver in the week before Christmas, which means this is the perfect time to renegotiate. By December 24th, the market goes dead until the New Year, when contracting spring begins again.

There is a longer cycle that can last up to a decade. The demand for contractors can mirror the growth – or lack of it – of the economy very closely, as contractors are the easiest people to hire, and the easiest to get rid of when times are hard. You're probably best off watching the growth of the financial markets, and looking out for a plateau, the edge of the bubble after which it's likely to burst.

As the market nears a plateau, start making plans to become less easily expendable. This might be a good time to go permanent, or to start looking at secondary sources of income.

As things start to warm up again, you want to be in a position to take advantage. If you're in a job that requires six months notice to quit, getting back into contracting might be difficult.

So always aim to be in the best position for any of the short, medium or long term contracting cycles, and you'll always be maximising the amount you can earn. Even when the economy is at its lowest ebb, there is always a demand for contractors, so use the lessons in this book to make sure you're always ahead of the pack.

11.

Managing holidays and absence

11.1 Taking time away from contracts

It is inevitable that at some point in your contracting career you will want to take some time away from a contract. There are any number of reasons to take time away, and specifics such has holiday, sickness and appointments are dealt with separately.

However, whatever the reason for taking time off, the process of arranging the time off with the client is going to be similar. Assuming your contract is outside of IR35 and you work through your own limited company, it very important to ensure that at no time you allow yourself to be under the control of the client.

Firstly, you must never ask a client for time away. This is a fundamental point, because by asking the client for time away you are implying that the client can say 'no', that they therefore have control over you, and that your 'outside' IR35 status is on very shaky ground.

However, you must agree in some fashion with the client that you need to take time off; for example, it could be that the project you are working on is at a crucial stage and you are needed to work for the next month without a break.

It is also a question of professional courtesy. How often have we all sat at home, having taken time off work to wait for a tradesman, only to have them not turn up?

You need, in as diplomatic way as possible, to 'tell' your client that you are taking time off. The way to handle this is by using an alternative close:

"I'm going to take half a day off next week to attend a medical appointment. Is Tuesday or Thursday better for you?"

You have quite clearly demonstrated that you are taking the time off, and the client is not in a position to object. However, you stroke the client's ego and extend basic professional courtesy by choosing to accommodate the client's requirements.

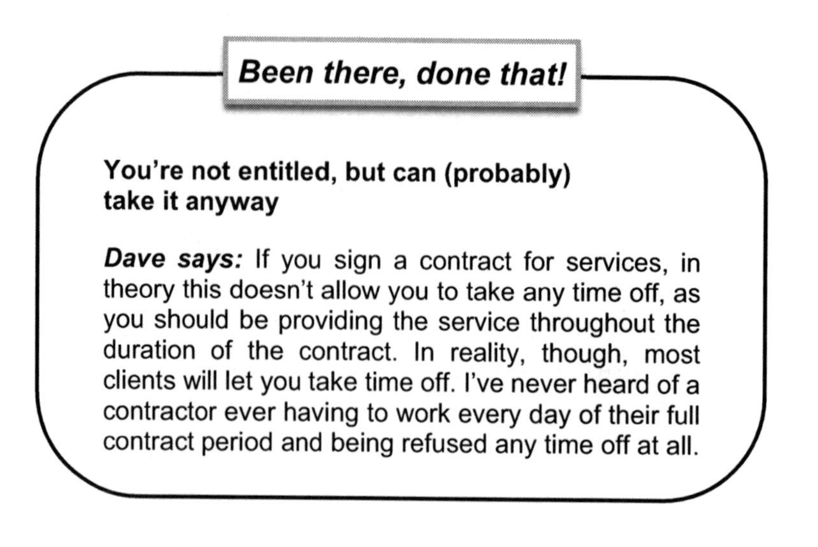

If your contract is inside IR35, then is it less important to keep to the process of not 'asking' or 'requesting' time off, and you should judge your approach according to the relationship you have with the client.

As a contractor working through an umbrella company, you will need to inform both your client and your umbrella that you are planning to take time off, as many umbrella companies hold back a portion of your pay in anticipation of holidays and sickness.

You need to check with your umbrella company for the specifics of their scheme, or if choosing your umbrella company for the first time make sure you add sickness and holiday pay to the list of questions to ask when doing your research.

11.2 Occasional absence – doctors and dentists

As long as you give your client plenty of notice and try to work around the project schedules and deliverables, then taking time off for medical and dental appointments is rarely a problem.

Remember, of course, to account for the time off on your timesheet as you will not get paid for and should not claim for any time you spend not working on your client's contract. Indeed, trying to negotiate pay for medical and dental appointments could make it look to a tax investigator as if you were acting as a 'disguised employee'.

It is best not to make a habit of taking too much time off as the client may get concerned that your frequent absences will impact on the project's timescales. Of course if you are unwell that cannot be helped, but as a contractor you have no employment rights and, technically, as your limited company is delivering a contract of services, if a client wanted to be awkward they could claim a breach of contract for your absence.

That is why it is important to have the client on-side and to arrange such appointments at the beginning or the end of the day to minimise the time you are not working on the client's project.

Alternatively, if you have arrangements with the client to spend time working on a contract in your own office, which may be at your home, then try to schedule appointments on those days.

It is still important to ensure your time sheet accurately reflects the time you have spent; if you lost a half day for a hospital appointment some distance away, don't try and charge the client for any of the time you were away, even though you are working from home. Of course it's not just doctors and dentists you may need to see on occasion. You could also need to have optician appointments or sessions with a physiotherapist, chiropractor or other medical practitioner.

The same principle applies – give the client plenty of warning as a courtesy and ensure your absence will not affect the project timescales or clash with a crucial project team meeting you should attend.

11.3 Holidays

As a contractor, you may take holidays, but you should never use your client's holiday booking forms or systems; to do so could be taken as evidence that you are a 'disguised employee'.

It is generally best, from both your and the client's point of view, to plan time off to take place during a future contract, during the contract renewal period, or before you start a new one.

Having said that, as a contractor working through your own limited company, you have the flexibility to take odd days off for holidays during the term of a contract. Naturally, though, such holidays mustn't adversely affect your work or the delivery of that contract. It is very rare that you will be required to work every day during the contract period, unless the contract length is less than one month.

If you take time off during a contract then it is very unlikely you will be allowed to take more than two weeks off at a time. If there are quiet periods during your contract then most clients will let you take ad-hoc days off at very short notice. This saves them money and does not affect project deadlines. But if you wish to take long periods away from contracting, one month or more, then this really is best done between contracts.

You are not limited to a certain number of days per year, because your time off is not paid by the client. You can take as many days off as you want, provided the client agrees that you do not need to provide your services during that time.

Taking holidays in no way changes the length of your contract. Contracts have a fixed start and end date. If the client wishes you to extend your contract for a few weeks, to cover for potential holiday taken, then you would need to sign a contract renewal. This is extremely rare though.

There are no set rules for how to book holidays when you are a contractor, although the key is to ensure you keep your client happy. Guidelines for dealing with existing clients include:

- If you want time off during your existing contract, or an agreed renewal, then simply inform your project manager that you are taking a break
- If you strongly suspect you will be offered a renewal which you will accept, then again speak to your project manager
- If you do not think you will be offered a renewal, or don't want to renew then go ahead and book your holiday – you are the boss!
- But to stay outside IR35, you must avoid acting like an employee – so never use any of your client's holiday booking procedures and do not allow yourself to be controlled by the client.

When you are looking for a new contract you might have holiday already booked, which you would need to take during that contract. Best practice includes:

- Don't plan on any holidays for more than a week within the first month of a new contract. This could affect your chances of securing the contract
- Wait until you have received an offer before you mention that you have holiday booked. Having holidays booked might not get you chosen for interview by the agent and you will fall at the first hurdle
- After receiving a contract offer, if you have holidays booked then check with the client that you can take time off before signing the contract.

If you wish to take time off for more than three weeks then this will probably need to be done between contracts. Bear in mind that on your return from holiday it could take between one week and a month to secure a new contract.

For this reason, if your planned holiday is less than three weeks it is better to plan it during an existing contract, so that you have something to come back to immediately.

If you did take holiday at the end of one contract you could attempt to line up a new contract ready for your return. However, most clients hire contractors on very short notice, usually less than one month, and the process can take a couple of weeks.

11.4 Sickness

If you develop a medical condition that means you are unlikely to make it into work with your client, then ensure you inform your project manager immediately. Most clients will be sympathetic for a few days absence but with any condition that requires you to take weeks off, you could be in danger of being in breach of contract.

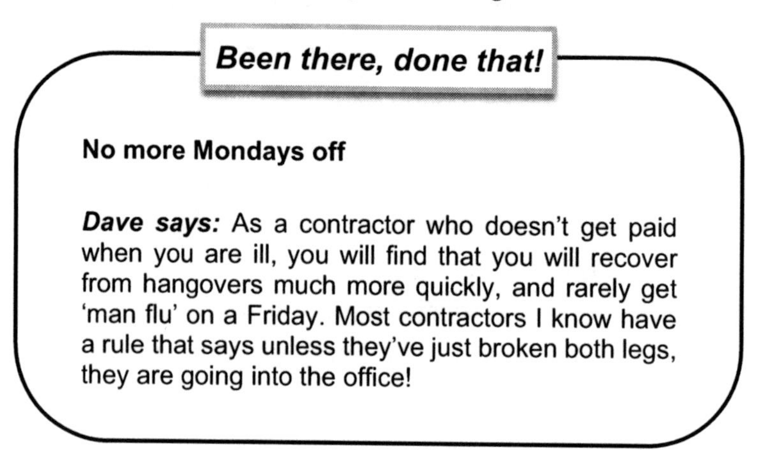

It may be that you can exercise your substitution clause and find a replacement, but in many cases this might not be practical. However, to protect your status as outside IR35 it is good practice to have a pool of colleagues who could step into a position if your condition means you need to take more than a few days off. Naturally, you would have to cover the costs of any training and for their time spent working for you on your client's project.

Some contractors invest in a private health insurance policy, so that they have a little more control over their access to medical treatment. If you have a condition that is likely to result in a procedure that will require time off to recuperate, private health insurance will make it easier to plan your health needs around your contracting, or vice versa!

Should you require ongoing treatment, it might be possible to negotiate a reduced schedule with your client, for example only working four days a week for a period. As long as this will not impact on the deliverables of your contract, most clients will be amenable. After all, they don't pay you when you don't work.

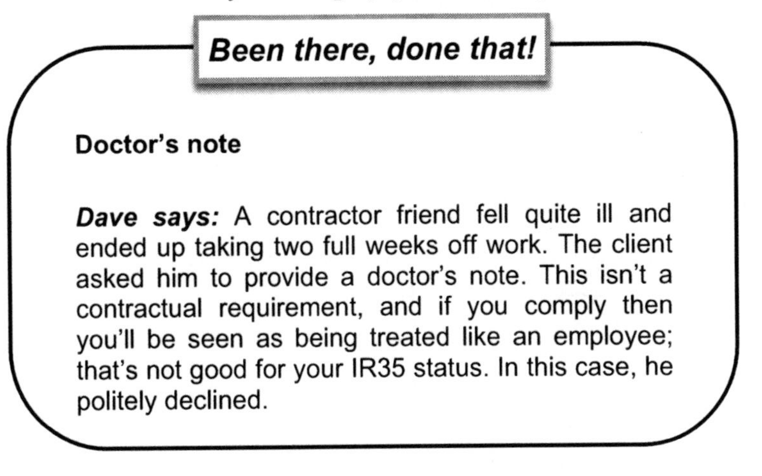

Been there, done that!

Doctor's note

Dave says: A contractor friend fell quite ill and ended up taking two full weeks off work. The client asked him to provide a doctor's note. This isn't a contractual requirement, and if you comply then you'll be seen as being treated like an employee; that's not good for your IR35 status. In this case, he politely declined.

Under no circumstances should you imply that you should receive sick pay from your client, as this indicates you might be a disguised employee. If you are signed off by your doctor as unable to work, you may be eligible for statutory sick pay but the sums involved are so small it is almost not worth the hassle. And you should not provide your client with a copy of your sick note as this implies you have an employee-employer relationship, which spells doom for your 'outside IR35' status.

If you are involved in an accident that was not your fault, then explore what options you may have for claiming loss of earnings from the party responsible for the accident.

In addition to private health insurance, you can also take out policies that may provide you with income protection. Chapter 12 covers insurances in more detail.

11.5 Long term absence

Should you have a medical condition that means you will be unable to work for a year or more, it may be a good option to make your limited company dormant, a process described in chapter 6. Similarly, you need to inform your umbrella company (if you are using one as your trading vehicle), as you may have been paying into a scheme to provide you with some pay during extended periods of illness.

If you make your limited company dormant during a long spell of illness, you can always reactivate it at very short notice when you are ready to start work again. If you have dissolved the company you have to go through the time and expense of setting up a new business all over again.

Making your company dormant is a last resort as it precludes you from earning any fees through your limited company. But the costs and time associated with keeping the company running may not suit your circumstances, and of course you may not be well enough to manage your limited company effectively.

Although not a topic many people would want to discuss before it happens, if you are seriously ill you should also make allowances for the fact that you may never return to work. This is where an income protection policy and private health insurance may justify the premiums you pay when you are well. Peace of mind comes at a cost, but it could be worth the investment, particularly if you have dependants.

Another worst case scenario is that if you do not have a termination clause, you may have to provide a substitute to take over from you.

If the client insists, then this includes training them and paying them from your contract fee.

The client is certainly within their rights to insist you provide a substitute if they want to; and if you don't comply they could sue you for breach of contract. If you are inside IR35, or working for an umbrella company, then you don't have to worry.

11.6 Compassionate leave

As a contractor, you are not entitled to paid leave of any kind. If the worst happens and you experience, for example, a close personal loss, then the same rules apply as for sickness – you don't get paid for time off.

Most clients will be very understanding and pleased to allow you a day away from their project for you to attend a funeral. However, to cope with longer periods of grief you may have to tough it out at work as you won't get paid and the client will be concerned about project deliverables.

It's difficult, but try and minimise the amount of time taken off for compassionate reasons in the same way as sickness. Clients will be understanding about a day or so, but any longer and they will start asking questions that might lead to you being found in breach of contract.

11.7 Financial planning for time off

Many contractors work out the cost of their holidays by calculating the cost of the money they won't be earning if they go away. This is a scary route to go down, which could stop you from ever enjoying a holiday or taking the rest you need for the good of your health!

To plan accordingly, so you have money set aside for when you take time off, consider the following:

- There are eight public holidays in each year
- You will probably take fewer days off sick than when you were a permanent employee and received sick pay
- You'll want to take the same, or more, holidays than your entitlement when you were a permanent employee
- If you play your cards right you should have few or no gaps between contracts.

With the above in mind, you should typically plan to be earning for 44 weeks in the year.

It is therefore prudent to estimate your annual revenue for 44 weeks paid contract work and then pay yourself a monthly amount that takes that into account. Don't forget to allow for savings for personal taxation. Your accountant or umbrella company will be able to advise on an exact amount to take each month.

If you are planning on taking an extended absence (say a whole year off) then try and cut back on the money you draw from your company the year before, whilst you are working, and spread the income over the time off as well – this will ensure you minimise the tax you pay.

Unfortunately, if you are using an umbrella you won't have this luxury as you are paid regularly by PAYE according to when you submit your timesheets.

12.

Personal finance for contractors

12.1 Why contractors are different

Contractors inhabit a space where they are not employed, yet they are not self-employed. For this reason, because they don't have the advantages that permanent employees enjoy, when seeking a mortgage, handling pensions, or considering how to make investments, contractors are different.

Because you are different, you must ensure you take proper advice from a qualified financial expert before making any decisions. The following chapter is only to be used as a general guide and is not to provide a substitute for professional advice.

Permanent employees rarely have a problem obtaining mortgages. They walk into a high street mortgage lender, show their pay slips and they are offered a mortgage based on the lender's standard, current criteria.

Contractors don't get the same reception, even when they may be earning several multiples more than the permanent employee. When a contractor goes to a high street mortgage lender and tells them that they run their own business, they typically get demands to see accounts for the past three years, and then all sorts of references get taken, and calculations get made, following which they are still unlikely to be offered a reasonable mortgage.

The whole process can be made worse because accountants, quite rightly in most cases, will advise contractors to maximise costs in the business and minimise profits. In this way the contractor's company is as tax efficient as possible and the contractor's net pay is maximised, usually because they take a fairly low salary and make up their earnings through dividends. This does not impress the banks and mortgage lenders, though, who like to see consistent healthy profits. This chapter will explain ways around what can sometimes seem like a 'Catch-22'.

Sometimes things work in favour of contractors, though, and not against them. For example, one of the pre-tax costs to a business can be payments into a contractor's pension fund – if the business invests in the contractor's pension, it can reduce tax to be paid and prepare the contractor for a flexible, early and comfortable retirement.

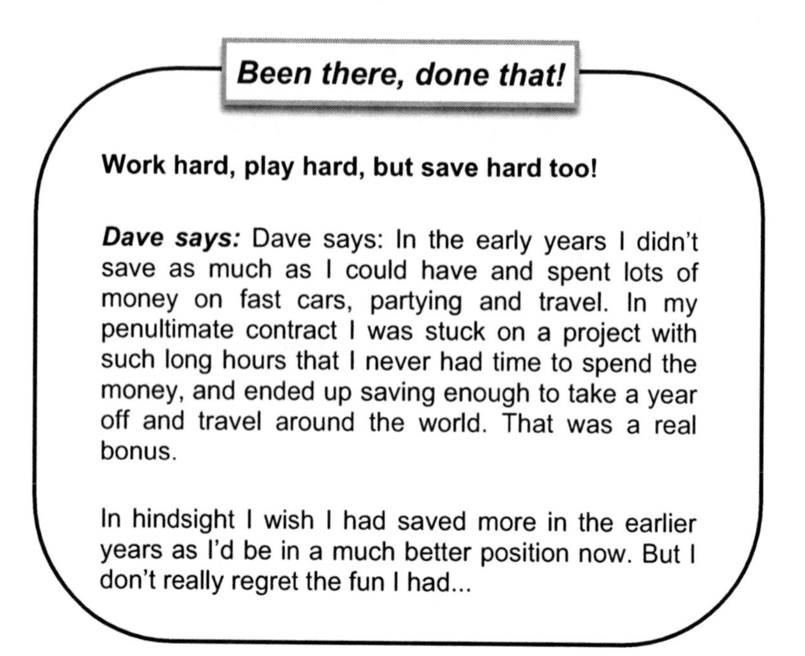

There are also financial services suppliers who have developed products specifically for contractors, for example by using multiples of the contractor's typical rate to calculate their borrowing limit. It is likely that these types of suppliers will increase as the benefits of lending to relatively solid, higher-income customers like contractors become apparent.

12.2 Mortgages

The problem for the High Street banks is that they lack the experience in understanding contractors. A typical contractor in IT, for example, earns close to £100,000 per year at the time of writing, so you would expect banks to be eager to do business with them.

But the lenders see only that it's not a 'regular salary' as they define them. Of course, job security even for permanent employees has declined to a point where many actually have less security than contractors, but the lenders do not yet acknowledge this.

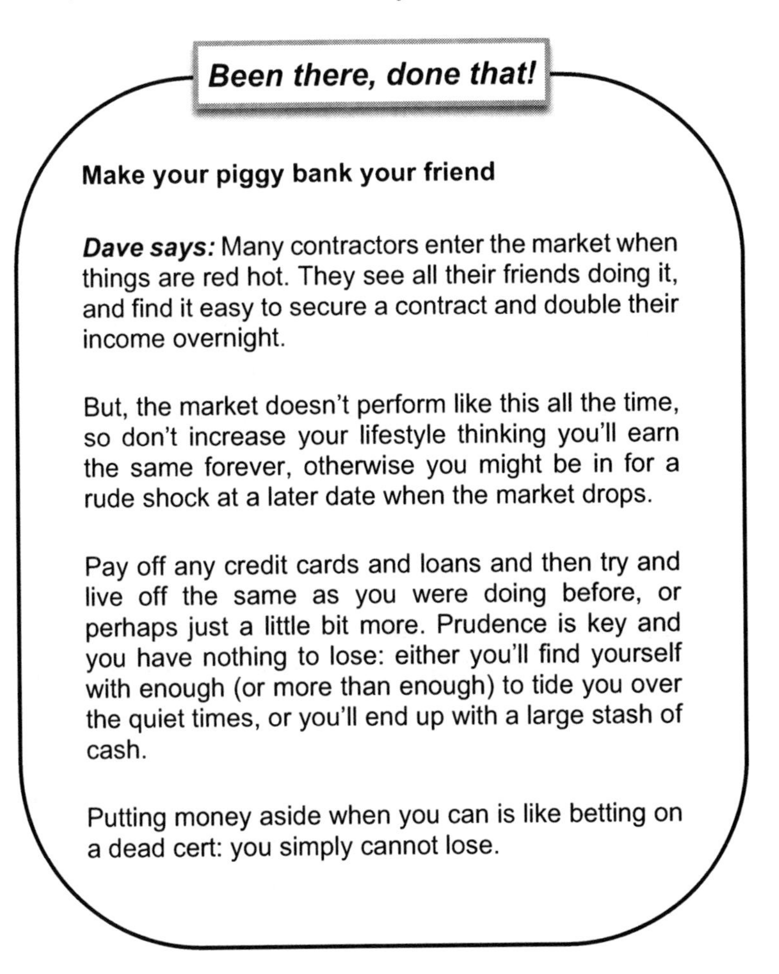

Been there, done that!

Make your piggy bank your friend

Dave says: Many contractors enter the market when things are red hot. They see all their friends doing it, and find it easy to secure a contract and double their income overnight.

But, the market doesn't perform like this all the time, so don't increase your lifestyle thinking you'll earn the same forever, otherwise you might be in for a rude shock at a later date when the market drops.

Pay off any credit cards and loans and then try and live off the same as you were doing before, or perhaps just a little bit more. Prudence is key and you have nothing to lose: either you'll find yourself with enough (or more than enough) to tide you over the quiet times, or you'll end up with a large stash of cash.

Putting money aside when you can is like betting on a dead cert: you simply cannot lose.

Fortunately, the contracting sector is so strong that it has made the financial services industry recognise its profitability and adapt to serve it. There are now specialised brokers who work with contractors, and they are well equipped to handle contractors' mortgage requirements. They are used to working with the lenders and to filling in the gap between permanent employees and contractors for them.

Independent mortgage brokers, who are usually qualified and regulated Independent Financial Advisers, know from experience what questions the lenders will want answered, and they have the contacts among lenders to present your mortgage request.

Brokers can also deal directly with the personnel at the lenders who actually make decisions about mortgages; these are the key underwriters within the lenders' centralised processing units. This avoids the involvement of high street branch employees, who are unlikely to have the right blend of knowledge and experience.

The broker will help you compile documentation to show that you have regular income and that you have contracts ongoing at a solid rate of pay. Obviously your personal credit rating, and your background have importance as well; but a good broker can even help you overcome obstacles like a poor credit rating.

The one thing you must be able to demonstrate is a good hourly rate of pay, as it appears in your actual contracts. This works as a kind of substitute for the pay slips that the permanent employee would be asked to present.

A good broker can also avoid schemes that have extended loyalty clauses and hefty associated fees, such as higher lending charges. And they can often obtain competitive rates, with smaller deposits required.

12.3 Pensions

Often the same IFA who helped with your mortgage can also advise on your pension.

Why should you set up a pension? Well, apart from the importance of providing for your future, it is one of the most tax efficient ways of saving money. It makes no difference whether you are inside or outside IR35; either way, you can put money into the pension fund and see it start collecting interest, and you won't pay tax on it.

At the time of writing, the amount of tax relief can be as much as 48%, meaning that for each £100 invested you only pay £52, while the taxman pays the rest.

Money invested in a pension fund can come from your limited company or umbrella company as long as you have put a pension fund in place. Umbrella companies are flexible in how they can continue to pay into any existing funds you have.

The only limit is that the funds be somehow related to trade, i.e. your contracting earnings through your limited company or umbrella company, and that they do not exceed your gross revenues. There is a limit on contributions but it is high; at the time of writing £235,000 per year.

Many contractors are concerned that if they set up pension funds for their contracting business, they won't be able to access them if they go back to permanent employment. But by choosing the appropriate provider, one that permits the appropriate flexibility, you can resolve this issue. The pension fund you set up should be something that you can contribute to for your entire life irrespective of whether you're contracting, not working, or working for a permanent employer.

It is also important to avoid companies that levy initial set up costs or have high charges. This ensures that the maximum amount of your contribution goes into your pension. This is crucial given the fact that your employment status may mean that you do not fund the scheme continuously for the rest of your life. In this way, even funding for a relatively short term makes sense as you have not burdened your investment with upfront fees and charges.

Any pension also needs to be flexible enough to reflect the fact that as a contractor your employment status is inherently changeable and you must have complete freedom to increase, decrease, suspend, restart and cease contributions completely, and on month-by-month basis if necessary. Any pension must be versatile enough to allow contributions regardless of whether you continue to work through a limited or umbrella company, are between contracts or a permanent employee.

The scheme must also be with a financial institution that has the financial strength and backing to remain the steward of your fund for the long term. Whilst previous performance is not an indication of future growth, you are likely to be better off with a provider that has a long track record and solid financial strength.

The variety of pension fund structures is a complex topic best left to the experts; you should contact a well-recommended Independent Financial Adviser to discuss all the best possibilities. Of course you will probably be better served by an Independent Financial Adviser who works regularly with contractors and understands the characteristics of the contracting market.

12.3.1 Pensions for limited company contractors

The deregulation of the pension market in April 2006 has resulted in considerably more flexibility for contractors working through their own limited companies. The major difference is that there is no limit on the contributions you can make from your limited company.

However, it is safer if the amounts you plough into a pension are not larger than your company's income for the year of the contribution, otherwise there might be questions from HMRC about whether the money was actually sourced from your trading activities.

Your limited company can contribute 'pre-taxed' company income to a pension. If you are a higher rate tax payer, instead of declaring the income as company profit and taking the income as a dividend, you can put the same sum straight into a pension.

For example, you have £100 worth of company income, and you are a higher rate tax payer, not caught by IR35. You can either put the £100 into a pension, or you can declare it as profit and take it as a dividend.

But if you choose the latter option and take a dividend payment, you pay:

- £21 in corporate tax on your £100, leaving £79
- 22.5% personal income tax on the dividend, which takes another £17.78
- Your total net take home is £61.

Choosing to invest in a pension, on the other hand, means that the whole £100 goes into your pension fund and then has an opportunity to grow in a tax efficient environment. £25 of your contribution represents the part of the pension fund that you can draw tax free when you retire. A further £36 of your money goes into the pension fund, together with the £39 that would have gone to the taxman (quite a decent initial 'return' on your £36). This £75 can also grow and be used to skim off an income at a later date, or buy an annuity.

12.3.2 Pensions for umbrella company contractors

If you are using a contractor umbrella company to manage your contracting income, you can get very significant tax advantages through pensions while at the same time building up a fund which you can start withdrawing from starting at age 50 (55 for younger investors). The principle is similar to a limited company but with key differences.

Provided your umbrella company has a pension scheme in place you can use 'salary sacrifice' to contribute 'pre-taxed' income to a pension. Most umbrella companies do have a scheme in place, and this should be one of your questions to any prospective umbrella company. So, instead of paying employers NI, employees NI and Income Tax you can put the whole sum straight into your pension.

For example, you have £100 worth of income, and you are a higher rate tax payer. You can either put the £100 into a pension, or you can take it as salary via your umbrella company.

But if you choose the latter option and take a salary, you pay:
£12 employers and employees NI, leaving £88.

A further £36 is paid as higher rate PAYE tax (Income Tax).

Your total take home is £52.

Choosing the pensions option means that the whole £100 goes into a pension fund and then has the opportunity to grow in a tax efficient environment. In reality £25 of your contribution represents the part of the pension fund which you can then draw out tax free when you retire. £27 of your own money also goes into the pension fund, together with the £48 that would have gone to the taxman (quite a decent initial 'return' on your £27). This £75 can also grow and be used to skim off an income at a later date, or buy an annuity.

12.3.3 Pensions for contractors caught by IR35

There are fewer financial benefits to contracting if you are caught by IR35. However, even if you are within IR35 your gross income can be invested into a pension scheme, before taxes are applied.

For someone caught by IR35 earning £40 an hour, each £100 drawn as gross salary (at the top end of their earnings) attracts £48 tax with only £52 ending up in their pocket.

Instead of drawing it as salary the whole £100 could be contributed to a pension. This reduces net income by £52, but increases a pension by almost double. This means contributions attract 'tax relief' of 48%.

12.3.4 How you can use your fund as you approach retirement

You don't have to buy an annuity until you reach the age of 75. Before that time you can skim a certain amount from your pension as income. Most annuities only pay around a 5% return, but remember you've only invested £36 yourself and with the £39 from the taxman it is paying off as £75. So even with the choice of an annuity your overall return is much higher because of the initial tax savings.

In the event that you die before you retire, if you've not taken an annuity, the whole of your fund can be passed on as an inheritance, completely tax free.

12.4 Savings

There are, of course, many sorts of investments a contractor may make apart from pension funds. On this topic, one thing should be made clear from the start: you can generally invest through your limited company in anything (legal!) you want to.

You will hear, from time to time, that the small companies run by contractors should not be used as investment vehicles. This is entirely false. If you want to spreadbet your revenues, if you want to invest in stocks listed only on the Baghdad stock exchange, then go right ahead... at your own risk, of course.

However, if you are contracting through an umbrella company, you are limited in what options you have to save because you take your income as pre-taxed.

12.4.1 Property

Contractors often find that they have to travel to a distant site on a regular basis for work. If this travel is prolonged, you may decide that it's easier to buy a place, through your company, to live near the site and to stay there during the working week.

You can do this and still retain your right to deduct travel and living expenses to the site for the first 24 months of work (until you 'know' that you are going to work beyond 24 months). You can, however, only do this so long as the property does not become your principal residence. If you move in full time, you have to stop claiming travel and living deductions, as no one gets to live free courtesy of HMRC (or at the expense of other taxpayers).

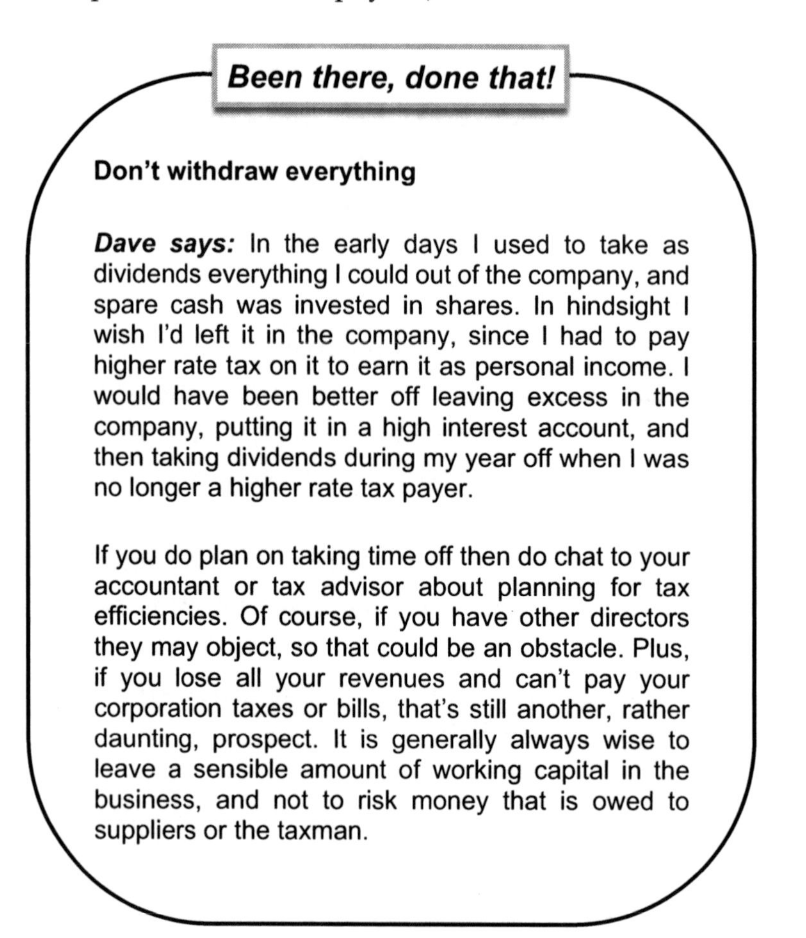

You can also buy the property through your limited company, and the maintenance is partly tax-deductible from your corporate profits. But be aware that any profit you make on any future sale is subject both to capital gains tax and to corporate income tax. Best check with your accountant from the start.

You can instead buy the property outside of your limited company with your own savings, and then it figures in your personal income tax. You will still have to pay capital gains tax on it if you sell it for a profit. Once again, check with your accountant early on, to find the most tax efficient way to proceed.

12.4.2 Individual Savings Accounts – ISAs

You can make significant tax savings by investing in Individual Savings Accounts (ISAs), especially if you take a long term view with your investments. ISAs are a highly tax efficient method of saving for retirement and you benefit from them in a number of ways. Unlike pensions, ISAs they don't attract the same upfront tax boost but are far more flexible in the way you can take out your money.

ISAs must be funded by your post-tax income so, unlike pensions, they cannot be funded using limited company income. However, there is no tax payable on the income received from ISA savings and investments.

You can invest up to £7,200 every year in ISAs and the total amount saved can mount rapidly. ISAs are offered by most major financial institutions and you can choose which option most suits you, although it is generally best to seek the advice of an independent financial adviser (IFA).

There are two main types of ISA you can invest your money into:

- Cash ISAs that generally have a variable rate of interest, with instant access and can run almost indefinitely. There are versions that have a higher rate over a fixed term, and some may have penalties for early withdrawal, or will revert to a variable rate at some stage in the future

- Equity ISAs, which can perform very well over the long term but have a risk associated because they depend on the performance of the financial markets.

Cash ISAs are like bank or building society deposit accounts, but tend to attract higher rates of interest because the financial institutions view ISA investors as long term savers.

Interest is tax free but the cash-based return can be low when compared with other options. The advantage of cash ISAs is that you can withdraw your money when you need it, although with some saving schemes this might result in a penalty.

With an equity ISA you can choose to invest your money in a managed fund or you can make your own choices about which companies to invest in. Managed fund ISAs invest in three broad areas:

- International equity funds
- Commercial property
- Corporate and treasury bonds.

You can specify which fund to invest in and can invest via a wrapper that allows funds from many different providers. Your money is actively managed by a professional and it is this manager's expertise that will aim to make money in both good times and bad, by selecting relatively high performing shares on your behalf.

It is also possible for you to have the option of investing in a tracker ISA, which benchmarks the FTSE 100 or some other share index, so the value of the ISA rises and falls accordingly. Alternatively you can have a self invested ISA, where you personally choose which shares to buy.

Stocks and shares ISAs are for contractors playing the long game, as the value of the investment can fall below the contractor's initial stake as markets fluctuate. Over time the markets rise again and the value of the ISAs will regain and surpass their initial value.

You can opt for investments managed by a number of different fund managers to maximise your investment and still remain within the tax free ISA wrapper. Using a range of fund managers within the tax free wrapper can also reduce your dealing costs if you opted for stocks and shares ISAs. Plus, you can choose to invest in other financial market items, such as gold, via specialist funds.

If you have the time and the skills, you can play the stock markets yourself within your ISA's tax free wrapper, using a fully self invested ISA. You can net a significant return, although there is also a significant risk of losing your cash, particularly if you are inexperienced in share dealing.

As their name suggests, ISAs are held by individuals; you cannot have a joint ISA with a partner in the same way that you can have a joint bank account. As a result you should do some inheritance tax planning because, over the course of your contracting career, the sums held in your ISA can mount up considerably; and as these accounts are held in your name, inheritance tax could become an issue.

The major advantage of ISAs is that you do not have to pay capital gains tax on the profits from your share dealing/dividends and interest. If you have consecutively saved £7,200 over several years and worked the money hard on the financial markets, the profits could be significant, and the resultant tax savings could be considerable.

12.5 Insurances

Business insurances, such as professional indemnity and public liability, are covered in detail in chapter 6.

However there are other key insurances that you should consider to protect your lifestyle and as a safety net if things go wrong.

As a contractor, when you can't work because you've had an accident or are ill, you don't have the benefits permanent employees do. But you can easily and relatively inexpensively protect yourself against such financial hardship.

In your last permanent job you probably had 'death in service benefit' of something like up to four times salary. As a contractor you have zero protection in the event of your death. If you have an outstanding mortgage then a policy covering you will ensure no debt is left for a partner, children or other family members should anything happen to you. And depending on the type of life assurance you take out, you may be able to make long-term provision for your loved ones after your death.

And finally, there is the risk that you are diagnosed with a critical illness, or that you suffer an accident, that prevents you from working. You can protect yourself from the potentially disastrous financial consequences of both of these scenarios.

There are a number of specialist companies that can offer a tailored range of specially selected 'contractor friendly' policies that reflect the unique way in which you work. This means that the protection can mirror that which is enjoyed by permanent employees.

The key insurances to consider include:

- Permanent health insurance, which provides a monthly income if you are unable to work
- Critical illness cover, which provides a lump sum on diagnosis of a critical illness
- Life cover, which provides a lump sum in the event of your death.

In addition, it may be worth considering a private healthcare policy that provides you with a higher degree of flexibility over when and how you get treated.

12.5.1 Permanent health insurance

Most permanent employees have the benefit of at least three months pay in the event of accident or sickness. However, as a contractor you are exposed to financial loss from the first morning that you are unable to arrive on site, fit and ready to work. Fortunately, there are ways that you can protect yourself and your family against this loss.

You can preserve your current standard of living by setting aside a monthly figure towards permanent health insurance (PHI). These policies will support you financially if you are unable to work and can even maintain your standard of living through to retirement if you suffer a more serious illness or accident.

When considering different policies, it is important to compare and contrast the following key elements of the policy:

- Deferred Period: The time delay before you are eligible to receive benefits, between one day and a year. The longer the period the cheaper the policy. If you have savings to pay your bills over this shorter term then you may choose to take a longer deferred period and have benefits starting after three or six months
- Protected Amount: You can protect up to 75% of your income. The higher the percentage the higher the cost of the policy. Try to be realistic when considering a required figure. Some costs can be cut back, whilst others will be more essential
- Nature of Income: It is vital that the financial advisor/insurance company understands the nature of your income. There are many policies that will pay out solely on salary. Check that dividends are covered if you are outside IR35 and running your own limited company

- Track record: Check that the company has a good track record of meeting past claims. Delays in or attempts to limit or avoid payments of benefits in the event of a claim are frustrating and very unfair. Ask for evidence/statistics of previous payments to clients
- Occupation Type: Ensure the policy will pay out benefits if you are unable to carry out your own occupation. This contrasts with a lesser definition that, if ill the claimant must be unable to carry out any occupation. This is an area that is often overlooked and could be used as a means of making a quote seem more reasonably priced
- Term: Ensure that policies should cover you to your chosen retirement date
- Inflation Proof: It is essential to inflation proof your benefit. £2000 per month today will have a fraction of the spending power in 10 years time.
- Premium Payer: This means the premium is personal or via your limited company. If you pay personally then benefits are tax free. If you pay via your company the benefits enter the company tax free but you pay tax and national insurance on any salary drawn. Paying into the company can help ensure executive pension premiums are maintained in ill health.

As with all complex financial products, you should consult an independent financial adviser who is experienced in dealing with the affairs of contractors before taking any decisions.

12.5.2 Critical illness cover

As a contractor you are at just as much risk from contracting critical illnesses, such as heart disease, strokes and cancer, as if you were a permanent employee, but you will have no benefits from an employer.

You can protect yourself from the potentially disastrous financial consequences of critical illnesses that leave you unable to work, so that a lump sum is paid on diagnosis.

This can help pay for a period of convalescence, changes to your home or car to accommodate a reduced state of mobility and go towards maintaining your independence. Without, perhaps, the burden of your mortgage and with money in the bank, you can then decide whether and when you need to get back to work.

Critical illness cover pays out a lump sum on earlier diagnosis (rather than on death) for a range of serious conditions. It works well in tandem with permanent health insurance (PHI). However, note that whilst PHI pays a monthly income in the event of illness, it stops once you are deemed healthy enough to return to work.

A lump sum from a critical illness policy would be yours to keep, regardless of a return to some measure of good health and could maybe allow for some changes to your work pattern and lifestyle.

When considering different policies, it is important to compare and contrast the following key elements of each policy:

- Company Longevity: will the company be around in 10 years time to meet any obligations?
- Meeting Claims: does the provider have a good track record of meeting claims?
- Conditions Covered: medical definitions of what is covered are very important and vary considerably between providers. These must be comprehensive enough to be of practical use to you in the event of a claim
- Affordability: premiums must remain affordable throughout, so that protection can be maintained as you get older and more likely to fall ill
- Term: you can cover yourself for a fixed term – eg until children grow up or a debt is repaid – or for your whole life

- Amount of Cover: you can choose 'level term', meaning the same amount throughout, or 'decreasing term', which reduces in line with a reduced liability, such as a repayment mortgage
- Payout Terms: lump sum, or paid annually (called 'family income benefit', or FIB)
- Premium Waivers: a 'waiver of premium' benefit is recommended to ensure premiums are maintained by the insurer if you suffer less serious illness that means you are unable to work for six months or more.

12.5.3 Life cover

Most permanent employees have some form of 'death in service benefit' of up to four or more times salary. However, as a contractor you no longer have this security and might want to consider arranging your own protection for your family.

If you have bought a property and have an outstanding mortgage this will need to be covered by life insurance, so that no debt is left for your family should anything happen to you. Ideally, there would then be sufficient left over to provide long-term security.

Policy aspects to consider are:

- Cover Type: 'Term cover' or 'whole of life', which means protection for a fixed length of time, or your entire life
- Payment Type: Lump sum or family income benefit (FIB) plan. Lump sum is paid in one go. A FIB plan pays a set income over a period of time
- Premium Waiver: You could consider taking 'waiver of premium' as a low cost option to protect your payments against you being unable to work through sickness after six months.

Some reasons and uses for choosing term cover are:

- To provide a lump sum for those close to you to place on deposit and draw off the interest to make up for your lost income
- To cover your life for the time that your children will be dependents
- To protect an interest-only loan, such as an ISA mortgage, so that you leave no debts for your family to pay.

Uses of a decreasing term assurance include:

- To cover a repayment (capital and interest) mortgage or a similar reducing debt.

Reasons and uses for a 'whole of life' policy include:

- To provide continuous cover until your death
- To back up an investment plan that can be cashed at a later stage.

Certain life policies have an investment element. It is important to understand that these investments are longer term in nature and that the value of investments and income from them can fall as well as rise. So check with your independent financial adviser before making any decisions.

13.

Contracting abroad

13.1 Advantages and disadvantages of working abroad

One of the great advantages of being a successful contractor is that you can find work almost anywhere. Your skills and experience are likely to be valued pretty much everywhere: Australia or the United States; China or the United Arab Emirates; Brazil or South Africa; Russia or India. Think of virtually any country, and there'll almost certainly be a thriving expat contractor community.

Many UK contractors go abroad – it's a great way to gain new skills, learn to approach projects in different ways, perhaps learn a language, or just experience all that another country can offer.

It is not especially difficult for a good contractor to arrange to work in most countries. But there are some hurdles to be surmounted, even in the simplest of transitions.

If you are a European Union (EU) citizen wanting to work elsewhere in the EU, for example, you won't require a visa or any sort of work permit. But you may have to find the correct legal format to work in another EU country. At the time of writing, for example, in the Netherlands, you must work through a Dutch registered company; while in Germany you are obliged to work only through certain agencies that have a particular registration with the Ministry of Labour.

As with many issues relating to contracting, this is an area where the use of professional support is likely to save you time and money in the long term. And because your net earnings should be so much higher as a contractor than a permanent employee, you should be able to comfortably afford the fees that professionals charge, even if they seem painful at the time.

If you have a transferable skill set in IT, engineering or construction, then there are many opportunities to work with client companies almost anywhere in the world. And it is now as easy to identify contracts in Australia, the Middle East or the USA, for example, as you can in the UK.

The downside is of course that you have to live apart from friends and family in the UK, but it's a judgement call you have to make. Some contractors choose to work abroad for three to five years to earn a substantial amount of money, sometimes paid tax free, that they will then invest on their return to the UK and possibly even semi-retire.

If you have a family, there are a great many logistical issues to consider, such as education and finding a family home, but none of these problems are insurmountable. And you could be offering your children the opportunity of a lifetime.

Just remember one thing – as a contractor abroad you are not an employee and thus have no safety net with the client company if anything goes wrong. Good planning is essential to mitigate any such risks.

13.2 Finding work abroad

It is possible to find work very easily using online resources and agencies that have international divisions. Most of the major agencies either have dedicated offices in key locations around the world, or they have reciprocal arrangements with indigenous agencies.

It is also possible to search online and apply for jobs directly in the country in which they are advertised. Language barriers aside, it is as easy to browse a foreign agency's contractor positions as it is a London based agency's ones.

However, the caveat is that going for interviews with overseas clients could potentially be very expensive. Some clients will subsidise costs, which puts you at risk of being branded an employee by HMRC, even though you are travelling to interview for a legitimate 'outside IR35' contract in another country.

Embassies and consulates can be a very useful source of information for both contract work and regulations about working in the country in question. Major importers of UK labour, such as Australia, Canada and the USA, also have lists of skills shortages.

13.3 Factors to consider

13.3.1 Don't work through your own UK company

One thing is certain: if you are going for longer than five months, you do not want to work through your limited company in the UK. In practice, for short assignments you are likely to face no difficulties working through your UK company. But longer than five months means an effective change of corporate location; what that means is that your company goes where its controlling executives are, and that can have a tremendous impact on how you are taxed.

For most UK contractors working through their own limited company, the controlling executive is the contractor themself, and typically a partner or spouse, too. So, by definition, when you move to work in Brazil, your company moves there too. And it gets taxed there. As the tax system in Brazil is very different to that of the UK, and the corporate tax rate is higher, you may well want to make specific arrangements for your work in Brazil. Or wherever else you choose to work.

The bottom line is that it can be very complicated and is not a task you can take on yourself and hope to succeed at. International tax experts are expensive, but they are worth the investment as the money you stand to gain as a result of their expertise far outweighs their fees.

13.3.2 Visas and work permits

Such is the demand for skilled workers today, that nearly every country in the world offers a special visa to make it easier for their national companies to find such workers.

This goes by different names depending on the country, for instance: in Australia, it's called a Skilled Australia Sponsored Visa; while in the USA, there's the EB-1, or the EB-2, or a myriad of others other names, depending on the skills required, the location of the contractor, and so on.

Staying with the Australian example, you should plan on spending a few months obtaining such a visa. Typically, an agency in Australia will make links with a client willing to sponsor you. Now the paperwork starts. You will have to provide extensive documentation of your work experience, your skills, and your education. You can do all this yourself, but it is a bit tricky, because the authorities demand very specific kinds of proof for all of this.

It is really well worthwhile finding a consultant or an agency that specialises in helping contractors who want to work abroad. A small investment will get you skilled help that tells you just how to apply for a visa, and what proof you need, and you'll save a lot of time and trouble.

You should be aware: if you are refused a visa for many countries, you will generally have to wait at least a few months, and sometimes a lot longer, before you are able to apply again. So expert help can really make a difference.

13.3.3 Fiscal systems and currency

Continuing with the Australian example, you will need to find a legal format for working there. Being self-employed is not an option, as most agencies and clients won't deal with you. You could start your own limited company in Australia, and if you do intend to stay for a long period, say five years or more, this could make the most sense.

Obviously starting a limited company in another country is time-consuming and complex, and you will of course have to handle all the administration and tax issues that arise from it. But, in Australia, you'll face another problem: contractors with limited companies do not enjoy all the same tax advantages as do those in the UK, so you may spend time and money setting one up to little result. They have a simplified version of IR35 which is based on the revenues coming from a single client.

If you do plan to stay in Australia for a long time, and you are considering a limited company, you should first contact the Independent Contractors Association for specifics as these vary from sector to sector and depending on circumstances. Likewise, in many other countries there are contractors' organisations and labour bodies that are able to advise you.

Using an umbrella

You will find that the simplest way to organise your work in Australia is to work with an international umbrella company. These are companies entirely dedicated to helping contractors arrive from abroad. Many will have offices both in the UK and in Australia and therefore can help arrange your visa and all your tax and administrative affairs to greatest advantage. Naturally there is a charge for such services, which will vary according to the location and local business practices.

Fiscal matters matter

One area in which such an umbrella can be particularly helpful is in arranging a tax package. There are a whole series of tax reductions attendant on skilled migrants coming to Australia, but you have to know how to tap them. A local umbrella, or a good accountant, can help with this. Wherever you're planning to work, a good rule of thumb is to find good local advice.

Currency risk

Whenever you work outside the UK, you work in a different currency. So if you plan on moving back to the UK, the worth of the currency you are earning becomes important. For example, if you were paid in US dollars, and you'd started work in January 2006 with the idea of returning to the UK in 2008, you'd have seen the value of your earnings with respect to the British pound decline by almost half. But choose a different set of dates, and the picture could be just the opposite.

Currencies work in what are called 'currency pairs:' the value of a British pound is determined with respect to the US dollar, or the Brazilian real, or any currency you care to name. Some countries have 'non-convertible' or 'blocked' currencies, which means they are for domestic transactions and not openly traded. If contracting in such countries, you are most likely to be paid in the convertible currency of another country.

Foreign Exchange (Forex) markets determine how much our money is worth, because money is traded in the same way that stockbrokers trade stocks. So you do need to watch carefully how the value of the currency you are working in is changing with respect to the pound.

Every major business newspaper will write endless commentary about these exchange rates, but you simply need to watch the major trends and make sure a major decline for the currency you are working in isn't in store with respect to the pound. If you think one is coming, try to beat it by changing your local currency into pounds before it hits.

It is also possible to hedge currency risk by changing your money into a variety of currencies, but this is fairly complex financial strategy, and you'll need to read up on it or work with an expert. A simpler strategy is to:

- Insist on payment in your own currency and push the risk onto the client
- Negotiate shorter contracts, which allows you to renegotiate if the currency rates move against you.

13.3.4 Different legal regimes

Different places, different laws. It is especially important that you find out about the legal regime in the country you are going to, the differences between its laws and the UK's, and how these will impact on you, your contracting and your life outside work, too.

For example, the UK's legal system is very similar in many respects to that of the USA, as both are based on a common source; yet there are still vast differences that could get you into trouble if you didn't know about them, or chose not to respect them.

Similarly, our law is very different to the laws of mainland Western Europe, which is based on the so-called Napoleonic code. Even though we share so much in common – not least the legal structure of the European Union – there are significant differences that will affect you.

So the upshot is, even if you're just contracting on the other side of the English Channel in France, make sure you are aware of the legal system there and, best of all, always seek local, professional assistance.

13.3.5 Moving from the UK

You may still be liable for tax in the UK even though you have moved abroad, particularly in the first year after making the move to another country. In addition to using local experts to arrange your affairs in your new location, it is important to ensure your UK accountant has done everything possible to mitigate any residual tax liabilities in the UK.

In addition, you may continue to be taxed in the UK on income you receive from UK sources, such as investments. It is also possible, depending on how you manage your tax affairs and where you are working, that you may be taxed on your overseas income.

It is therefore essential that you plan the move and do your homework to ensure the most tax efficient arrangements. The complexities of international taxation treaties are such that you will need a professional to make sure you get the best deal. So assume that you will need expert help and source it accordingly.

13.4 Working in the United States of America

For reasons of language, cultural similarities and, above all, because of the great opportunities for contractors in such a large economy, working in the USA remains very popular among UK contractors. But you do need to work your way through a very complex visa system.

The most painful way to get into the US is to go to the American Embassy or consulate nearest you, and to enter the 'Green Card Lottery'. A Green Card is a work permit, and every year a very small number of foreigners win the draw and obtain a Green Card in this way. Most of those who enter the lottery lose, of course, so it's not wise to depend on this method.

More promising, of course, are the American versions of the skilled migrant visa, known in the USA as EB-1 and EB-2 visas. But these are limited in number, and most of them get grabbed by certain companies – there is even an ongoing debate in the US about which companies should get most of them.

But there are other alternatives. It is possible to start a limited company in the US, and then to request a visa to run it. But this possibility, as well as some others, like short-term skilled migrant visas, involves going through a lot of very complex paperwork.

If you are determined to go to the US, and you can't find a company with an EB-1 or EB-2 visa for you, then your best bet is probably to start a US limited company. But you will almost certainly need the help of a US-based immigration lawyer if you are going to try it. There is good advice for this sort of thing to be had across the Atlantic. And, despite their perceived great wealth, American lawyers tend to cost much less than their UK counterparts.

13.5 Working in the European Union

For UK contractors who seek work abroad, the EU is entirely open and does not require any visas or permits. But you will need to look carefully at whether earning in euros or in the local currency changes your fee expectations. You should also consider your tax status carefully, as the entire system of taxation is different from country to country, and varies wildly once you get into the EU countries of Eastern Europe.

What is important in working in the EU is to understand the specific regimes that govern contracting in each country. For example, agency work is closely regulated in Germany, while conditions for contracting in France are not too different from those of the UK, although you will not be able to work through a limited company in France unless you have more than one client.

Needless to say, you will want to find a local accountant, lawyer or umbrella company to help you deal with the vagaries of taxation and administration in the different EU member states. There are simply too many different variables, not only from one country to another, but sometimes even from one national province or borough to another within Europe.

13.6 Working in Eastern Europe

Things can get even more complex when you get into Eastern Europe. Many of the former 'Eastern Bloc' countries are still at various stages of economic, financial and legal reform. For example, Hungary simply adapted the German civil code and made it the law of the land, whereas others are still adapting their former communist structures.

Law, theory and practice can be widely divergent in some parts of Eastern Europe, so if you plan to work there, you should definitely get some local advice about how to handle your business. Conditions are improving throughout, but it's always advisable to know what to expect and the best way to make your contracting and your business work.

14.

Growing your business

14.1 Introduction

You can have a great time being a contractor, and many contractors take full advantage of the lifestyle: good money, work when you want to do it, time off to do the things you really enjoy, amazing flexibility, and few of the niggles, hassles and worries that permanent employees have to face every day. It all adds up to make contracting a hugely worthwhile choice.

But inevitably, after a while, you start asking yourself, 'Where is all this heading?' Because, in order to enjoy the benefits of contracting, you have to work really hard, much harder than permanent employees do in many cases.

So sooner or later you come to ask yourself if you want to keep doing this same thing for the rest of your life. Some contractors are just fine with that. But many others decide that they want to build something more out of their contracting career.

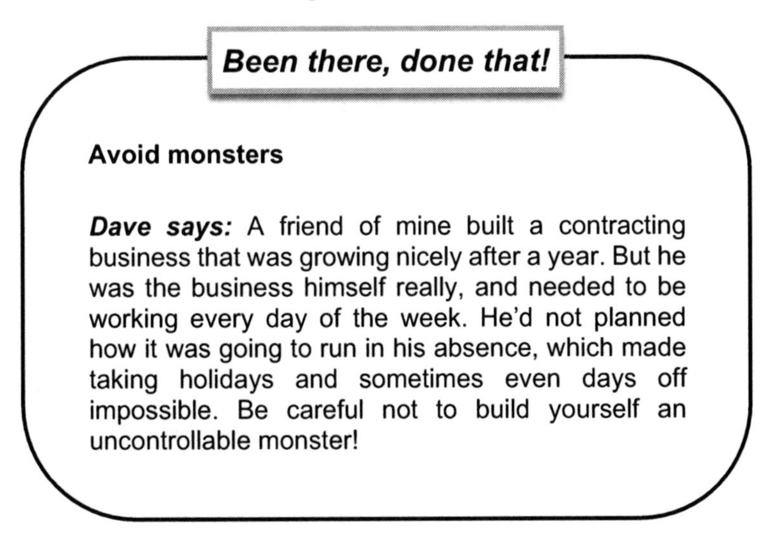

Been there, done that!

Avoid monsters

Dave says: A friend of mine built a contracting business that was growing nicely after a year. But he was the business himself really, and needed to be working every day of the week. He'd not planned how it was going to run in his absence, which made taking holidays and sometimes even days off impossible. Be careful not to build yourself an uncontrollable monster!

They consider building a truly self-supporting business – one that doesn't depend on a single person. They want to escape the 'time for the money' equation that most contracting depends on, because you eventually reach the ceiling of earnings. This ceiling is your day rate multiplied by the number of days you are prepared or able to work.

For the typical UK contractor, the upper limit is likely to be around 220 working days.

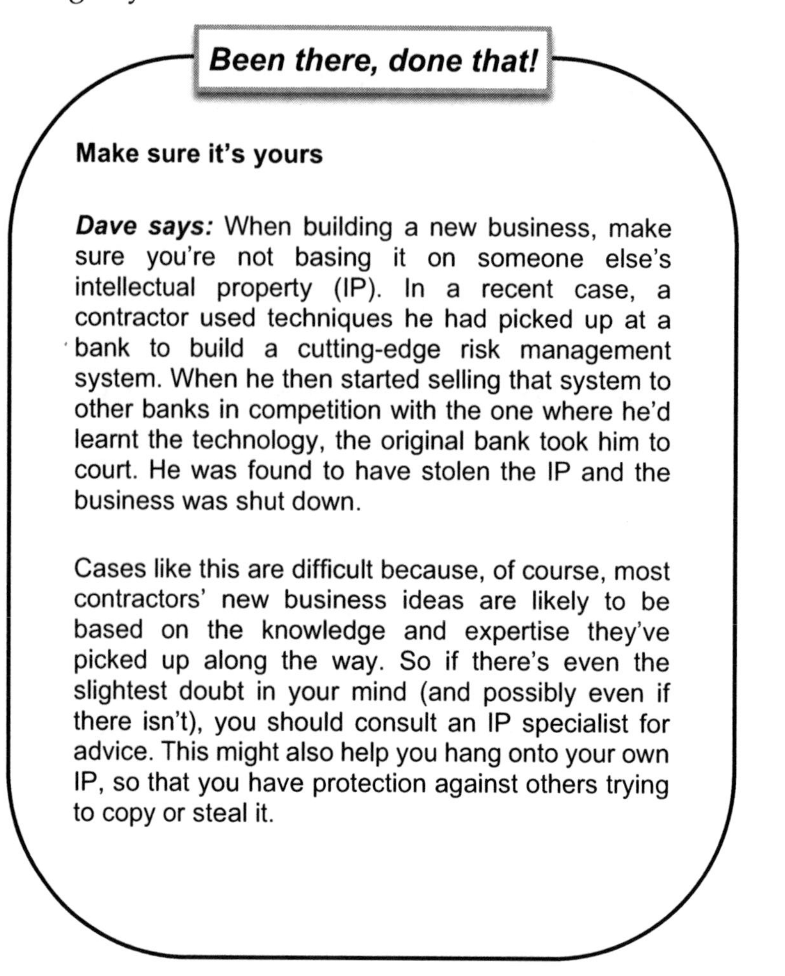

Been there, done that!

Make sure it's yours

Dave says: When building a new business, make sure you're not basing it on someone else's intellectual property (IP). In a recent case, a contractor used techniques he had picked up at a bank to build a cutting-edge risk management system. When he then started selling that system to other banks in competition with the one where he'd learnt the technology, the original bank took him to court. He was found to have stolen the IP and the business was shut down.

Cases like this are difficult because, of course, most contractors' new business ideas are likely to be based on the knowledge and expertise they've picked up along the way. So if there's even the slightest doubt in your mind (and possibly even if there isn't), you should consult an IP specialist for advice. This might also help you hang onto your own IP, so that you have protection against others trying to copy or steal it.

You might find yourself wanting to build a self-supporting business after a couple of decades of contracting, or it might be your ambition from the start, and one of your reasons for going into contracting in the first place. Either way, you'll have to start thinking like an entrepreneur.

A typical example is a contractor who found that he really liked working with small businesses, and was able to add tremendous value to them. So he marketed his ability to work with such clients, then began hiring other contractors and later employees to undertake the actual projects for him. After a year, he had a full-scale dedicated consulting business up and running.

But consulting is only one obvious option. Another example is an engineering contractor who developed a patent for a drainage process and began to sell the rights to it. Before long, she had an industrial design business growing up around her.

There are plenty of opportunities if you have the motivation. And if you have been contracting through a limited company you already have a trading vehicle ready made for your new business.

14.2 Business development and strategy

Whatever your situation, and whatever your preferences, if you want to go down the route of building a business, you will need to do some serious business planning. A contractor can go footloose and fancy-free, as it were, from one contract to another. You can't do that if you're planning to build revenue dependent on multiplying sales, particularly if you might start employing people and taking on other overheads, like premises.

If you're ready to take this step, start by writing a business plan that will help shape your thoughts and provide you with some tangible actions and targets. But you may wish to put a bit more research into what is, after all, a major career step, and there are many business plan guides and plenty of planning software you can use to develop this.

In addition there are a great many enterprise support organisations, such as Business Link, which can provide independent, impartial and often free advice and support. This government-funded organisation is often a good starting point, as it has access to a wealth of market research, offers brokerage services to put you in touch with relevant professional advice, runs relevant training courses and in many cases will provide free one-to-one business support and mentoring. You've paid the taxes to support the service, so you may as well use it!

Whatever your approach to your new business, you will need to think about marketing it: who is your target market, how will you reach the largest possible section of this group, who else is competing for the attention of the same target group, how are you different to and better than them, etc.

In all of this, what you have learned as a contractor will be the best guide. You've seen what clients want most from you on the job, and you've seen how to get their attention. So use what you've learned as a contractor to build strong foundations for your business.

The principles are the same, only instead of the product being you and your skills/services, it's your new business model.

14.3 Diversification from contracting

Contracting is a very successful business model, but it does have limitations. Unless you intend to diversify, the business will always be limited by the maximum day rate you can command and the number of days you can work.

Top consultants and business gurus bill up to £5,000 a day or more, sometimes very much more. But the chances of you being able to generate such a day rate are limited. The number of working days in the UK is usually calculated to be around 220. So if you do the maths, and it's not likely you will be able to charge more than £1,000 per day, this limits earnings to about £220,000 per year.

This of course is a fantastic salary, but you will have to work extremely hard to sustain it and not take any time off. However, it is possible to change your business model to maximise your day rate and/or expand your revenue streams by charging out other contractors or developing products.

The three obvious options that may be relatively easily available to you include:

- Personal consulting, in which you do what you do as a contractor for a number of clients at the same time, and at a much higher rate
- Product development, in which you create some intellectual property and sell it
- Consultancy services, in which you hire out other people like yourself and manage and market their efforts.

These three routes are discussed below.

14.3.1 Consultancy

What's the difference between a contractor and a consultant? It's simple: a contractor builds something for the client, and the consultant tells or teaches the client how to build something.

Let's take an example from the experience of a corporate writer, who became an editorial consultant. When companies need content on their websites, they call in a corporate writer who writes something for them, gets paid for the piecework, and goes away. The contractor produces a product.

Or, the company could go to an expert on website content, and say, 'how can we build a team that will produce the content we need on the website whenever we need it?' The consultant helps hire workers with the right experience, finds a manager for the team, and provides the client with planning so that they can do the necessary research and produce the content themselves. The consultant shares know-how.

You will read endless jokes about consultants and their 'consultant-speak' in the business press, but the fact is that businesses need consultants to survive. They cannot possibly obtain all the know-how they need by hiring new people – the budget would burst at the seams!

Instead, they bring in a consultant who provides the know-how they need and shares it with the people they have. A good consultant saves money for the company, or adds value to it. The consultant's fee is therefore paid for out of the money saved or the increase in revenues and profits.

An obvious example where a consultant can save money is a good tax consultant, who will save a company 20% on its taxes, and then charge the company 10% in fees. In effect, the company hasn't spent anything on the consultant, but has saved 10% on taxes.

In your work as a contractor, you will often see knowledge gaps that you know you can fill yourself. If you have the motivation, there's your opportunity. Your great incentive is that consulting is highly paid: the best consultants earn upwards of £1,000 per day. And instead of being dependent on a single client, you'll build up a portfolio of clients who call you in again and again.

You will want to make yourself an acknowledged authority in your field, for example by publishing papers and 'working the conferences'. It's an extremely effective and quite agreeable way to market yourself, since you will often meet all your competitors at the same conference and you can enjoy the ensuing debates. More importantly, you will be meeting prospective clients, potential future employees or sub-contractors, and generally getting your and your company's name out there.

Consulting can have the added advantage of placing you well outside of IR35, as you are clearly in business in your own right, are not controlled by your client, can supply a substitute and so on.

All in all, it can prove a highly profitable, enjoyable and satisfying way to earn a crust!

14.3.2 Product development

There is one classic story about a contractor who became a fantastically successful product developer. He worked in radio as a sound editor. When he edited tapes, he obviously made them shorter or longer as needed.

This genius discovered one day that he could use the same techniques he used in editing to effectively get more 'stuff' (that is, more content) into the same time period. In other words, when an advertiser paid for a minute, the contractor could squeeze a minute-and-a-half's worth of content into it.

The contractor patented the process, and became extremely wealthy in the space of a couple of years. Every single advertiser on radio wanted to use this product. It's still being marketed more than a decade later.

All this sounds terribly unlikely and/or difficult; yet in fact, contractors see opportunities like this all the time. Going from contract to contract of the same type, you see each time that a certain kind of process, or a bit of code, or some very specific skill, resolves an important issue. You use it, you know it works and the demand for your services as a contractor proves that there's a genuine demand.

It's not really a great step from there to marketing that product yourself. You do need to think about how to reach the target market, and in some cases how to retain your hold on the intellectual property.

Build your business plan around those two aims, understanding the market need and creating a product to fulfil it, and you could create a thriving business.

14.3.3 Hiring contractors

This is an option for people who consider themselves good managers and who know how to delegate, explain, support and encourage.

The basis of this business model is that if you can win work based on your skills and expertise, you can pay someone else to do that work and take part of their earnings. You find them work, you coach them on how to do it, and you get some of the money without spending a great deal of your own time.

Needless to say, a lot of hard work goes into building a consultancy of this type. Again marketing is the key, and you will benefit from what you've learned about the companies you've worked for yourself.

But managing people and marketing to companies are skills that do not necessarily come to all contractors, so ask yourself if you have what it takes, and even if the answer is 'yes', find ways to improve your management and marketing skills.

Obviously, there are many issues to be confronted with this type of business that don't really enter into contracting. Just because you are a good programmer or engineer, for example, you may not have the skills required for running a business that involves a whole host of specialist business skills: hiring, managing, administration, marketing, finance, etc.

But if you can make it through the skills gap, you will enjoy one advantage that contractors don't have: you'll have a business that is sustainable on its own, one that doesn't depend on you personally to generate billable hours.

The advantage of each of these approaches is that you are adding value to the business – it is not just dependant on you personally.

That means you are not necessarily essential for its continued success, which means you have the opportunity to go through a transaction, which may be a trade sale of the business or floating in a financial market. And that's where you will really make your money.

15.

Coming to the UK

15.1 Living and working in the UK

The UK can be a great place to live and work. Like any country, it has its pros and cons and so it is largely down to personal preference as to whether it offers an acceptable alternative for the duration of a contract, or series of contracts.

The benefits of contracting are covered in detail in chapter 1, and these benefits also apply to non-UK residents currently living outside the UK. In addition to the greater earnings potential and flexible lifestyle, there are a huge number of other factors that make the UK attractive to workers from overseas.

For those looking to test their skills and further their careers, for example, the UK offers many of the world's most exciting and leading-edge projects to work on. And for those interested in 'seeing the world', the UK's tourism opportunities are equally exciting. Once thing is certain, though: contractors from outside the UK are unlikely to come for the weather!

15.1.1 Before you leave

Doing your homework before you come to the UK will really pay off. In fact, what you discover may heavily influence your decision to come, where you choose to accept a contract, and where you live.

For example, it may be that you live and work in a country with few business regulations and low taxation, and that you might find the situation in the UK less attractive from that point of view. Whilst the UK is not as heavily regulated as some European states, it does have a reasonably high burden of business red tape, and individuals and companies are relatively highly taxed.

However, in many sectors the UK is one of the leading nations in the world in terms of opportunity, and this is certainly true of contracting opportunities in the IT, financial and engineering sectors, among others.

A vital task is to ensure you can qualify for a visa that allows you to work. Largely due to the security issues that have come to the fore in the last decade, immigration has tightened up considerably and contractors who attempt to work in the 'black economy' without a proper visa will almost certainly get found out and may face fines, imprisonment and deportation.

Section 15.2 covers visa issues and the main lesson is to enlist professional help, even though it is expensive, to ensure you can work in the UK legally.

Your local British embassy or consulate is a good place to start your research and there are numerous business and enterprise support agencies to assist companies from overseas who wish to relocate in the UK.

15.1.2 Travelling and relocating home and family to the UK

If you are single with no dependants, then coming to work in the UK could be as simple as packing a bag and getting on a plane. However, if you have a home and family that will be coming with you, it is a major exercise in logistics to ensure everything goes smoothly.

Good quality accommodation, and in particular family accommodation, is scarce in some parts of the UK. This is particularly true in the large capital cities, such as London, Edinburgh, Cardiff and Belfast, as well as other major cities like Birmingham and Manchester, where there are concentrations of contracting opportunities.

In such areas hotels and other temporary accommodation can be prohibitively expensive, with prices driven up by a combination of under-supply and high demand from leisure, tourism and business customers. So the answer is to ensure you have, at the very least, an affordable, short term accommodation solution in place before you get on the plane.

There are also significant regional variations in the UK which impact on the availability of contracts and quality of life. For example, the financial sector is focused mainly in London and the South East of England, and the bulk of higher paying IT jobs in the financial sector can be found there.

Oil and gas contractors will find work is mainly in Scotland, particularly Aberdeen, and in Humberside and East Anglia.

However, many oil and gas work contracts require offshore work, so it actually does not matter where the contractor is based as long as transport links are good.

15.1.3 Living in the UK

There are any number of online guides and books about life in the UK. Again the key lesson is to do your research. Your research checklist should include:

- Visa issues
- Other documentation, such as professional qualifications and health records
- Your financial arrangements, such as savings, banking and insurances
- Where in the UK to live and finding accommodation
- How you plan to get around, as public transport is poor in some rural areas and you may require, for example, a hire car for your first few weeks
- Healthcare
- Education, if you have school age children
- Starting a business and regulatory issues
- Finding a contract, preferably before you arrive in the UK
- Where to go for help if things go wrong.

The UK has a well developed public sector and this includes free healthcare at the point of delivery for all and compulsory full time education from ages five to sixteen, soon to rise to eighteen.

However, the quality of state services is variable and there are options available in the private sector that some contractors may wish to consider.

15.1.4 Doing business and working in the UK

Previous chapters have covered in detail what options contractors have for starting their UK based contracting career and a basic introduction to the UK legal system. You will almost certainly need an accountant, or an umbrella company, when you have won your first contract and they can help you negotiate doing business successfully in the UK.

There are also numerous business enterprise support agencies that can assist people starting a business. These services are typically free or heavily subsidised and can usually be found via the state funded organisation, Business Link.

The workplace for highly skilled and professional contractors is generally quite informal and relationships between contractors and their clients tend to be quite relaxed, as long as everything is going well.

Workplaces are heavily regulated, with much health and safety and employment regulation in place to protect workers. But remember that, as a contractor, you are not an employee of the client and do not have any employment rights in the client's workplace. This does not mean your client does not have to provide a safe environment for you to work in, but it does mean you will not be entitled to enjoy all the employment benefits and protection given to permanent employees you might be working alongside.

Although it is moving towards the litigious society prevalent in the United States, the situation in the UK has not got to the stage where every issue or conflict must be resolved in court. The UK courts are quite keen on Alternative Dispute Resolution, and if you end up in court without having exhausting non-litigious avenues the judge is likely to be unimpressed. This leads to a much more consensual workplace, where people and companies tend to work more constructively towards a solution that benefits all.

Although there are reasonable levels of union membership in the UK, industrial unrest tends to be low and in most environments contractors from overseas will find themselves with little or no disruption as a result of union activities.

The major industry body which protects contractors' interests is the Professional Contractors Group. Originally created as a single platform lobby group against tax legislation, the PCG has become a fully-fledged industry body, just short of being a chartered professional institute.

Having said that, the majority of its membership is made up of contractors running their own limited companies, rather than those working through umbrella companies. Nevertheless, the PCG's activities are aimed at protecting and enhancing the working lives of all contractors.

15.2 Visa issues

There is always a demand for highly skilled contractors in the UK, although naturally the range of skills and numbers required fluctuates.

Contractors from countries inside the EU can come to work in the UK without the need to go through immigration procedures. It is a very good idea, however, to have a strong command of English if seeking contracts in the UK.

There is plenty of room for skilled workers from outside the European Union (EU) to take a share of the action.

Coming to the UK to work just became a lot easier for workers outside the EU, because the former process of obtaining visa and work permits was a bit chaotic. Now the rules and procedures are much clearer under legislation that was adopted in 2007, and which has come into force in the spring of 2008.

From 'Highly Skilled Migrants' to 'Tier 1': Formerly, the UK, like many other countries, offered a special working visa for contractors with skills much in demand.

Now this visa has been replaced by a system of immigration based on points. Contractors who seek to enter the country can seek a Tier 1 visa which, as the Immigration Service has it, is for highly-skilled migrants, entrepreneurs, investors, and foreign graduate students.

Tier 1, in other words, is designed for people living in countries outside the European Union – top talent who can contribute the most to the UK economy.

Migrants coming to the UK under Tier 1 visas do not need a job offer or a sponsor and are free to seek employment anywhere in the UK. You can stay for three years, and you can also renew a Tier 1 visa if you choose to. But to get in, you must successfully score 75 points under the new points-based system.

Tier 1 is meant for a variety of highly skilled individuals, but the part applying to contractors refers to highly-skilled migrants. These are highly educated people with the right skills and experience. You also need about six months worth of living expenses in the bank to fit into this category.

It would also be possible for contractors to enter the UK by setting up a business or by taking one over. This category, referred to as 'Entrepreneurs,' does however require that you have £200,000 pounds in capital to invest.

For both of the above categories, applicants must show English language ability, which is worth 10 points. Your six-months worth of living expenses is also worth 10 points.

The rest of the 50 points you need are allocated with respect to three factors:

- Having a skill that is in demand
- Work experience
- Any previous experience living, studying and working in the UK. If you've lived and worked in the UK before, you get some points because you've shown that you can adapt to life here.

But even if you haven't lived in the UK before and if you have a skill that is high up on the list of skills in demand, a list made public regularly by the UK Border Agency, you will earn a substantial number of points. You must be able to document your skill thoroughly.

Then, work experience which shows that you will integrate well into a UK company is the other quality that scores points. Again, very thorough documentation, along with serious references, will be sought.

The downside of this kind of visa application is always the need to prove equivalences. The UK does not necessarily accept diplomas and qualifications from the country you come from. This means that you may have to prove that your diploma and your work qualifications are actually equivalent to those issued in the UK.

This is a tedious process involving legal translations of university transcripts, declarations of equivalence from recognised industrial organisations or trade organisations, recognition by professional organisations and so on. Sadly, there is no quick fix for all this.

Having described this system in some depth, you should recognise that you will need expert help in applying for this visa. There are any number of agencies and lawyers to help you obtain it, and your sponsor or agency will also be able to provide help. A dedicated umbrella company would provide another alternative.

Contractors who arrive with a Tier 1 visa in the UK can work anywhere they choose, and so can run their businesses exactly in the same way as a contractor with British citizenship would.

You should be aware that you will be taxed as a UK resident and if you choose to form a limited company here, you will need to pay tax both on your corporate and your personal income.

You may have read about the possibility of working in the UK without being domiciled here. This is rather difficult for migrant contractors to do, because the 'non-dom' status means that you live most of the time outside the UK.

If you can arrange to spend less than 90 days in the UK while working as a contractor, then you may consider this option, which permits you to keep the largest part of your income outside the country, and to pay no tax on it.

You do pay something on what you bring in. Also, if you remain for longer than seven years, as a 'non-dom' you will have to pay a substantial annual sum in taxes; at the time of writing this was at least £30,000 per year.

Acknowledgements

There are many people to whom I am grateful for advice, ideas and encouragement offered during the development of the *Contractors' Handbook.*

My friends and loved ones deserve special mention, for their unfailing support and incredible patience over more than a year as I have spent late nights, weekends and even holidays staring into my laptop as this book has taken shape. For all the parties and special occasions I've missed, the get-togethers I've had to leave early, and the last-minute changes of plan – I'll make it up to you!

I would like to thank those experts within the contracting sector who have so generously given of their time and offered freely their advice and opinions on the wealth of guides developed on ContractorCalculator.co.uk, and which form the backbone of this book. My thanks go, among others, to John Brazier and John Kell of the Professional Contractors Group, the late David Royden, Adrian Marlowe, David Colom, Simon Sweetman, the team at Qdos Consulting, Tony Harris, Rob Crossland, Barry Roback, Sid Home, Ann Swain, James Fraser and Roger Sinclair.

Huge thanks go to the team at Copestone Copywriters, whose help has allowed this book to become a reality. Many others have also contributed – you know who you are!

In particular, I would like to thank the contractors, from every sector, who have contributed to this book in one way or another: some because I've had the pleasure of working alongside them and developing friendships for life, and others whose brave fights with HMRC and HM Treasury have established important principles that have helped all contractors.

But the true impetus for this book, over and above all others, has come from the hundreds of contractors who have sent in queries – from the basic to the bizarre! – to the Contractor Doctor on ContractorCalculator.co.uk.

To all of you, my heartfelt thanks.

Dave

Lightning Source UK Ltd.
Milton Keynes UK
29 October 2010

162093UK00002B/2/P